The
ABCs
of
Writing for Children

The

ABCs

of

Writing for Children

114 Children's Authors
and Illustrators Talk About
the Art,
the Business,
the Craft & the Life
of Writing Children's Literature

Compiled by Elizabeth Koehler-Pentacoff

Printed in the United States of America

Published by Quill Driver Books/Word Dancer Press, Inc.

1254 Commerce Way

Sanger, California 93657

559-876-2170 • 1-800-497-4909 • FAX 559-876-2180

QuillDriverBooks.com

Info@QuillDriverBooks.com

Quill Driver Books titles may be purchased in quantity at special discounts for educational, fund-raising, business, or promotional use.
Please contact Special Markets, Quill Driver Books/Word Dancer Press, Inc. at the above address, toll-free at 1-800-497-4909 or by e-mail: Info@QuillDriverBooks.com

Quill Driver Books/Word Dancer Press, Inc. project cadre:
Doris Hall, Susan Klassen, Brigitte Phillips, Stephen Blake Mettee, Linda Kay Weber

Third Printing

To order another copy of this book, please call
1-800-497-4909

Cover illustrations by Sarah Wilson

ISBN 1-884956-28-9

EAN 9781884956287

Library of Congress Cataloging-in-Publication Data

Koehler-Pentacoff, Elizabeth.
    The ABC's of writing for children : 114 children's authors and illustrators talk about the art, business, the craft, and the life of writing children's literature / by Elizabeth Koehler-Pentacoff.
        p. cm.
    Includes bibliographical references (p.) and index.
    ISBN 1-884956-28-9 (Trade Paper)
        1. Children's literature—Authorship. I. Title.
PN147.5 .K64 2002
808.06'8—dc21

2002005138

For Stephen Mooser and Lin Oliver

Contents

Introduction

Rumor has it a famous neurosurgeon saw Dr. Seuss (Theodor Seuss Geisel) at a party. The neurosurgeon said to Geisel, "I write children's books as a hobby."
"I too have a hobby," replied Geisel. "Brain surgery."

Have you ever dreamed of writing a best-selling children's book? Ever fantasize about what it's like to live the life of a published children's author? Although writing and illustrating books for children is not as easy as it looks—an acquaintance once said to me, "Writing children's books looks so easy, I think I'll write one this weekend."—new authors and illustrators are being discovered and published all of the time.

Even if you're not planning a career in this field, learning how authors and illustrators work can lend new insights and appreciation to their art. The same ideas and inspirations that help authors and illustrators of children's books, may encourage students, teachers, librarians and other creative artists in their literary efforts.

While gathering at a writer's conference recently, several of us children's authors and illustrators shared anecdotes about our profession. We reminisced about the years it took each of us to learn our craft, market our manuscripts, and learn to deal with rejection before we became published authors. Then we discussed our lives after getting published.

Many of our concerns are still the same. We still strive to grow as writers, respond to today's sophisticated child reader, deal with the chain store mentality that permeates the publishing market, and be true to our creative selves. The old cliche, you're only as good as your next book, is true, so that even after you've "broken into the business," you may be faced with the same challenges: getting the next book bought by a publishing house, publicizing your books so they don't go out of print, and making a living with your career.

Just as there are over one-hundred authors and illustrators quoted here, there are as many ways in which to create a children's book. Among these pages, you'll see a wide-range of philosophy, know-how, talent, and opinions. You'll discover how other authors and illustrators work, what inspires them, and the various situations they face in their careers. You'll learn many 'dos and don'ts' for creating children's books. You'll see what works for one author, may not for the next. And you may just learn what will work for you.

Acknowledgments

I'd like to thank all of the authors and illustrators in this book, who graciously took time out of their own projects to give me phone interviews and correspond with me via e-mail and mail. Everyone I talked to was willing to share their know-how to help others discover their own voice in the field of children's literature.

I'd also like to thank my editor Steve Mettee, my agents Andrea Brown, and Laura Rennert, author-illustrator Sarah Wilson for her delightful art on the cover, and authors and friends: Ellen Leroe, Susan Hart Lindquist, Susan Taylor Brown, Karen Cushman, Marilyn Singer, Caroline Arnold, Patricia Polacco, Loretta Ichord, Lee Wardlaw, Ginger Wadsworth, Tricia Gardella, Joan Holub, David Lubar, and Virginia Kitteridge for their enthusiasm, encouragement, and guidance.

Those of us creating books for children face a solitary existence; we usually work alone in our home office or art studio. But it is essential for us to share our experiences and connect with others in our field. This book is dedicated to Stephen Mooser and Lin Oliver who, in 1968, began the Society of Children's Book Writers, now called the Society of Children's Book Writers and Illustrators (SCBWI).

Through Steve and Lin's hard work and leadership, the organization has grown from a small group of local writers into a world-wide organization make up of thousands of people who write, illustrate or share an interest in children's literature. SCBWI publishes an excellent newsletter and many other helpful publications, presents invaluable national and local conferences, generously gives awards and grants to its members, and lobbies the government for issues that face our group.

Steve and Lin have given children's authors and illustrators an extraordinary gift. SCBWI is the reason many of us, within this field, are published. Perhaps more important, because of Steve and Lin's nurturing guidance, the membership is made up of a network of caring individuals, who are willing to help each other succeed within this highly competitive field of children's literature.

First Times

Getting published in the field of children's literature is a difficult feat. However, with persistence and hard work, it can be done.

Believe in Yourself
"I started writing in 1983 and was first published in 1997. Fourteen years of writing!"
Franny Billingsley

Lost and Found
"My first book was *101 Black Cats* published by Scholastic. I sent it off in 1973 and didn't hear from them. So I retyped the manuscript and sent it to thirteen other publishers. The thirteen publishers rejected it. A year and a half later, I received an acceptance letter from Scholastic. They had lost the manuscript and found it in the process of moving."
Stephen Mooser

Magazine Success
"I sold my first short story in 1978 to *Highlights*."
David Lubar

Slush Pile
"I wrote *Corey's Fire* in 1982. Three years later it got plucked from the slush pile."
Lee Wardlaw

Eight Years
"I started writing and submitting in 1988. The first book I authored and illustrated was *Pen Pals*, published in 1996."
Joan Holub

Path to Success—Read!

"I wrote as a child. I've been writing ever since! As an adult, I became a librarian. They asked me if I liked children and I said yes, so they made me a children's librarian. After I read all the children's books, I could write them. It took me ten years to get my first book published."

Marilyn Sachs

Late Bloomer

"My story is different from other people's. I didn't start writing until I was forty-one. My art helped me join Society of Children's Book Writers and Illustrators. We had a vibrant group in the San Francisco Bay Area. They taught me the nuts and bolts of how things were done. When I finished my stories, my mother bankrolled a trip for me to go to New York. She went with me. We had the most glorious time! The hayseed was sticking out of my hair. Who cares, I thought. It was a great adventure!

"I did my homework. I made appointments way ahead of time and sent photo bios, mailing material, so they'd know why I was there and who I was. I had sixteen appointments in one week! That meant four portfolio reviews a day. I saw editors, not art directors. The editor is the only person who can acquire anything. I think I saw Patty Gauch at Philomel on the second day. Simon and Schuster took *The Keeping Quilt*. Philomel took *Raschenka's Eggs*. Dodd Mead and Bantam took other books."

Patricia Polacco

Research Helps

"My first editorial letter leading to a sale came when I'd been writing nine months. It was beginner's luck! But I had been a children's librarian for umpteen years. I was already aware of children's books; I had done my research."

Suzanne Williams

The Five Year Plan

"It took me seven years to get my book about Julia Morgan published. I made a deal with my husband. He would work for five years to support me. When I didn't sell anything, I became a teacher's aide to help out. The first book I sold was *Julia Morgan, Architect of Dreams*. Although I loved being a teacher's aide, I didn't have the energy to do that, write, *and* be a parent to two elementary-aged boys."

Ginger Wadsworth

From Diapers to Romance

"Once I had kids out of diapers, in 1986, I went to a writing class at a college and I found a local romance writer's group. I joined it and jumped right in. The first year, I wrote for adults. But when I wrote a kid's mystery, it clicked. I knew then that this is what I was meant to do. After I sold the book, it wasn't actually published until three years later."

Linda Joy Singleton

Different Time Frame

"The 1970s were a different time. My first picture book was accepted six months after I submitted it. People were more will to take a chance and costs were lower. Lists weren't overcrowded. Nobody expected minimum sales of 10,000 books."

Marilyn Singer

Worth the Wait

"I didn't start writing until 1989, when I was in my forties. I had a licensed day care in my home, so I spent a lot of time reading to the children. My first short story was published in a magazine in 1992, and I sold my first book in 1994. *Covered Wagons, Bumpy Trails* took two years to write even though it was only 150 words long. It took three and a half years to sell it, and then I had to wait six more years until it was published!"

Verla Kay

Graphic Background

"My background is art and I eased my way into children's books by working as a graphic designer, and then creating puzzle and coloring books. In the 1970s I went to New York every year for six years, trying to get *Chickens Aren't the Only Ones* published. No one was interested; full color was very expensive to print, nonfiction picture books were rare and I was an unknown author. It was coincidental that my first book, *Chickens Aren't the Only Ones*, was finally published at the same time that California schools were introducing science to kindergarten."

Ruth Heller

Three's a Charm

"I've been telling and writing stories since I was in the third grade. But I didn't start (writing for publication) until my kids were born. I started writing for magazines first. I didn't sell anything for a long time. Then I read an article in *The Writer* by Mary Calhoun that talked about focusing. It talked about the core of three. Three episodes. *The Three Billy Goats Gruff* pattern. I decided to try it and that achieved my first sale. It took me a year and a half before I published."

Sue Alexander

Success and Scratch Paper

"It didn't take me long to get published. I sold my first story to a magazine for twelve dollars. I was hooked! My first book was published in 1958. Here's how it happened. I had sent a book about building a harbor, Redondo Beach, to a Los Angeles publisher. The editor sent it back and said it was too narrow, but invited me to see her. I did so, and I brought a long list of ideas to fit the California State Social Studies Framework. We agreed I'd work on two of the ideas. One became my first book. The other, scratch paper!"

Ruth Radlauer

Heaven Help Us

"It was easy to get my first book, a picture book, published. And virtually impossible to sell a second manuscript. I'm not sure why the first one sold so easily. The first publisher I sent it to asked me to revise and send it back. I didn't like the revision suggestions so I sent it to a second publisher who bought it. Sometimes I think my father, who has been dead for many years, pulled some strings from heaven. But after that, I had to work my hind-end off!"

Gennifer Choldenko

Early Poet's Fans

"I had my first poem published in a newspaper when I was seven. It was about spring. My family was living in Maine at the time, and spring had been very late in coming. The newspaper didn't pay anything for the poem, but people who read it wrote me letters and sent money in envelopes!"

Sarah Wilson

Good Friend

"Depressing as this is, it took me nine years to get published. I was more inclined to do the work than do the self-promotion, so I sent out samples to publishers about once a year, if that. Unfortunately, aggressive assertiveness is not one of my character traits, but fortunately perseverance is. I finally worked up the courage to send my work to Thacher Hurd, who was a friend of some friends of mine, to ask for his opinion/advice. He referred me to Nicole Geiger at Tricycle Press, and then if finally happened...two long years later."

Eve Aldridge

Thanks to Society of Children's Book Writers and Illustrators . . .

"I started writing seriously in 1984. I was living in England and one of my flatmates published a children's play with Samuel French. I thought if he could do it, I could do it! I racked up a stack of rejection letters there. When I got back to the United States, I happened upon Sue Alexander at a library's Meet the Author Day. She told me to join Society of Children's Book Writers and Illustrators and two years after that, I had my first book accepted."

Bruce Balan

A Ghost of a Chance Turns Real

"I was eight years old when I sold a stained-glass drawing to the *American Girl Magazine*. (It was a Girl Scout magazine then, different than the one today). I wrote and edited a college newspaper and it was a great training ground. After college, I worked for *Houston City Magazine*. I was turned off by the editorial slant, so I decided to write books for kids. I took the Institute of Children's Literature course and sold four of my assignments to children's magazines. It's where I wrote the first draft of *The Ghost Cadet*. Although I graduated from ICL in 1984, and began sending *The Ghost Cadet* out immediately, I didn't sell that book until 1990."

Elaine Marie Alphin

Biography

"I wrote when I was a child, but publishing came as a mid-life career. Before that, I worked in medical research, worked in schools and in libraries. I had worked with children's books forever, but I still didn't know how to write them. So I took a class on how to write for kids. It still took five years for me to learn how to write a biography that would get published."

Beverly Gherman

A Believer

"I had an agent who kept sending my first manuscript out for six years before it got published. She really believed in my work, even when I didn't!"

Kathryn Reiss

Going Crazy After All These Years

"I had been trying for ten years to get published. I was teaching school when I found out. I yelled, 'Yabba yabba Doooo!' The class thought I was nuts!"

Wendelin Van Draanen

California Hippie?

"My first book was published in 1988. At that time, art directors at publishing houses said my stuff looked spirited but unschooled. I had sold crafts professionally, toys, tapestries, dolls and painted eggs before this, but I hadn't any art school. An agent showed my first book to editor Anne Schwartz, at Knopf. She liked the uniqueness of my voice, but she thought the art looked unfocused and too wild. What is ironic, is that I show children now what the early dummy looked like and they like it better! The editor said my art looked 'very California.' When I asked her to explain that, she said it looked 'psychedelic.' I have sympathy for unknown talented authors and illustrators. Don't get bitter at this difficult, marketing-driven career."

Elisa Kleven

Important Element

"It took me about two years to find a publisher for my first novel, *The Sara Summer*. One editor said she liked the girls in the story, but, at the moment, her company was looking for mysteries. Could I add 'the element of mystery' to my manuscript?"

Mary Downing Hahn

Take Two Aspirin

"It took me about six years to get published. My day job in advertising, while living in Florida, kept me pretty busy so I wasn't terribly aggressive, at first, about submitting manuscripts and sample artwork. Never the less, I gradually gathered a folder of rejection letters. At one point, with the help of a friend, I managed a meeting with a publishing agent, the very gracious Edite Kroll. I later learned she confided to my friend that one of my manuscripts gave her a headache, a comment I have always valued!

"With recommendations from her, I took a week off from work, flew north and pounded the pavement, getting face-to-face meetings with editors in New York City and Boston. Though no contracts resulted from that trip, two of the editors I met with asked to see some revisions on a couple of my stories. It energized me and I suddenly felt that this dream to publish a picture book was within reach! Finally, I was introduced to a gentleman, Peter Elek, who became my agent. After six years of gathering rejections on my own, he obtained my first contract within three months. Perhaps I would have been published eventually. But Peter certainly accelerated the process and he continues to work with me today."

Tedd Arnold

To Write or Not to Write

"People should think long and hard before they start a book. The competition to get a book published is intense, so make certain the story you want to tell is unique and that it will be fun for you to write. Then look at the story and make notes. Is there a story beyond an interesting incident? Is there an ending? I'm good at opening scenes due to my film background, but when I have not planned, I have sometimes painted myself into a corner. When you enter the tunnel, make sure you can see the light at the end."

Stephen Mooser

2

Writing Tips from the Pros

Give Yourself Time

"A writer's first book tends to be derivative of things they have read. Write until you get past this to find your *own* voice. That means you'll write things that won't be published or *shouldn't* be published."

Bruce Coville

It's Simple as 1, 2, 3...

"There are three things you have to do to be a successful writer. Read a lot of children's books, write a lot, and rewrite what you do. I can almost guarantee anyone, that if they spend years learning, they will publish a book. It just requires learning and persistence."

Stephen Mooser

Mavis, where are you?

"Learn to type."

David Lubar

Best Inventions

"Post its! Post its! Post its! And...

"I have a four- by eight-foot dry-erase board hanging on the wall of my office. When I'm planning, scribbling on it encourages me to think freely, in broad, bold strokes. Later, when I'm in the midst of my story, and even after I've finished a draft, I use it to help me link cause and effect, to map setting and to visualize plot sequence, dramatic tension, and character development. Something about being able to stand back and look at the whole thing fools me into believing I'm in control."

Susan Hart Lindquist

Friends

"Read your work aloud constantly. Listen to the rhythm of your words and sentences; *do you trip up anywhere? Are you boring yourself?* Get into a children's writer critique group and have *them* read the story aloud. Then you'll hear it cold—not with the enthusiasm and drama that you would put into it—the way an editor would. Then analyze it: *what works and what needs work?* Characters are everything. You must know her as well as you know your best friend; better yet, as well as you know yourself."

Lee Wardlaw

Upside Down, Inside Out

"This is a good tip for when you're stuck in a story line, or when your characters stubbornly refuse to engage in original behavior, or when the outcome of a chapter or a book seems trite and stereotypical, and you're fresh out of ideas. I call this burnout zone, 'playing solo racquetball' because you're batting the same old tired ball back and forth to yourself without a partner to give you fresh perspective and impetus.

"When this happens and I'm stuck, I think of one of my favorite quotes from Ray Bradbury's *Fahrenheit 451*. 'If they give you ruled paper write the other way.'

In other words, look at your problem inside out, or literally turn your idea upside down by inverting the norm. For instance, if you're working on a picture book about a child terrified of the dark who runs to Mommy for comfort when the monsters beckon, make the kid *bully* the night monsters in his closet. Or don't have the little brother and sister be insanely jealous of the newest addition to the family; have that child smother the baby with love. Play with point of view and tell the classic fairy tales from the viewpoint of the gingerbread cottage in *Hansel and Gretel*, or the red cape of *Little Red Riding Hood*. Be different, be bold, be original. Do as Ray Bradbury commanded and 'write the other way.' It might not clinch a sale, but I guarantee the editors will take notice."

Ellen Leroe

It's Gotta Be Fun

"Your function as a writer is to tell a story. You can sneak a message in, but you can't get away from the fact you're there to entertain."

Marilyn Sachs

Jack LaLanne and Michael Jordan

"Read a lot and write a lot. Pay attention to the things around you. It's just like playing basketball. You have to exercise those muscles."

Karen Cushman

Imaginary Friend

"The first thing my editor told me was to pretend you're telling your story out loud to a kid the age of your readership."

Deborah Norse Lattimore

Ask for Directions

"I have found, for me, once I have figured out who the characters are, and vaguely what my story is about, then I work out the ending as close to the actual wording as I can get. Because that's my road map. It tells me where I'm going."

Sue Alexander

Try for the Prize!

"Enter contests. If you win, it helps you to get published."

Ellen Jackson

Be True To You

"Read your own heart. We know joy, grief, hope, despair. All of those things are the truth of the story. The circumstances of the story don't matter, as long as you convey the honesty of the feeling of the story. Don't be afraid to put down weakness and talk about it. People like to be reassured that they aren't so different. If it's unpleasant, it helps to hear about other people going through it. And everyone has family traditions. And if you think you don't, you can start a family tradition this week!"

Patricia Polacco

Get Excited

"Henry James says you can tell good writing by strong specification. If writers can bring up strong details, then it's exciting for the reader. And writer. I jump out of my chair when something works! I close my fist and say YES! That's exactly what I want to see on the page. Either you have it or you don't."

Gary Soto

Keep On Keeping On

"Don't stop trying. Once you stop, you have failed."

Debra Keller

Love Thy Book

"Read. Pay attention to why you like something (in a book). What about the style appeals to you? Explore it in your own writing. If you care deeply, that passion will shine through."

Elaine Marie Alphin

Day By Day

"The best professional strategy for writing and publishing children's books, is to do some kind of writing work every single day. It could be writing, researching, editing, responding to editors' queries, scheduling author visits, or just looking at children's books in the bookstore or library to see what's being published."

Deborah Lee Rose

The Bottom Line

"Want to know my secret? BIC. That's right. BIC. Butt in chair. There is no other single thing that will help you more to become a writer."

Jane Yolen

Brushed Your Teeth? Write About It.

"Write it all down! Keep that loose-leaf notebook next to you. I wrote so much before I was published. It was my learning ground. Something I actually wrote when I was fourteen and finished in college, eventually became a book of poetry, called *The Other Side: Shorter Poems*. Your early work means something."

Angela Johnson

Read this Book and Lots of Others

"The trick is to read a lot! That's better than any kind of textbook. Don't just read one author. Read all kinds of authors and soak up their styles."

R. L. Stine

Good Advice

"The most important trait for realizing a dream of writing for children is persistence."

SuAnn Kiser

All the World is a Stage

"Playwriting is a genre for wordsmiths, for it is dialogue alone that must convey the thought of the play, unlike a novelist's narrative description or an essayist's detailed background information. Plays are a far more verbal form than visual, as distinct from film. Only the words of the play and the author's terse stage directions last in the published form. The concrete visual elements: the sets, costumes and lighting are ephemeral, disappearing at the end of the run. Each time the play is mounted, these visual components alter as do the sound effects and the specific casting. This brings an extraordinary vitality and a collaborative creativity to the experience.

"My advice to any playwright, is to read, read read plays—classics and contemporary and to attend as much professional theater as possible. If you're new to this genre, join a reputable amateur theater group, or sign up for theater classes at a local university or community center to experience all different aspects of mounting a show.

"If your play gets produced, watch the production to make sure that the spirit of your script is intact, and the text hasn't been altered without your permission. The latter happens more often than you'd think, despite the Dramatists Guild regulations and copyright laws. Also watch the audience to see what impact the play has on them, and try to hear what they say afterwards."

Joanna H. Kraus

Get Organized

"I figure my priority for each day, each week. I'm usually working on many projects. For instance, this week I finished a *Cam Jansen* and sent it off and worked on a rewrite of a biography. One of my outlines for a future book is at my publisher now. As soon as it comes back, I'll get to work on that book. I haven't asked my editor for the notes on the outline. She thinks I am very patient. I'm not. I'm just very busy! But all the time between rewrites is good for my work. Each time I come back to a project, hopefully I'm able to give it a fresh look."

David Adler

3

You've Got Writer's Block! Now what?

Have you ever stared at an empty page or blank computer screen, without being able to write? Ever write yourself into a sticky situation where you couldn't get out? Have you ever thought you were lazy, undisciplined, or lacking talent? Well, stop the self-name calling and check out what these children's writers have to say about the subject.

The Sound of Music

"Music helps me feel creative. A couple of years ago, I attended symphony open rehearsals during the day, to help my writing. While musicians practiced on stage, I wrote in my notebook.

"Now, as soon as I hear classical music, I feel the compulsion to write. I've conditioned myself to write with the sound of music."

Elizabeth Koehler-Pentacoff

Maybe or Maybe Not . . .

"I don't think I have it, but sometimes I have periods when I don't write because I'm discouraged. That's me looking at every available excuse not to write. I'm so involved with the Society [Society of Children's Book Writers and Illustrators], I'm here all day stuffing envelopes. It's so much easier to stuff an envelope than it is to start a book. Intellectually, writing is fun, but the starting of it is painful."

Stephen Mooser

So What?

"If I have writer's block, I write anyhow."

David Lubar

Don't Got It!

"I never have writer's block. I have more ideas than I have time to develop. The hard part is turning them into the beginning, middle and end. Ideas are easy. Now see if you can turn them into a book!"

Joan Holub

Who Are You, Anyway?

"If I don't know my character well enough, then I'll have writer's block. That's a clear sign I haven't delved deep enough into the personalities of my characters. You have to completely understand their motivations. Not only *who* they are, but *why*. I have a character questionnaire; I ask myself thirty-five questions about each character, filling pages and pages with ideas. Other times I'll sit down and step into the head of the character and have her write to me, telling me about herself. If neither of these activities works, then I know the story isn't important enough for me to tell."

Lee Wardlaw

I Think I Can, I Think I Can...Puff Puff Puff...Choo Choo...

"Most of us don't feel good unless we're writing. Try to write if you can, but if it is unbearable, then read and find your inspiration in the work of other authors. Or read something you can say, *I can do this*. I remember Tennessee Williams said, 'For every one successful play I've written, I've written ten rotten ones.' "

Marilyn Sachs

Leftie

"I ask writing friends and kids, what did I do that you like? Then I start scribbling or walking. I also write with my left hand. It's something that is very difficult for me to do."

Deborah Norse Lattimore

What's It About, Alfie?

"Before going to the computer, I take a good look at what's really the central theme of a story and try to work it in different ways. Even the early, early idea-scraps and pieces (on envelopes, paper napkins, whatever) go into one large story folder, usually with a few thumbnail sketches. I've found that the more pre-thinking and pre-planning I do, the less I seem to get stuck. For desperate times, though, I have a beautiful little daybook for scribbling down questions and frustrations about particular projects—and thoughts about writing, in general. It's been an invaluable tool."

Sarah Wilson

A Different Kind of Angel . . .
"I'm lucky. I'm not working on a deadline. If I'm stuck, I write something else, do laundry, or take a nap. Sometimes changing the channel like that will help. Writing feels like pulling teeth. Another author once wrote about writing: 'It's like an angel that sits on your shoulder.' I told Sharon Creech, for me, It's more like a tapeworm!"
Karen Cushman

No Such Thing
"I don't believe in writer's block. It's just a matter of sitting down and telling yourself you're going to write. I keep ideas in store for later. I scribble something on a piece of paper and stick it in my ideas file. If I'm stuck for a story idea, I can go through that file. I write on at least two stories at a time."
Suzanne Williams

Frying Pan Motivator
"I never had blocks. When it was time to write something—remember the frying pan? That took care of any possible block! It's important that you *not* be critical of what you're doing. Sit down and do it. You can go back and correct it."
Ed Radlauer

Finally—Someone Just Like Me!
"Yes, I get it. It is triggered by rejection which paralyzes me. Sometimes I cry. Sometimes I suffer through until the paralysis goes away. I don't cope successfully. I wish I knew how! The books I read don't really help me."
Sue Alexander

Misery Loves Company
"I get miserable! I drive my wife crazy. If I had advice I'd listen to myself! I keep all my work on the computer. Every story has its own folder. I start clicking through things I haven't sold or finished. I clean them up a little. It gives me a great feeling of accomplishment."
Bruce Balan

Cleanest Author Contest
"Retype what you wrote yesterday. Sometimes I change gears from nonfiction to fiction. Take a shower! I'm the cleanest author in La Habra. It relaxes the tension you feel. Take a walk. Ed and I dreamed up a whole series of books on a walk. "
Ruth Radlauer

Call 911

"I don't have writer's block. I have *life* block. I'm terrified I'll be glued to my keyboard one day and the house will burn down around me and I won't even notice."
Gennifer Choldenko

Take My Book...Please . . .

"I may have a hot idea and not be able to have time to write it, since I'm often busy with other writing related chores. New writers don't realize that you spend a lot of time promoting the book, selling it, reviewing royalties, doing paper work. Also, I'm working on more than one project at a time. That helps writer's block. If I am blocked, I put the manuscript away and come back to it another time. Many of my manuscripts don't make it into final version."
Ellen Jackson

In the Groove . . .

"I get illustrator's block. I have a love/hate relationship with illustrating. I think I love it best when it's all done. The best advice I can give on getting over any kind of block, is to stay seated at your worktable. Do not go look in the refrigerator. Do not snip off your split ends one by one. Do not decide that now would be the best time to clean out that kitchen drawer. Just stay seated, stay focused, and have faith. Sometimes that is extremely difficult, having faith, but by simply sticking it out and staying there, ideas do start to come through, images do start to look the way you want them to, and suddenly you're back in the groove and happy to be doing what you do."
Eve Aldridge

Soccer Is the Cat's Meow

"Illustrator's block crops up about two seconds after I've signed the contract for a new project! It's merely that terror of the blank page that many creatives face, and I know I'll get over it eventually. For me, having a few simple preparation rituals helps. I'll straighten my work area, make sure I have the materials I'll need for the project at hand and then thumb through my reference files for things I might use for inspiration. At that point I'm ready to settle down to some brainstorming and rough sketches. Some of the initial sketches often become paper balls that I use to play "soccer" with my three cats. As to advice, try on work habits of other artists or writers if you wish, but don't walk around in them if they pinch you about the neck or if they puddle around your feet and make you trip."
Nancy Barnet

Money Talks

"I've never had the luxury of having writer's block. When I do, I think about my mortgage! No words equals no income. This isn't to say that there aren't times when I'm almost pulling out my hair or banging my head on my desk, but I support myself through my writing. Sometimes I'll try something new, get a massage, treat myself to a day at the movies, go on an extended bike ride, read a book and not allow myself to return to the computer until I finish it. I would also suggest reading Julia Cameron's *The Artist's Way* and practice its advice."

Larry Dane Brimner

Crunchy Clue

"I have a wonderful husband! When I get stuck, or try to tie things together, we brainstorm. In *Sisters of Mercy*, I put in a carrot-chomping dog. The carrot is thrown like a stick. When no one throws it, the dog will eat it. Sammy hated throwing the carrots, they were so slobbery. I knew it [the carrot] had to have a purpose. It drove me nuts. Finally, I took a carrot out of the refrigerator. I sat down and held the carrot! It was cold. It turned out to be a major clue. The carrot started as a tool and wound up developing into a clue. I really had to think about it."

Wendelin Van Draanen

Free Associate

"I never have illustrator's block. I can always illustrate. I never have writer's block, either, because I free associate. Now whether it's good or not, is different. If I have a story-making block, I put the story away and try not to think of it consciously. I get ideas when I take a walk or when I do the dishes. Sometimes I make snippets that don't form a story, but they are compost for another story. Keep thinking. Stop working! Let your unconscious help you. If you're REALLY blocked, stop thinking AND stop working. Look at a picture and think *what if* about it.

Elisa Kleven

Click Your Heels and Say Three Times...It's Just a Rough Draft...

"I'm familiar with two kinds of writer's block. The first I struggled with for years—this was before I began to write for children. Looking back, I can see clearly that it was a lack of confidence in myself that made it so difficult to work. This happens when my internal critic is too active. I now use a kind of mantra while I'm working: It's just a rough draft, it's just a rough draft....

The other kind of writer's block is when I am stuck at a particular place in a novel and something is just not going right. I usually turn to another project for awhile—I've always got several going at once. When I return I find the problem is still there, but it's simply 'the right time' to plough ahead until I see my way clear.

"With three children and many volunteer activities competing with my writing time, I don't really have time for writer's block. On those rare times when I'm stuck, or the words aren't coming quickly, I just sit down at my computer and write —even if I only write a paragraph or two a day."

Debbie Duncan

Yep—Those Murky Middles

"I get writer's block, but it's not exactly the way most people think of it. When I write a long novel, I will sometimes get stuck and I can't see how to get myself out of whatever I got myself into. I will puzzle and puzzle. I'm lucky, for I can leave it and start a picture book that's been in my mind. I do something else and pretty soon my block goes away and I can go back to it again."

Eve Bunting

More Middle Muddle

"If I get stuck in the middle, I put the story aside for awhile, and start brain-storming ideas or questions for myself around the "stuck" part. Why does my character want to do something? I free-write on this question."

Suzanne Williams

Middle Muddle Solution

"Write hooks and chapter leads. The first and last line of each chapter will help you map out your plot. It helps those soggy middles."

Susan Hart Lindquist

It's Okay, You're Okay

"Trust the process. Acknowledge your doubts and then write anyway. Every-one goes through it. You're in good company when you experience doubt—we've all been there. Read. Especially books that are similar to your own style. Nothing gets me out of that murky valley faster than reading a good book. It inspires me. I think, 'I can do that!'

"Understand the structure of a story, know how the plot works. The murky middle is nine tenths of the book, not just one third, so you better know the me-chanics of story."

Mary Pearson

Maui Anyone?

"I live in a constant state of writer's block. It's only with the greatest struck of good luck that a story muscles its way through my defense mechanisms.

"If you have illustrator's block, go to a really new environment. Change the scene! I grew up on the East Coast and that's familiar to me. So I went to the Southwest. I loved the light and the different plants and animals and red rock. It gives me different smells and flowers and light. Hawaii is wonderful, but I haven't been able to use it yet, to write it off on my taxes!"

Ashley Wolff

Dirty House = Great Book. Clean House = Writer's Block

"Writer's block has never been a problem until recently. I've become so critical of my own writing, I have difficulty writing a sentence without rewriting it at least twice and often more, before I move to the next sentence. Sometimes I can't think what will happen next and I abandon manuscripts. Sometimes everything I write seems dull and trite. I either work my way through the block or take time off to do other things—like scrub the kitchen floor or clean out the closets. A visitor can tell at a glance how my writing is going. If the house is clean and orderly, the writing's in disarray—and vice versa!"

Mary Downing Hahn

To Every Season

"After my father died, I went through a dull, gray period. My writing stopped. Concerned, I asked an artist whom I respected, what to do. She invited me to her flower garden. The earth was brown and bare and crusted.

"I looked at her blankly. 'I don't see anything.'

'No, but in a few months it'll be a riot of color. The garden needs fallow periods. So do we,' she said."

Joanna H. Kraus

Around the Block

"I've found that immersing myself in other creative pursuits—without any pressure to write—is most helpful. Reading, for me, is also a block buster. Words jazz me up and I feel like I just *have* to write something when I read. Usually, I'll write in my journal and that will eventually be a springboard to a new project, or help me get unstuck on a stalled project. When all else fails, I walk and walk and walk. Walking is great tension relieving, head clearing, spiritual boosting activity—and it keeps you fit too."

Maureen Boyd Biro

Feel the Burn?

"I like to run, but walking or any other kind of repetitive physical movement works for me. Very often, those switches flip back on, the doors in my mind start flying open, and my biggest problem becomes remembering all the ideas that came while running."

Ann Manheimer

Computer-ease

"I always start a writing project by creating three to four documents on my computer disk, where I'll keep a novel. I make a separate subdirectory per novel. One document is the manuscript, the novel or picture book itself. I make numbered copies for each major revision. One document is called my 'journal,' another is my 'workbook,' and sometimes a fourth is called 'research.' Then I begin writing.

"I believe the best way to rid yourself of writer's block, is to write anything that comes into your head. So what if it's not relevant to your story? If I don't know what to write next in my book, I turn to my journal. The journal is the main 'anti-writer's block' document. That's where I brainstorm the story when I'm starting off. It's also where I put my mini-outlines. I don't write from an outline, but when I'm into the book, I often know what's coming next, and I can outline as much as I know. Most importantly, it's where I rid myself of blocks. I write how I'm feeling about the book, or myself, or about anything. As long as I'm writing, I'm stimulating my creative subconscious and breaking through the block.

"If I'm working through a scene that's not turning out quite right, rather than stare at the screen and risk getting blocked, I go ahead and write out the scene in my 'manuscript' document. If I hate it or it's not quite right, I lift it out and place it in the 'workbook' document, just in case I change my mind and want to use all or pieces of it. I date it and note the draft number and page. Then I rewrite the scene. Sometimes I have to do this several times. I use this process a lot when writing picture books, especially rhyming books. I keep all the versions of a stanza, even the awful ones. The continuous process of writing, even if the writing is bad, is what keeps me from getting blocked."

Marisa Montes

Remember What?

"If I'm stuck on a story, I go back and remember what I was trying to do originally. Usually I'll find that without meaning to, I've gotten away from my original premise."

Joan Bauer

The Beatles were Right—Let It Be

"A couple of years ago, I went about eighteen months not writing anything. I really couldn't force myself. I just left it alone. I think if you actively try to deal with it, you aren't doing yourself any good. One day I just started writing again—I think I wrote a poem. And it all came."

Angela Johnson

Bad Books Aren't so Bad After All

"I work on different projects. I've got five books in progress right now, and if

I'm blocked on one, I move to another. They're various genres so they take different thought processes. If that doesn't work, I reread one of my favorite books, something that inspires me with its great writing. Sometimes a poorly written book will inspire me, too. I think, 'Yuck, I could do better than that!'"

Linda Kay Weber

Make a Splash!
"I get lazy about writing, the way I get lazy about anything, like cleaning house or flossing my teeth. The only way to cope is to jump in and do it."

Janet Wong

We All Scream for Ice Cream
"Scream. Eat. Scream some more. Call a friend. Eat again. Quit writing. Eat some more. I have three or four projects going at once so I try to make a change from fiction to nonfiction or from picture book to novel. Sometimes just going back and doing some research will trigger a new thought and get me rolling again. If I'm having trouble with a particular aspect of writing on a project, say scenes or dialog or something identifiable, I'll often pull a few writing books off my shelf and see what they have to say about it. If it's close to the end of the work day, I'll stop and give myself a sleep suggestion about the problem before I go to bed. Often that will wake up my subconscious so that in the morning I can break through the block."

Susan Taylor Brown

Fiction Friction
"When I get stuck on a scene, I'll ask my character an important question. Often, it's about fear. *'Why are you afraid to argue with your mother?'* None of us really likes conflict, but that's where all the story-juice is."

Kathleen Duey

Sweet Dreams
"Lynn Reid Bank has said, when she's blocked, she asks herself what the essential question is just before she goes to sleep. *'Often, by morning, I have the answer,'* she says.

"There is a magical unconscious process that doesn't happen in a state of stress or suffering.

You get rushes of creativity and you feel you're entertained by your own mind. You have to be patient for that to happen. For me, that doesn't necessarily happen at eight o'clock every morning."

Lin Oliver

4

Story Starters

Need some ideas to write about? Here they are:

Suspense
"Drop a character into a dangerous situation where the wrong information, leaked out, will cause trouble."
Stephen Mooser

Free Write
"Open a newspaper, book or magazine and pick a word. Start writing from that word. No second picks! If you pick a second pick you're already cheating."
Ed Radlauer

Nonfiction
"A good nonfiction exercise would be to take a topic and write five sentences, with one sentence for each of the five senses."
Caroline Arnold

Outline
"Practice writing nonfiction outlines. You really need them to sell your idea to an editor and then to work from as you write your book. You may end up changing things around, but at least you have something to guide you along the way."
Loretta Ichord

Personal Experience
"Write regularly in a journal, to help find your writer's voice."
Sneed B. Collard III

Rich Language
"The writing exercise I like to use most often with children is one in metaphor and simile; I ask kids to turn a person into a plant, animal or object. Metaphor and

simile are poetic techniques that most people use daily, without effort—'that busy bee,' 'stubborn as a rock.' It's easy to use these techniques in prose, to modify and build on them."

Janet Wong

Fresh Ideas

"One of my favorites for helping students discover what they want to say to young readers: Complete this thought—*If I could tell the world just one thing....*

"It sounds simple. But my students lose all track of time as they passionately scribble about not just one, but *every* thing they would tell the world. By the time they are done, they have explored enough themes and life lessons to keep them in writing ideas for a long while."

SuAnn Kiser

Merrily We Go Along

"...take a nursery rhyme or song that you are familiar with and rewrite it with your own words."

Susan Taylor Brown

Method Acting

"While doing writing exercises, write them from the point of view from a character in the novel you're writing."

Elizabeth Koehler-Pentacoff

Cinderella's Novella

"Look at a long list of words in the rhyming dictionary. *Can a story could be written from them?* Example: A Little Novella about Cinderella. She had two ugly stepsisters Stella and Della, and very mean stepmother, Queen Isabella."

Teri Sloat

Setting

"...pick a mundane location, and then try to describe it as thoroughly as possible, using all five senses. You'll find there's no such thing as a mundane location, if you describe it effectively."

Neal Shusterman

Featuring Sid Fleischman

Sid Fleischman is a screenwriter as well as an award-winning children's author. His books include the McBroom series, *Bandit's Moon*, *Bo and Mzzz Mad*, *The Ghost in the Noonday Sun*, the 1987 Newbery book, *The Whipping Boy*, and his autobiography, *Abracadabra Kid*.

In your autobiography, The Abracadabra Kid, *you mentioned that you heard your first tall tale from Professor Fait, a magician who told a tale of a canoe that threw him like a bronco. Since that time, you've written several tall tales over the years, and have perfected the art of the tall tale. What have you learned about this art of exaggeration that might be helpful for writers who'd like to write them? What makes a good tall tale?*

"Tall tales are highly specialized humor. You need to be awfully good, for the classic tales you compete with are superb. Take Jim Bridger (he really lived) who discovered that it took eight hours for an echo to return from a distant mountain. He turned it into an alarm clock by shouting "Wake up!" before he went to bed. The next morning, eight hours later, the echo returned and woke him up. What distinguishes that comic fantasy from nonsense is the bedrock of reality—echoes are real. Can more be done with the echo idea? Of course. You have to think around it and up over it and so forth. That's how I found my way to the additional tales in my *Jim Bridger's Alarm Clock and Other Tall Tales*. And, of course, the tall tale teller must never laugh at his own jokes. He must narrate the tale as solemn truth."

You've said, "Like classic fantasy, comic fantasy has its taproot in the real world." In McBroom's Ghost, *it was so cold "...Polly dropped her comb on the floor, when she picked it up the teeth were chattering." Do you brainstorm on the themes of your tales to come up with original comparisons? What exercise could writers try to encourage their own outlandish comparisons?*

"Yes, I mull over the theme to see what can be squeezed from it. I first try to find all the traditional material on a subject and take off from there. Windy? So windy, what? Finally: a wind blows off hats—reality. A bronze statue of Abe Lincoln—the wind blew off his hat. This tall tale conceit appears in one of my books somewhere.

"If you attempt to write a tall tale, don't expect miracles. Tall tale humor is the head-scratching-est form of comedy to write."

When you visited Truckee on your magician's tour, and you thought about that long ago Donner Party, you said your "sense of living history was launched." Do you have any advice to give about writing or researching historical fiction?

"Drama is an equal opportunity writer's migraine. Historical fiction is distinguished from regular fiction only by all those out-of-date clothes. You still have to come up with characters who engage us and scenes that carry us along. In researching, I keep an eye out for the revealing or odd and interesting detail. For example, in country stores of the past, shoes were sold in barrels. There were no right and left shoes until modern times. Only once you wore them did the shoes shape themselves. How to use a detail like that? That's an opportunity for the historical novelist.

"I create a notebook for each book I write, and fill it with details, from research. That includes sections for the price of things. What did a pair of shoes in a country store cost? You need to know stuff like that. But beneath all that, in historical as well as contemporary fiction, are the demands of structure, pacing, rhythms, etc."

When you wrote Mr. Mysterious and Company, *you said "...it was the first sustained comic writing I have done. It fixed my style and gave me a literary voice of my own." Upon reading your autobiography, I was struck by how you managed to capture your own, unique voice within that work of nonfiction. I believe I actually heard your voice telling me your life story in my ear! That illusive term, voice, is most difficult for writers to grasp. Can you define voice and give some advice or suggestions on how writers can develop their own voice?*

"We all have one [literary voice] even if we're so new at writing that our voice hasn't yet changed. I don't think you find voice. *It* finds *you.* I have never worried about it. I suppose when I first began to write I tried to impress the reader with my lubricious and unshorn adjectives. I would never do that today. My voice has changed."

You are known for your fabulous humor in your books. What humorous techniques are your favorites, and how can other writers encourage their own humor?

"I know nothing about the techniques of humor, except the use of surprise. As far as I know, the writer is able to make comic connections. For example, in writing about the 1994 Los Angeles earthquake in *The Abracadabra Kid*, I said that the shake had straightened all the pictures on the wall. That was a connection."

In your autobiography, you say you "write the first page once, twice, ten or twenty times before I get everything as right as I can. Only then do I move on to the second page and the third....When I reach the last page, the novel is done—almost done." If you don't rely on plot on outlines, how do you keep all of your subplots and threads straight?

"Writing without an outline is not as difficult as it looks. Even though you are improvising from day to day, you stay alert. As the direction of the novel begins to reveal itself, you make sure that the scenes follow the arrows. You toss out extraneous stuff as soon as you recognize blind alleys and detours. But this writing method is not for everyone. For those who use an outline, I would have to ask with the same sense of mystery: how in heck do you stick to the outline?"

You've said, "Imagery is powerful shorthand." How can writers deepen their own writing with figurative language?

"It's hard to think up fresh figures of speech at first—but it gets easier. You develop something like muscles for it. But it's still hard."

Easy Readers

Doug Cushman has illustrated over eighty children's books, writing about a dozen of them, including the Aunt Eater and Inspector Hopper easy reader series. Some of his other books are *Hello Red Fox*, *Flora and the Tiger* and *From Head to Toe*. As a teenager, as he made comic books about his teachers, selling them to his schoolmates for a nickel a piece.

What comes first when you begin a project?

"I usually start with a character, sketched out in one or five or six sketch books scattered around the studio (and my various travel bags). I like to think my books are character driven; everything begins and ends with a strong character. A setting may set off an idea for a book as well. In many books, the setting is really the main character. (Think of the Mississippi River in *Huckleberry Finn*.) In *Inspector Hopper*, Hopper was the first character I developed. (I loved his long legs and goofy fedora in my first sketches.) But as I worked up the bug-sized setting, more and more ideas appeared. The insect world has many, many varied creatures. The hard part was to pick and choose the best ones."

Does being an illustrator help your process?

"Many decisions are visual, which ones would be the most fun to draw? I'm an artist first. I like to see things. One of the funniest drawings I think I've done in a book is one where Aunt Eater is hugging her sister Eliza. There are these two round little characters hugging with their long noses arching off in opposite directions. It's a hoot."

So how do you write an easy reader?

"Lillian Hoban once said that writing an easy reader is like giving someone

EASY READER MARKET RESEARCH

"Don't tell too much. Make it short and simple. Some editors don't really understand beginning readers as well as someone who has taught. We tested our subject matter. We ask children to let us know what they like. By letter, they've told us what they like to read. My husband [author Ed Radlauer] used to stand around a magazine rack and see what kids were reading. Don't forget librarians and school teachers. They can tell you what they need. Study curriculum guides. Know what social studies includes in the different grades.

With easy readers, my talent is simplification. It's important where you break your lines, how you use repetition."

Ruth Radlauer

directions to your house. It's a 'first you do this, then you turn here, then you turn there, and finally you arrive at my house' thinking process. It's linear. No flash-backs, no pausing for reflections. It's all action and dialogue. I like to say that I write what I can't draw. For instance, why would I write, 'Aunt Eater watched the red sun set behind the purple hills as she pondered her latest mystery' when I can draw a red, setting sun, purple hills and Aunt Eater thinking? Then all I would need to write is, 'This is a real mystery,' said Aunt Eater."

What has inspired your Aunt Eater series?

"Many books come from my own love of reading. I love mysteries. Agatha Christie's Miss Marple was an inspiration for Aunt Eater. And I love terrible puns! At that point in my career, I was sick to death of drawing cute little bunnies and bears and mice. I wanted to do an odd creature. An anteater fit the bill. I sometimes outsmart myself, however. As I was working up the dummy for the first Aunt Eater, my editor pointed to a drawing and said, 'Can you make Aunt Eater happier in this picture?' *I thought, how do you make someone without a mouth smile?*"

How will a writer know if their book fits a reading level?

"I've had many discussions with my editor about reading levels. I don't believe in them. It's purely for marketing in my opinion. A good book is a good book no matter what reading level is attached. I've had so many parents say, 'Oh this is a level two book. My child is a level three.' I can almost hear the 'nayah, nayah, nayah' in their voices! Their child is missing out on some great literature. I'm not just talking about my own work either. I don't bother with reading levels when I'm writing. I just try to write a good, entertaining story. The best judge is to look and study what's been done. Anything by Arnold Lobel, James Marshall, or Lillian Hoban for example. Study the rhythm of the language. And the pacing. Most authors are clueless regarding pacing in a picture book and easy reader. It's hard to explain. Study the masters."

What's your favorite easy reader that you've written?

"I don't have a favorite easy reader that I wrote. They all work on different levels for me. Aunt Eater has done very well for me and kids seem to like her. The first *Aunt Eater, Aunt Eater Loves a Mystery*, has a warm place in my heart because she started it all. *Inspector Hopper* is new. There's more that can be done with him I think."

How do you submit your easy readers?

"After twenty years I still submit a full blown dummy, text, sketches, and everything. It's more work, but it's the best way for the editor to understand what I am trying to do. I set the pace, the pictures and words in the dummy. Each element must play off of the other, work together like an orchestra, or better, a trio or quartet. One element is not more important than the other. If an author thinks her words are so damned important, why bother having pictures in the first place? The same with the artist. Too many books are out there with beautiful pictures and no story, no real story, just a thinly realized plot to hang a bunch of gallery paintings together. That's not book making. It's vanity."

What are some specifics regarding format?

"I always submit my *I Can Read* manuscripts in the short line format, double spaced, the whole works. My manuscripts are usually twelve to fourteen pages in length. I break up the story in chapters, so I might end a chapter on one page and start another one on the next page. Thus one manuscript page may have only three or four lines.

The basic format of the *ICR* is thirteen lines per page, thirty-six characters per line (including spaces and punctuation). The separations are usually between clauses, but if one reads a few *ICRs* you'll get the idea. *ICRs* are usually sixty-four pages but there are some with forty-eight. My manuscripts usually run about fourteen pages or less for a sixty-four page book. Anything beyond that is too much. There are forty-eight and thirty-two page formats now. As my editor says, 'Just write a good story. We'll go from there.'"

What Is the Best Writing Advice You've Ever Received?

Take the Plunge

"Don't censor yourself up front. Let all ideas come out no matter how bizarre. As you go through the process of creating and building your story whether in words or pictures, the ideas that really don't work will drop off. Some ideas that you discarded in the beginning, may turn out to be the best ones."

Eve Aldridge

Sensual Music

"My poetry teacher, Philip Levine, said, 'Each line should sing on the page.' If your eye gazes over a line of prose and it doesn't do anything to your senses and it doesn't do anything for you, that's weak writing. Don't allow abstract language to tell your story."

Gary Soto

Time and Time Again

"Multiple submissions work. Who has time to wait for responses one by one? Life is too short."

Angelica Carpenter

Let's Hear It for Nonfiction

"Caroline Arnold told me to consider nonfiction as an avenue into publishing."

Larry Dane Brimner

Writing Responsibly

"Listen to your readers and pay attention to their reactions. When I was young and arrogant about my writing, I assumed if the reader didn't get something, the reader was at fault. It was quite a discovery to realize that, if communication fails, it's more the fault of the writer than the reader. I've found this incredibly helpful. Writing is an art, but it is a form of communication. If the communication fails, then the art has failed."

Elaine Marie Alphin

Best and Worst Advice

"Possibly the best and worst writing advice I ever got was the same advice from the same person: Thacher Hurd. When I was just starting out, he advised me to write chapter books instead of picture books, because they were easier to sell. I ignored him and went on to publish a good number of picture books—but now I'd like to write chapter books and novels, and I wonder whether I would have done better to follow his advice!"

Aaron Shepard

"The best advice I ever received was, 'Don't be a children's writer. You'll never earn a living.' It was also the worst advice."

Alexis O'Neill

♥ *Your Writing*

"'Write from the heart.' I believe if you write from your heart you will find, or make, a market for your work."

Wendelin Van Draanen

Aim High

"The best advice for writing for children's magazines I ever got, was from Rob Criscell, my former editor at *Highlights for Children*. He said, 'When you write nonfiction, shoot for the top.' He meant go to the most shining, best respected expert you can find and ask for that interview. To my great surprise, even as a fledgling writer, those sources usually said yes."

Kelly Milner Halls

Audience First

"Please yourself, but don't forget that you are writing or illustrating for children. Remember what you loved as a child."

Elisa Kleven

More than Prose

"Myra Cohn Livingston told me, over and over, 'You must read.' I remember saying, I *am* reading in a very defensive way, and she answered, 'you need to read more.' She gave so much good advice. Much of it is in her book *Poem-Making*.

'Can you put a little music into it?' 'How is this not just arranged prose?' I think of her lessons often."
Janet Wong

Channeling

"Dancer Martha Graham once said something to the effect, that every artist has a unique message to convey which no one else in the world can relay to our society, and our job as artists, is to 'keep the channel open' so that the message can come through us. This has been very helpful to me when I was tempted to compare myself to other writers."
Katherine Sturtevant

Just Do It

"Write every day. Write what you know."
Debbie Duncan

"Write every day. Paul Fleischman told me he writes seven days a week—even if it's only for a little while on weekends. That advice has stuck with me and I aspire to be a seven-day-a-week writer!"
Caryn Yacowitz

"Write every day—it's like exercise. It keeps you toned."
Tricia Gardella

"Write all the time. Write every day. Don't edit yourself in the first draft."
Linda Kay Weber

With a Twist

"The best sentence I ever heard is 'Write what you know.' My personal best advice to anyone would be, write what you're hungry for."
Margaret O'Hair

"I guess the advice I was given that I didn't like was, to draw and write about what I know. I didn't want to hear that. But you can take what you know and tweak it."
Ashley Wolff

"Write what you know. If you take this to mean that you should learn everything you can about your subject matter before you write about it."
Kevin Kiser

"Write from your heart."
Mary Downing Hahn

She Said Loudly, Shrilly, Glaringly, Noisily, Piercingly...

"Technically, I love the trick I learned from poet, Adam David Miller. Always question your use of adverbs. Few are worth the space they take. For nonfiction, from my editor, Pam Zumwalt, 'Watch out for your own point of view. Let your readers draw conclusions for themselves.' For fiction, from novelist Franny Billingsley: 'Make sure what your character wants cuts through the whole story like a blade.'"
Suzanne Morgan Williams

Mine the Memories

"Write what you know. I would expand that to write what you've *felt*. Go back to your childhood. Were you ever the new kid? I was not. I went to the same schools with the same kids for thirteen years. But the thing I felt, was being labeled and not being able to shed my image for a new one. So I could write about being stuck as the smart kid or the shy kid or the dorky kid, because I was all of the above."
Susan Middleton Elya

No Rest for the Writer

"After I sold my first book, another writer congratulated me and in the next breath said, 'Now, get busy writing the next book." *What? Wait a minute! I want to sit and rest on my laurels a bit!* But I followed her advice anyway, and now I've come to realize that getting a book published isn't the end all of everything. Getting four, or ten or twenty books published isn't the end all. It's the writing and how you grow with each book. I'm so glad I followed that advice and got right back to a writing routine."
Mary Pearson

No Way to Say it Better

"'Write a shitty first draft,' from Ann Lamott's *Bird by Bird*."
Karen Romano Young

"The best advice I've ever come across for any kind of writing is from Anne Lamott's book, *Bird by Bird*. She says to write just one inch at a time. I love that! It's so easy to be overwhelmed by a big project, but if I only have to concentrate on one inch, and only hold myself accountable for one inch, well, that I can handle. Eventually those inches will be feet and yards and whatever it takes to make a book. This is true for research, too, which can be overwhelming."
Maureen Boyd Biro

HA HA!

"I spent a week in New York and Boston pounding the pavement for face to face meetings with editors. I was carrying both manuscripts and an illustration portfolio, hoping to become published on the merits of one or the other, but ideally, both. The best advice came from a meeting I miraculously obtained with the great editor, Walter Lorraine at Houghton Mifflin.

"I sensed right away that he was wondering why he had agreed to see me. And I didn't know whether to thank Edite Kroll for the recommendation or to curse her for getting me to drive from New York City to Boston for what was clearly going to be a three-minute meeting, if indeed I could somehow drag it out that long. Walter promptly dismissed my folder of manuscripts and flopped my portfolio onto the heap of papers strewn across the desk. He flipped through my artwork fast enough to stir a breeze in his office.

"Suddenly, he paused at one drawing for a nanosecond and said, 'That's funny!' Then, more quickly than ever, he was through the portfolio and through with me and I was out the door. I don't know whether 'That's funny!' constitutes advice or not, but I remembered it as if he had said, 'Do that!' The drawing he had liked was from a short poem of mine about a little girl who awakens to discover she's green. Years later, I turned that poem into my book, *Green Wilma*."

Tedd Arnold

Five Tips

"The hardest part about writing is simply to *begin*.

"Do three things a day to further your writing career.

"It's impossible to know what a book is 'really' about until the first draft is finished. Once you start adding layers of depth and discovering connections, the book's true theme emerges, and often, it catches you by surprise.

"Trust the process and let it happen.

"Listen to suggestions, and your inner editor, and don't balk at rewriting."
Dian Curtis Regan

Take It Seriously

"The best advice came from an instructor in a class on travel writing, who said a personal rejection letter meant the editor liked your writing, wanted you to send her other things. It made me look at rejection letters as a stepping stone to a success, rather than a failure."

JoAnne Stewart Wetzel

Calm and Collected

"Put the scene you just feverishly finished, away for a few days. Come back to it. Read it aloud and revise with a surgeon's detachment."

Joanna H. Kraus

When the Going Gets Tough

"Be thick-skinned. Not everyone will love what you do. Persevere! Don't let a bad review or a rejection slip discourage you."

Daniel San Souci

"Writing success comes to those with a little talent and a whole lot of bone-headed persistence."

Ann Manheimer

Follow the Rules

"There are many rules on what you must do to write a good book. None of them is right."

Marisa Montes

Any Time Is the Right Time

"Write when you feel like it and write when you *don't* feel like it. Sit your butt in the chair!"

Joan Bauer

That Ticking Clock

"The best advice I ever got came from the science fiction writer, Kate Wilhelm. Speaking as one married female writer to another, she said, 'Set aside a block of time every day just for writing and guard it ferociously.' If I didn't stick to that advice, I would never produce anything, because every single day I deal with hundreds of other demands on my time. Most of those demands come complete with people who are ready and willing to make my life immediately and acutely unpleasant if I don't meet them. Whereas, since I prefer to write on spec, nobody cares if I don't write except me."

Nancy Etchemendy

A Novel Experience

"The only advice anyone has ever given me was from Cynthia Rylant. She said,

'It's time for you to write a novel.' Then I *did* write my first novel. I didn't think I'd ever write one! I thought picture books were the only things I'd ever do."
Angela Johnson

"Enjoy the process."
Susan Taylor Brown

Out of the Zone

"The best advice I was ever given was by my professor, Oakley Hall, at UC Irvine. He told me to expand into other genres. To try writing everything. If you're focused on science fiction, then do a romance next. If you're into historical fiction, then write a fantasy. Master as many different genres and as many different types of writing as you can, because the more well-rounded you are as a writer, the better a writer you'll be. Force yourself out of your own comfort zone!"
Neal Shusterman

Style is Everything

"After high school, I took a portfolio to New York and spent the day going to various publishers. A Random House editor told me to stick to my own way of drawing and work on telling stories in my own style. The trade editors were not so encouraging because they spoke about my cartoony way of drawing and how it wasn't their style."
R.W. Alley

No Question About It

"When my daughter, Louisa was just a few months old, in a moment of creative frustration, I expressed doubt to an online children's authors group that I would ever write again. Jane Yolen was kind enough to post supportive words: 'Haemi, you will write when you are ready because you are a writer, and that is what you do.' Simple and straightforward, those few words helped me put things in perspective and enjoy my new daughter."
Haemi Balgassi

Empty Well

"Myra Cohn Livingston, who taught a UCLA poetry class for many years, said, 'Give the well time to fill up again.' She was talking about those horrible times most of us experience when the writing well runs dry, when the ideas stop flowing and nothing you put down on paper is worth a thing. That permission to rest, to give the well time to fill also gives me an excuse to spend that time reading. In fact, it's often in the process of reading, when I'm lost in admiration for the brilliance of someone else's writing, that I become so jazzed about the whole process that I can't wait to get back to work myself."

Alice Schertle

Go for it!

"Sid Fleischman once said, 'In writing, nothing is wasted but the paper.' I think of that all the time. You don't want to rewrite. You think, *that's such a good idea, I'll leave it in.* Don't be afraid to cut it out, because you have to throw away things that aren't good. Or you might be able to use it somewhere else. Writing is part of your life process. It makes you amenable to change."

Lin Oliver

Young Readers

"Ask children you don't know to read your manuscript."

Jacque Hall

7

What's the Worst Writing Advice You've Ever Received?

One person's 'best advice' can be another's 'worst.' You be the judge.

"The worst advice is write what you know. We should qualify this. It *should* be write what you care about."
Bruce Coville

These authors agreed with Bruce. Here's their twist on 'write what you know':

"A nonfiction author can find out! A fiction writer needs personal experience with emotions. Facts can, and must, be discovered and checked."
Suzanne Morgan Williams

"Write what you know is the worst advice, because people misinterpret it to mean fiction is no more than slightly disguised autobiography."
Mary Downing Hahn

"As writers, we need to grow in our knowledge. We need to research. When I wrote about growing giant pumpkins in *Squashed*, I had to find out how to do that. And I'm telling you now, I had never grown a vegetable that lived! But I knew about growing a big dream, so I layered that onto my story."
Joan Bauer

"None of my books would exist if I hadn't followed the best advice and ignored the worst."
SuAnn Kiser

Ode to Joy

"People who say you must write every day no matter what. What a depressing concept. E.B. White once said, *'One should jump into a story the way one jumps into the ocean. Prepare to splash about and make merry.'* If you aren't joyful, why do it? Writing is a discipline, but it's really important to take time off. Cruise around the world. Enjoy your children! Cook a meal. Be intuitive, so when you *do* sit down to write, you're not bleeding. That's another lore about writing, that you have to sit down and open a vein. I don't want to be a suffering writer."

Lin Oliver

Money Talks

"Don't be an illustrator. Be a bank manager!"

Eve Aldridge

"Don't write unless you are getting paid for it."

Susan Taylor Brown

Welcome Change

"Never let anyone change your work. Actually, writing is about change and revision."

Gary Soto

Find Your Rhythm

"If you want to be a writer you have to get up every day and write for four hours in the morning. I think that's terrible advice because everyone works on their own rhythm. I do my best writing in the late afternoon or evening. Some people may only work on weekends. It's important to experiment to see when your best time is. Another piece of worst advice came from Hemingway. He said any writer worth his salt would never use a thesaurus."

Bruce Balan

To Market To Market

"'Look in the stores and see what sells and do that.' Egad! Can you think of worse advice for advancing an art form?"

R.W. Alley

"Don't do multiple submissions."

Angelica Carpenter

"'Don't multiple submit.' Ignore this very outdated advice! 'The minute your rejected manuscript returns, have another mailer ready to send it out again.' Never

do this. Always give the piece a fresh read-through. I guarantee that you will re-edit, revise, or completely revamp it."
Dian Curtis Regan

"Write to trends."
Elaine Marie Alphin

"Write for the market."
Wendelin Van Draanen

"Change an ending you know is aesthetically right, to make it more marketable."
Joanna H. Kraus

"'You have to write what the market wants.' That simply doesn't work. You can't predict what the market will want, and if you try to pander to that, rather than to your own heart, you'll end up pleasing no one, because your story won't feel authentic. Don't write what you think the readers will want to read, write what you're passionate about writing."
Neal Shusterman

Whatever Works
"'Work from an outline.' If it works for you, great, but for me it destroys my spontaneity. Then my work isn't coming from intuition. Good writing has to be intuitive. However, outlining for a basic plot is different. For picture books though, outlines for me don't work."
Elisa Kleven

Celebrate Diversity
"What has hindered me the most has been the host of generalizations that are made about writers. 'Writers are really observant.' 'Writers are loners.' 'Writers are driven to write.' I used to torment myself with these kinds of sayings, wondering whether I was a 'real' writer because they didn't seem to be true of me. When I talk to young writers, I now stress the fact that every writer is different, and I urge them to have confidence in themselves."
Katherine Sturtevant

Follow Your Passion
"Start out with magazines. I was writing a young adult novel and was told, 'You'll never break into that market. Start with something easier like magazines.' I think that is a bit insulting to all the talented magazine writers out there. Different types of writing are just that—different. Writing for magazines takes a certain kind of talent and passion

that I am not blessed with. I do, however, have a passion for YA. And I think that is always the key. Passion will keep you going in the face of rejection."
Mary Pearson

Mass x Volume = Frustration
"Write ten pages a day."
Larry Dane Brimner

Growth Spurts
"Write every day. Nothing induces more guilt for me than feeling mandated to write every day. I can't do this. I write in spurts—great bursts of creativity with long dormant times in between. This is just what works for me. The dormant times are usually 'thinking' times or times of alternate creativity—cooking, traveling, gardening, and/or letting a work 'season.' If I wrote every day, I'd write a lot that should never be read!"
Maureen Boyd Biro

"'Write every day'—ooh, the guilt when you don't!"
Tricia Gardella

"'Write something every day.' There's days when that just doesn't happen. That's okay because if you are hungry to write, you will experience days where your appetite will be unquenchable...thus the days, feast or famine, balance out."
Margaret O'Hair

SOS Parents
"'An adult shouldn't be present in children's stories.' Not all families are dysfunctional. Some parents *are* involved in their children's lives. To actually cut them out isn't good advice."
Jacque Hall

Cliché
"The worst advice came from my week-long series of meetings in New York. Another editor liked a story of mine about twin princes vying for the throne of the elderly king. This editor suggested I try a more traditional formula and have the twins competing for the hand of a princess. Basically, he was saying, 'Go for the cliche!' Despite my better instincts, I tried, because I was just so pleased that someone was even halfway interested in anything I had done. It was a mistake, and a dead-end, but it took me months of work to realize it *and* to realize that, meanwhile, the editor had lost interest anyway."
Tedd Arnold

CRUEL AND UNUSUAL PUNISHMENT

"The worst advice I ever received came from the members of a six-week workshop I attended one summer when I was still very close to the beginning of my career. The workshop consisted of twenty-four rank beginners and a different instructor each week. We spent every morning critiquing each other's stories in a round-robin fashion, where all of these young idiots who were there because they didn't know the first thing about what makes a good story, tore people's manuscripts to bits like dogs in a pit. The mortified and writhing writer had to sit there and listen in silence, because it was against the rules to defend yourself until everyone else was finished with you. The advice received in this fashion was predictably contradictory and so general as to be useless. *'I just hated this story. I don't know why.'* Even though I had already had one novel published at the time, it took me years to re-cover my confidence.

"My advice to writers who are considering joining a workshop is to proceed with great caution. A bad workshop can be far worse than no workshop at all."

Nancy Etchemendy

Musty Thinking

"The worst advice starts with 'You must . . .' For example, 'You must write everyday. You must start with a complete outline. You must know your characters intimately before putting pen to paper.' If I had to do each of these, I would never have written a word of fiction."

Marisa Montes

The Impossible Dream?

"*Don't even try to get poetry published.* I can't tell you how often I was told that. We all have dreams. To be a poet was mine. Kick the word 'never' out of your vocabulary."

Rebecca Kai Dotlich

Where's That Muse When You Need Her?

"When inspiration comes, when the muse sings, write. If I waited for my muse, I'd write about twice a year!"

Caryn Yakowitz

8

Story Behind the Story

How do authors come up with ideas and turn them into books for children?

For: **Louise the One and Only** *by Elizabeth Koehler-Pentacoff*
"Louise was born on a soccer field. While watching my son at soccer practice, I eavesdropped on a conversation between two mothers. One of them was a kindergarten teacher.

"She said, 'I am so exhausted. What a day I had!' The other mother asked her what happened. The kindergarten teacher replied, 'All of my students decided to change their names today. Lindsay was Michelle, Michelle was Jennifer. Kevin was Chris, and so on. I couldn't pass back papers or even take roll call. It was a mess!'

"At that moment, a little girl popped into my head. She said, 'I'm not Louise.' From that moment on, Louise wouldn't leave me alone. Every time I volunteered in my son's kindergarten classroom, I saw the world from a five-year-old's perspective."

For: **Monster Road** *by David Lubar*
"I had written a short story, and gave it to another author to read. She said, 'You need to say what happens next. This should be a book!" So I turned it into my chapter book, *Monster Road*. It is now my favorite book that I have written."

For: **The Thing Upstairs** *by Stephen Mooser*
"When I was ten, I took a trip with my aunt and uncle to visit the Grand Canyon. On the way, there were signs advertising THE THING. The first sign said, 'See THE THING—1000 MILES.' Later, the next sign said, 'THE THING IS COMING! 500 MILES.' The signs got bigger and bigger as you got closer to

the destination. By the time we got to THE THING there was no way we weren't going to stop!

"We pulled into this dusty desert place and inside, we found THE THING upstairs. THE THING was a shriveled body in a glass case. I'm pretty sure it was a mummified Indian put on display. Once we were up there, a thunder and lightning storm broke. The four of us were trapped in this room with THE THING! It was a funny experience I never forgot. It was the basis for my book, *The Thing Upstairs*. It's about a kid who wants to be a writer and puts on a play. He can't think of endings. The play goes nowhere until there's a thunder storm and a mummy, stashed above, falls out of the ceiling. That incidence gives him his ending."

For: **I Have a Weird Brother Who Digested a Fly** *by Joan Holub*

"I overheard a kid at a library asking his mother, 'Besides birthdays, there's a Mother's Day and a Father's Day. Why don't I get a Kid's special day?' So I wrote *Happy Monster Day*, a book about a young monster who creates his own special day, and learns to appreciate all that he has.

"When I was growing up, my older sister and I used to pick on my brother. Once, while we stayed at a hotel, our parents square danced while we got into mischief in our room. We dared my six-year-old brother to go down the hall and touch the Coke machine, while in his underwear. He did it. Then we locked him out! How mean! Another time, while traveling in a car, my brother was laughing with his mouth open. The windows were down, and in wooshed a bug. My sister and I nicknamed him Bug Boy for a few weeks. *I Have a Weird Brother Who Digested a Fly* is dedicated to my brother, Paul."

For: **101 Ways to Bug Your Parents** *by Lee Wardlaw*

"*101 Ways to Bug Your Parents* was inspired by a newspaper article. Many years ago, a teacher had a tough time with her own kids at home. When she got to school, her students needed a topic to write on in their journals. So she told them, 'Write ten things you've done to bug your parents.' The class came up with 101 ways and the teacher wrote them all down on the blackboard. The aide copied them from the blackboard and sent them to a local newspaper. When I found it, I thought, *what kid could resist that title*? I called the school and interviewed the teacher. After the list appeared in the paper, the editor received lots of nasty letters, which he published. The teacher was afraid she'd lose her job. But her principal had a great sense of humor and he laughed it off. Then I thought—*what if she had gotten into trouble and lost her job?*

"In another article, I read about a kid who had invented a glow in the dark toilet seat. I played *what if* again. *What if he needs money? What if he writes a book and sells it on school property? What if he gets into trouble—and the teacher gets in trouble?* Hence, the birth of *101 Ways to Bug Your Parents*. In the book, I thank the teacher and the class in the acknowledgments. In the sequel, *101 Ways to Bug Your Teacher*, I had four sixth grade classes come up with the list."

Five Ugly Monsters by Tedd Arnold

"My book *Five Ugly Monsters* was inspired by a group of children who wrote to me. Before my scheduled visit to their school, a class of third graders wrote me a letter about how they were looking forward to my appearance. They all drew pictures of bed-jumping because they liked my book, *No Jumping on the Bed*. But, because they had made their drawings just before Halloween, instead of drawing children jumping on beds, they drew Halloween monsters jumping on beds.

"When I opened their mail and looked at all their drawings, the first thing that popped into my mind was, 'Hey! No more *monsters* jumping on the bed!' which reminded me of the old rhyme about five little monkeys. I have always felt that, while monkeys are cute, monsters are *cool!* Why not rewrite that old rhyme?

"I contacted the teacher and let her know that her students' drawings had inspired an idea. And asked if I could keep in touch with them. I then called my editor at Scholastic who loved the book idea. After that I wrote to the children throughout the publishing process, first when I signed the contracts, then when I delivered the first sketches to my editor, and so on. Meanwhile, it seemed like every time I wrote them, the kids would send back more monster drawings.

"By the time the first press proofs came out, the children were in the fourth grade.

"When they received the proofs they saw that *Five Ugly Monsters* was dedicated to all of them and their third grade teacher. When the book was finally published, the kids were in the fifth grade. They had to be tracked down and gathered to a special assembly to receive their signed copies. Representing a final step in the publishing process, I sent them a packet of the great book reviews *Five Ugly Monsters* received from various magazines. The book is additionally special to me because it, in turn, inspired an entire series of books for *Scholastic* starring Huggly, the little green monster who lives under the bed."

For: Peacebound Trains and Tae's Sonata by Haemi Balgassi

"It's been different for each story. In my sophomore year of high school, I wrote an essay, 'War Child,' for the school literary magazine. 'War Child' was based on my mother's and grandmother's rooftop train ride in the first winter of the Korean War. I didn't realize it then, but it was the first draft of my picture chapter book, *Peacebound Trains*, that would come to life more than a decade later.

"The process for my middle grade novel, *Tae's Sonata*, was entirely different. The book's word count is ten times longer than *Peacebound Trains*, but from conception to final draft, it came to life much more quickly, taking months, not years like the first book did. I suppose Tae's voice had been living inside my head ever since my own middle school years. This isn't to say that I am Tae, or vice versa. Tae is her own person, with her own life and history. But, she and I have traveled some of the same roads."

For: **A Pocketful of Seeds** *by Marilyn Sachs*

"I met a woman named Fanny Krieger at a PTA meeting. All of her family died in Auschwitz. *A Pocketful of Seeds* is loosely based on her story. I asked her to speak to me every week. I brought a tape recorder, and the first time she spoke two or three hours, I had forgotten to turn the tape on! But I took notes, and found I didn't need the tape recordings anyway.

"I never visited France. I knew nothing, so I read all the books I could on this country. Fanny showed me pictures of herself and the town."

For: **Christmas in the Big House; Christmas in the Quarters** *by Patricia and Fredrick McKissack*

"Our editor at Scholastic Publishing, Inc. asked for a Christmas book. We talked about it for a long while before actually committing to write one. Then Fred and I began asking ourselves many questions about when, where and how the first American Christmases were celebrated. After gathering this material for awhile, we decided to narrow our topic to the Tidewater area of Virginia, 1859, where the first American Christmas was celebrated by both slave and master.

"Using a Triple-A guidebook, I contacted the Shirley Plantation and the owner was kind enough to share a lot of information about his family with us. Then we went to visit the plantation. We toured the house and many other houses in the area. We read more diaries, read books, looked at journals, record books, and much more.

"Back home, we drafted *Christmas in the Big House; Christmas in the Quarters*. I wrote it in the present tense, as that the action is now, the time frame is immediate, and the reader experiences everything as it is happening. I like that book very much. It was fun to write, and we especially enjoy John Thompson's artwork. His images seem to leap off the page."

For: **Librarian Lil** *by Suzanne Williams*

"I wrote *Librarian Lil* because I was working with third graders. I wanted them to write their own tall tale. I thought about Pecos Bill and Paul Bunyan. One was a cowboy, and the other, a logger. The students' parents didn't have those kind of jobs. Maybe it would be easier if they wrote a tall tale about a character with an occupation similar to one their parents might have. So I did a demonstration story, and since I was a librarian, I made the main character a librarian, too. I asked myself, *what kind of strengths would a librarian need?*"

For: **Julia Morgan** *by Ginger Wadsworth*

"My thirteen-year-old son wanted to be an architect. I knew very little about it, so I took a class on architecture and that led me to learn about Julia Morgan. I hadn't realized I was surrounded by her work, all the years I've lived in the San Francisco Bay Area. I learned that she had respect for the land. She was like a modern day environmentalist, but years ahead of her time. Asilomar [conference center Morgan built in Monterey, California] is a good example. She worked with the natural setting. Many of the buildings [at Asilomar] have fireplaces made out of beach stone. The buildings are only one or two stories high and have views of the Pacific Ocean. Every Sunday, I check the homes for sale in the San Francisco Bay Area, and if one is listed as a 'Julia Morgan home,' I go to the open house. It's always lots of fun. Once, I met some adults who had lived in a Morgan home, but as children, and they showed me some cubby holes she had designed for them where they could hide from their siblings or store treasures."

For: It's Hard to Read a Map with a Beagle on Your Lap *by Marilyn Singer*

"The way the book *It's Hard to Read a Map with a Beagle on Your Lap* started literally was with a beagle on my lap! We had a beagle named Eubie. In the car, my husband, Steve, asked me to look something up on a map. I said, 'It's hard to read a map with a beagle on your lap!' We laughed. I wrote that down and thought it would be funny to write ridiculous dog poems. Because I like the couplet, I thought it would be good to punctuate the book with couplets."

For: Tattered Sails *and* Homespun Sara *by Verla Kay*

"My editor asked me if I'd write a book on the early colonials. I tried to write a story about a little girl who left her home and sailed to the colonies; then her daily life in the colonies, but I had a difficult time. It just wasn't working. One day I sat down and drew up a time line. Then I realized my character was leaving England in the early 1600's and living in the colonies in the mid 1700's. My seven-year-old girl was about 100 years old! So I broke the book into two and wrote them simultaneously. I ended up with *Tattered Sails* and *Homespun Sara*."

For: A Sea Within a Sea: Secrets of the Sargasso *by Ruth Heller*

"One of the plants I learned about from the research I did for *Plants That Never Ever Bloom* was Sargassum Seaweed. The animals that live in this seaweed all look so much like the seaweed that they are perfectly camouflaged.

"This information gave me the idea to do a series of books on camouflage. My book published in 2000 was called *A Sea Within a Sea: Secrets of the Sargasso*. This is an excellent example of how one idea inspires another and another."

For: I Hate to Go to Bed! *by Katie Davis*

"*I Hate to Go to Bed!* was inspired by my son who got out of his big boy bed the first night thirty-seven times! That book was blood, sweat and tears. First I had written it about different nights. It was too scattered. I had her catching the parents doing stuff they tell her not to, like leaving dirty laundry on the floor, jumping on the furniture, running with sticks. She didn't even go to bed at the end! Not so smart for a bedtime story!

"I thought *Who Hoots?* would be easy to plug in the pattern established by *Who Hops?* Not true. Following the original pattern of *Who Hops*, I asked myself, what are three animals who meow? Etc. I couldn't do that. So then I thought, what if I switch it? Who doesn't? It became a better companion book."

For: Nadia the Willful *by Sue Alexander*

"My brother died and my father wouldn't let us talk about him. I knew my father was wrong, but I didn't know how to tell him that. Since I've been in the fifth grade, whenever I had a problem I wrote about it. So when I realized I had to write this story, I recognized I couldn't live through writing it in the here and now. I needed to set it in the past with another culture. Anywhere I could control the writing and not get caught up in my emotions.

"And that's when I remembered the Bedouins. In the fifth grade I discovered the Bedouins. My parents took me to see a stage play in which the Bedouins were the characters. I became fascinated with the idea of a nomadic people who seemed, in that play, so romantic. The play had nothing to do with the Bedouins in reality, but I didn't know that at the time. I went to the library and read everything I could about them, because I was utterly fascinated. So to write my book, I went back to the library and read about the Bedouins all over again. The names of my characters and the setting of *Nadia the Willful* came from the reading I did.

"I gave my father a copy. Shortly after that, he began to talk about my brother."

For: National Parks Series *by Ruth and Ed Radlauer*

"I wrote twenty books on national parks. Before going to a park, I spent several weeks studying it. I wrote to the park's visitor center for a reading list, bought some of the books, and then I worked up an outline. We'd go to the park with a tape recorder and a ton of camera gear. The cheapest part of the trip was film, so we took many rolls. We took hundreds of pictures to get the few that went into the book. If we couldn't get a good shot, we'd get it from a historical society or an angel; someone who's there almost year round. I'd go through all the museums talking into my tape recorder. I took many ranger interpretive hikes and brought home a mountain of stuff and reduced it to a forty-eight-page book with half the pages given over to photographs.

"I knew how many lines of text and the number of characters per line there should be. I'd write it out and then compact it. I had to choose information that would be interesting to children. Having taught school, I knew that students study the states and national parks in fifth grade. Our books fit nicely into that curriculum. I have a sense of what children can read at that age.

"On my very last national park book, *Shenandoah National Park*, I had to write yet one more page on wild flowers. I said, '*What can I say that is different?*' That weekend I took a seminar of poetry. and my usual walks in the woods. Then I wrote the best wildflower page of the whole series.

"One of my editors just loved us because we sent her a package that was easy to work with. We almost designed our own books. We had a professional looking manuscript with slides all labeled and in protective slide pockets."

For: Pursuit School *by Ed Radlauer*

"One of the nicest experiences I had was when I was writing a book called *Pursuit School*. It was a school for highway patrol officers. I called a racetrack in Atlanta, Georgia, where they had the first school for this kind of training. The person in charge told me he'd reserve a hotel for me. He said I'd get to ride in the patrol car and take all the pictures I wanted. It was marvelous. A month before that, I had wanted to write a book about a clown college. I called Ringling Brothers in New York and asked to attend their college in Florida. They said absolutely not. What a contrast!"

For: Notes From a Liar and Her Dog *by Gennifer Choldenko*

"*Notes From a Liar and Her Dog* came in part from ding letters—rejections from some of my other manuscripts. I was mad that I kept getting letters which seemed to categorize my work –'Not another (fill in the blank) book.' I decided I wasn't being taken seriously, and I wanted higher quality ding letters, so I dug down as deep as I could go and I wrote *Notes From a Liar and Her Dog*. The first two ding letters I received were each two pages long. The third letter was an offer."

For: Almond Cookies and Dragon Well Tea *by Cynthia Chin-Lee*

"There are a lot of autobiographical elements in *Almond Cookies and Dragon Well Tea*. It's set in my grandparents' Chinese laundry. The main idea comes when a Chinese American girl who invites a European American girl to her house. When I was in elementary school I invited a Caucasian girl to my house. Her mother came over to inspect our house! I guess she found out it wasn't an opium den, so she let her play with me."

For: Sarah's Story *and* Hurry Granny Annie *illustrated by Eve Aldridge*

"With my first book, *Sarah's Story*, I found that the reference material I'd been gathering for years wasn't enough to help me accurately draw her. I needed a model. The only child I knew who was in the age bracket was a seven-year-old boy. He was such a good sport, totally willing to sit, stand, lay down, roll over and shake, make faces, etc., that the drawing took on an authenticity based on his personality. One of the "secrets" I share with kids is that nobody knows that Sarah is really a boy. He is the 'Miles' the book is dedicated to.

"Along that line, the agile, sneezing Granny from *Hurry Granny Annie* was based on an upside-down photograph I took of my old boyfriend holding a frozen somersault pose, butt to the sky, in the middle of a public park. Who'd have guessed?"

For: **Buoy: Home at Sea** *and* **What I Saw at Sea** *by Bruce Balan*

"I was delivering a large motor boat with my uncle. We sailed from Long Beach to Marina Del Rey. It was at night and we were going around the Point Fermin Bell Bouy. We passed it around midnight. It was very calm and the moon was up and it was rolling slowly, all by itself. As we went by it, it seemed very much at home. I said to my uncle, 'It's amazing that things and animals just live out here all the time. This is their home.' And he said, 'There's something to write a story about.' It took me five years to write *Buoy: Home at Sea*.

"I was sailing across the Atlantic Ocean and I was on watch at dawn. The sun came up and it was beautiful. I looked up and there were these clouds and one looked just like a giant duck flying so fast, that there was smoke coming from its feet. So I jumped down the companionway, grabbed a pad and pen, and sat in the cockpit and wrote the first draft of *What I Saw at Sea*."

For: **PaperQuake** *by Katherine Reiss*

"*PaperQuake* started with a contemporary mystery about triplets. The main character, Violet, age fourteen, starts receiving letters from the past, every time there is an earthquake. The letters are dated 1906. How could they be written to her? I find the idea of earthquakes scary, and I've always been interested in multiple births. I read an newspaper article where two babies were born right away, but because of medical problems, the third was born several weeks later. A part of a set, but yet set apart. Outside the set interests me. The story is also about sisters and siblings. I have an interest in history at the turn of the century, so all of these elements percolated in my head for a while. I like the idea of following a paper trail to link events in the past. In order for the mystery to be solved, the reader finds out about the past. Pieces of the puzzle have to be put together. In solving the story, Violet comes to terms with her own sisters. It's a family story too."

For: **The Sammy Keyes Mystery Series** *by Wendelin Van Draanen*

"The books I originally wrote were really adult books. I wrote what I felt like writing and the books turned into four hundred page novels! Then I read *Dandelion Wine* by Ray Bradbury. It reminded me of my life as a girl growing up with boys. So I wrote *How I Survived Being a Girl*. I didn't know it was a children's book. I thought it was for adults. I sent it to an editor at Harper who told me to cut it in half. In the time I was waiting for the editor to get back to me, to keep the lines of communication open, I sent her a sample of a mystery I was writing. I asked her if she knew anyone in the adult market. She didn't, but she said she'd love to see a mystery for kids.

"I took her suggestion and ran with it. I thought of what I liked when I was a kid and I knew she [Sammy] couldn't be a protagonist like Nancy drew, because life for kids is a lot different now. As a teacher, I had a lot of kids from broken homes in my classes, so I thought if I wrote about that, it would be helpful. My husband and I brain-stormed and came up with the idea that Sammy would live with her grandmother in senior housing. I put her in seventh grade, because that was the most terrifying time of my life for me.

"When I was three quarters through [writing the first one] I was already thinking about the second mystery, *Sammy Keyes and the Skeleton Man*. I sent the first one, *Sammy Keyes and the Hotel Thief* and was two thirds through *Skeleton* when suddenly, *Sammy Keyes and the Sisters of Mercy* sang in my head! *Who are these sisters? Why are they singing in my head?* After I wrote this book and a fourth one, I took a break. I didn't write *Sammy Keyes* for two months. The publisher decided to buy *Skeleton* but not *Hotel Thief*, nor the others. So I turned them down. My editor wound up going to Knopf and then they bought all four. I'm glad I turned down the first offer, for eventually *Hotel Thief* won the Edgar Award!"

For: The Folk Keeper *and* Well Wished *by Franny Billingsley*

"It's hard to know where *The Folk Keeper* came from. I had just read Susan Cooper's picture book version of the selkie story. I was running one day and it came to me to write a story with a half-selkie half-human, and it would be a journey of self discovery.

"I started writing this book in March 1993, when *Well Wished* was getting rejected. When I started the story, there were no Folk. I hadn't given Corinna enough of a story. There were weird things about her, but I didn't know how to put narrative energy into the story. I wanted her to be strong and interesting. She ended up being a jerk! She was a little too twenty-first century. I didn't like her or the story, since there was no story.

"Then I took a year off to revise *Well Wished*. I sent *The Folk Keeper* to my editor, Jean Karl. She said, 'The problem is, we don't know what Corinna really wants.' *Well Wished* had been out long enough for me to know that kids liked the Wishing Well [a magical well that gives people one wish each], which is sinister and unpredictable. So I thought I'd give my character an obsession and a history to give her a motive. I got to know her better. When I tracked her history to find what it was that made her want something so much, she started to speak to me. In the fall of 1997, I put in the Folk [evil gremlins who cause harm to others], and she became a different person. Equally unlikeable, but unlikeable in a way that was organic to her upbringing, not superimposed by me. I did four drafts and it took me ten months to write a completely different book."

For: Toothworms and Spider Juice: An Illustrated History of Dentistry *by Loretta Ichord*

"For my books *Toothworms and Spider Juice: An Illustrated History of Dentistry*, I had a high interest in dental history because I've been a dental professional for sixteen years. I had read a large book on the history of dentistry and though it was beautiful and wonderful, I felt there was a need for a smaller book on the subject for children and even the lay-person who is unfamiliar with dental facts and history. I wanted it to be fun, informative and grossly interesting!"

For: **At the Sign of the Star** *by Katherine Sturtevant*

"Ideas for novels don't burst upon me, but develop bit by bit, often in very prosaic ways. I knew from the start that I wanted to set my first middle grade novel in Restoration London, because I'm interested in that time and place and had already done research into it for other projects. My basic plot—the idea of a daughter losing her expected inheritance to a stepmother—came from materials about the era which revealed this to be a common problem. It struck me that it was a new slant on the problem of step-families, which is a problem children still have to struggle with today. Next, I needed to decide what kind of family my character would come from. I wanted to pick a trade that women were sometimes actively involved in. When I saw that bookselling was one of these trades, a light went on. I knew the book trade would be a rich background for my character. As I was researching, I saw what kinds of books were published in the era. That's when I got the idea of focusing each chapter on an actual book published during the Restoration. That idea DID kind of burst upon me. I felt like I'd just found a hundred dollar bill being blown along the sidewalk. I loved it. I gloated over it!"

For: **Art Dog** *by Thacher Hurd*

"*Art Dog* started out as a book about frogs in a swamp. I worked on it for years. It slowly turned into another book called Ultra Dog. I did up a rather elaborate color dummy and I showed it to my wife, Olivia. She didn't think much of it, so I put it away, discouraged. Then one day I was driving on the freeway and suddenly the thought came, 'What is ultra backwards? ART! Suddenly, the whole thing snapped into place for me. I knew the book should be called *Art Dog* instead of Ultra Dog, and from there, the book fell into place.

"But I still had to do five or six dummies with different versions before I knew it was right. Finally, I had a story that worked. But there was one last touch that needed to be added. By chance, one day, a friend was visiting, and I showed the latest dummy to her. After reading it she said, '*Art Dog* needs a home, a job, a place to start from.' And she was right. It was just the touch the book needed.

"I think people don't realize how communal these efforts are. The books happen through a number of different people contributing to them. It's like putting together a performance!"

For: **Animal Dads** *by Sneed Collard III*

"The story of *Animal Dads* is an interesting and instructive one, perhaps. I was speaking at a Society of Children's Book Writers and Illustrators conference in Pennsylvania, when an editor walked up to me and said, 'Sneed, I have two words for you: Animal Dads.' I knew it was a great idea and told this editor to return to New York and I'd write it for him. I knew I wanted to keep the book very simple and my biggest challenge was to make it flow without making it rhyme. After throwing out six or seven rhyming versions, I finally hit on the right rhythm and, after a couple more drafts, sent it to this editor.

"He rejected it.

"Fortunately, I knew he was making a big mistake. I sent it to an agent, who sent it to Houghton Mifflin with the suggestion of Steve Jenkins as an illustrator. They snapped it up and got it out in thirteen months. (Still a record for me!) It's also by far, my most popular book."

For: **Fly Away Home, Smoky Night, The Wall** *and* **How Many Days to America** *by Eve Bunting*

"Quite often my ideas come from something I've read in the news. I read about homeless people living in Chicago's O'Hare Airport. I put a child there and thought about what it would be like to be homeless and in an airport. [*Fly Away Home*] With *Smoky Night*, I was here in Los Angeles. [During the riots of 1992] *The Wall* took me three years to write because I had not been there. I did read a lot of photo essays about it in magazines, though. I knew I wanted to write a picture book, because I could visualize it. I woke up one morning and got the first couple of lines. Those set the voice and tone for me. I think we [writers] get [inspiration] because we think about these things as we go to sleep.

"The first serious-topic picture book I wrote was *How Many Days to America*. It's a Thanksgiving book. Jim Giblin, my editor at Clarion, was willing to take a chance. The book did well, so he accepted *The Wall* with no qualms at all. *Fly Away Home* was a Clarion book too."

For: **Lost in Death Valley** *by Connie Goldsmith*

"The idea for *Lost in Death Valley* came from a newspaper article telling about a man who was trying to recreate the journey of these '49ers through Death Valley on foot. I located the man through the Internet, and told him I was interested in learning more about these Gold Rush pioneers. He gave me the name of a couple of books and it took off from there."

For: **Video** *by Karen Romano Young*

"Most of the things in *Video* really happened to me, although in different ways. A man really did expose himself to my sister and me at a pond near our house. Because I spent so much time in the woods and wetlands –with and without friends— it concerned me. It's an odd thing, but since *Video* came out, many people have shared their similar experiences with me. Both men and women. The number surprised me, but it shouldn't have, because it happened not once, but several times to me. People are so shy about these things, especially around kids, but these things are happening to kids.

"Although that's the central drama of *Video*, it's not the only thing that's real-life for me. The two main characters are based on kids in my sixth grade class. They were people I'd always been curious about, but didn't know very well. It was my opportunity to sort of make them up from scratch and figure out what might have made them tick, and how they'd act under certain circumstances. Some of the events and settings—the horrible dancing school, for example—really happened to us."

For: **Wait Till Helen Comes** *by Mary Downing Hahn*

"*Wait Till Helen Comes* is a good example of serendipity. I love ghost stories, but as much as I wanted to write one of my own, I couldn't come up with a plot. Then one day my daughter, Kate asked me to drive her to a friend's house. The girl's family had bought an old church in the country and converted it into a home. They built an addition in which they lived and used the church itself as a gallery where the mother sold her pottery and her friends' paintings. When I parked my car, I realized you get something extra when you buy a country church—a cemetery in your backyard. Remembering my childhood fear of graveyards, I decided to write a book about a family who encounters the wicked ghost haunting the old burial ground. Staring at the crooked tombstones, I actually invented the entire plot of *Wait Till Helen Comes*. Serendipity—if I hadn't visited that church, I wouldn't have stumbled unexpectedly on the idea for one of my most popular books."

For: **Parts** *by Tedd Arnold*

"The idea for *Parts* occurred to me when my first son, Walter, was five years old. I found him lying on the couch, looking pale as a ghost, like he was sick or frightened. He clutched a Bible to his chest—he was praying! When I asked what was wrong, he wouldn't answer. In fact, he wouldn't even open his mouth. It was clamped shut. My wife, Carol, came in and finally coaxed a response from him. He pointed to his mouth.

Carol exclaimed, 'You have a loose tooth!' Walter's eyes nearly popped out with fright. But when he saw us both smiling, he relaxed a little. We assured him that it was perfectly okay for his tooth to come loose and that a new one would soon replace it. But Carol and I looked at each other, wondering if, despite all our efforts to be good parents for our first child, had we somehow completely forgotten to warn Walter that teeth fall out? And had he somehow missed all the relevant Sesame Street episodes? I almost laughed aloud when it occurred to me that my son was lying there on the couch, scared to death, because he thought he was falling apart! I made a little note about it in my journal. Ten years later, I expanded that memory into my book *Parts*."

For: Two Bear Cubs *by Daniel San Souci*

"*Two Bear Cubs* has an interesting story. It goes back to the time when my brother Bob and I were kids. We went to Yosemite and heard a Miwok Indian Storyteller tell this story at the base of El Capitan. He pointed to some scratches part way up the mountain, and he said that was where the mother bear had tried to claw her way up the mountain, to reach her cubs! '*Oh my goodness,*' I thought. '*This must be real!*'

"Then, a few years back, we were at a convention and the Yosemite Association asked if we'd work with them. He said they wanted a book about the story of the two bear cubs. Of course, we just jumped at it.

"The irony is, that the Yosemite Association is a smaller publisher. I thought it was a nice story, but too regional to have any grand expectations for its success. But it's been my best-selling book! It has won many awards, and it sells well in the national parks and at Disneyland's California Adventure Land. The story is on the California Recommended Reading List and Native American unit lists. I really wanted to do this book for a personal reason, as I loved it as a kid. Now I see that it's a timeless story and it will be around forever."

For: The Thing That Bothered Farmer Brown *by Teri Sloat*

"When I wrote *The Thing That Bothered Farmer Brown*, it was based on my husband waking everyone in the cabin while he killed a mosquito one night. After the story was written, it was funnier to picture animals waking up to each swat, which in turn made the main character a farmer, and naming him Farmer Brown gave him a name that so many words rhymed with, that the narrative story turned into rhyme."

For: The Babe and I *by David Adler*

"I struggled ten years with *The Babe and I*. I had the story in my head for that long or longer. I didn't know if it would be a book for older or younger children. I wrote first paragraphs for eight years before I found one I could use. Every six months I'd try again. The voice has to be consistent. So if the first paragraph doesn't have it, the book doesn't have it.

"Once I had the voice, it came smoothly. For that book, I went back and looked at newspapers from the 1930's. Baseball was different then. Teams played an almost two-week homestand. I knew the story would take place over several days. I found when the Yankees were home for an extended period of time, in 1932. Then I went through microfilm and read the newspapers."

For: **Rules of the Road** *by Joan Bauer*

"The interesting thing about *Rules of the Road* is that ten years before I wrote young adult lit, I was a screenwriter. I created Harry Bender, the world's greatest shoe salesman, for a movie I was going to write. I had a rough car accident, changed writing careers, and began to write novels. But I kept this character in my idea file. When I decided to write *Rules of the Road*, I knew it was time to address the alcohol issues I had experienced with my dad. I began with that theme, and then the shoes came and I remembered Harry and I yanked him into it. The story changed, as I adapted Jenna and grew her into this family and the crazy milieu of the shoe business.

"My father was an alcoholic, my grandmother had Alzheimer's Disease, although they called it 'hardening of the arteries' back then. People may think the book is autobiographical, but it's not. You can put your experiences into your story character, but it's important that you have enough distance so the story isn't emotionally bleeding.

"I'm always looking for a metaphor or a symbol that will hold the book together. Selling shoes wouldn't be anything to aspire to. But I thought, what's it like to kneel down at people's feet all day? I thought people who would do that would be very humble. It's also funny to care a great deal about something ordinary. I use passion and obsession quite a bit in my humor—passion for pumpkins, passion for selling shoes, passion for food service. Find a symbol that has meaning and push the envelope with it."

For: **Things I have to tell you and You Hear Me?** *Compiled by Betsy Franco*

"I have two anthologies written by teenagers: *Things I have to tell you* and *You Hear Me?*, written by teenage girls and boys respectively. I was inspired to compile the girls' collection when a teenage friend of mine shared some difficult experiences with me. I thought it would be helpful to hear from teenage girls firsthand. The purpose of the book was to give hope but not at the expense of honesty. I collected submissions for several years from all over the country. I used the Internet, ads in magazines such as *Poets and Writers*, telephone networking, and much more. Eventually I found a publisher at a writing conference."

For: **The Power of Un** *by Nancy Etchemendy*

"*The Power of Un* came from one of those ideas that cooked on the back burner of my brain for years and years—over a decade—before it turned into anything suitable for consumption. One of the peculiar aspects of being a writer is that I tend to look at everything as a possible story idea –bits of conversation, faces on a bus, lovely but nameless vegetables in the produce section. The idea for Un began with my first glimpse of a Macintosh computer. It must have been 1983 or '84, because Macs were totally new on the scene at the time. I was walking down University Avenue in downtown Palo Alto, and saw this completely unlikely computer in a shop window. It was small enough to carry around; images on the screen were black on white, rather than the more familiar neon green or orange on black; there was a picture on the screen, of all things! I'd never seen a computer with anything except letters and numbers on the screen. I was looking at one of the very first graphical user interfaces, and oh, I thought I had died and gone to a wonderful heaven where grown-ups get to play with the toys of their dreams. I went into the shop and started messing around with the display model.

"Instead of keyboard commands, it had this funny little box with a cord attached which you moved around on a pad, and it moved an arrow on a screen. I didn't even know the name for it was 'mouse.' There was a menu bar, where I discovered you could choose something called 'undo.' Any mistake you made on this computer you could erase, as if it had never happened at all. The peculiar power of that idea lodged in my mind like a burr, and I found myself mentally playing with it at odd moments. Eventually, that process of 'play' resulted in the story of a boy who can undo any mistake and do it over as many times as he likes.

"So *The Power of Un* started with an idea. This isn't always the case for me. Sometimes stories seem to appear out of whole cloth, complete with not only a good idea, but characters, plot, and setting to go with them. Other times, the process seems more dependent on conscious thought. A compelling character will show up without any story or setting; or a setting will appear, just waiting to be populated with people and plots.

"One thing that's always true of my work, though, is that it begins with play—from rather aimlessly messing around with whatever has my attention at the moment. That was definitely true of *Un*. It started with my spending half an hour playing in a computer store. It progressed through many hours of happily imagining plot scenarios centered on the powerful possibility of undoing mistakes at will. At the very end, I spent about a month working out plot details and a synopsis, and the book itself came rolling out in a very natural way over the next four months after that, which is very speedy for me."

For: Lyle Lyle Crocodile *by Bernard Waber*

"When I was in art school, I sketched animals in a zoo. I have a weird sense of humor and crocodiles amused me, so I drew them for my art portfolio so I could get a job. Later, when I had children of my own, I read picture books to them and the idea of writing and illustrating a picture book appealed to me. So I invented Lyle and put him in a book. He was kind of a family character."

For: **The Dark Side of Nowhere** *by Neal Shusterman*

"About *The Dark Side of Nowhere*: When I feel compelled to write something, it's usually the underlying issues and themes that come first, and then I find an arena in which to tell the story. Several years ago, I sat before my television, transfixed by the Oklahoma City bombing. The fact that it was an American who was the culprit, made it all the more horrifying.

"I began to think about how the greatest threats don't usually come from the outside, but from within—within ourselves, and within our communities. I also began considering the mentality that develops when the influences in one's life are limited to a few skewed points of view. That kind of limited perspective leads to everything from cults to Neo-Naziism, and led to the mind set that advocates acts such as the bombing. I knew I wanted to tell a story that was an allegory for all of these things, so I came up with the character of Jason—an every-kid in middle America, who takes his life for granted, and in the course of the story begins to lose his humanity, both literally, and figuratively. By the end of the story, he has to come to value what it means to be human, and fight against those that would destroy humanity.

"My writing process for *The Dark Side of Nowhere* was an unusual one for me. I had a back injury at the time, and for most of the time, was lying in bed. This made it very difficult to write or type, so most of the first draft was dictated into a microcassette recorder!

"**My involvement with the movie version:** The entertainment industry is a funny place—they have lots of money to buy film rights and pay writers, but when it comes down to it, it takes many millions of dollars to actually make a movie. Very few of the projects that get bought and paid for, get made. My working experience with Dark Horse Entertainment was a positive one. I wrote two drafts of the script, and then two more writers were hired for further drafts. They're still very excited about the project, and every day I wait for that phone call, telling me that it's going into production! Right now, however, my novel *Downsiders* seems to be the most likely project to go into production next, with Disney."

For: **Francie** *by Karen English*

"*Francie* started out as a picture book. I was doing some research and I came across how women did laundry. They used a big kettle, over the fire and put bluing in their wash. They did their whites on Monday. [So I titled it] Blue Monday. It was about a little girl who helped her mother do laundry for a woman named Miss Beach. Miss Beach's cat was called Treasure. The little girl's favorite thing was to sneak into the parlor and play on the piano. She was on her way through the kitchen and came across an open can of salmon. Miss Beach had put it there for the cat. The little girl tasted it, and liked it, so she ate half of it! Miss Beach accuses her and she lies. Then her mother sends her home.

"A couple of editors said it sounded like a beginning of a novel, so I made her thirteen and set it during the pre-civil rights area of the late forties. It took a year before Farrar, Straus & Giroux bought it.

"The first time around, the novel was more character driven. I let my husband read it because he's a plot man. He said, "There's no real plot here." So I decided to add Jessie. I read something a long time ago. It said, 'Fiction is like a basketball game. There's a goal and you have obstacles.' So I gave Francie a goal and obstacles.

"I wasn't raised in the south. I deliberately set the novel in southern Alabama. I'd visited my best friend in Alabama to get a feel for the place."

For: I Am The Cat *by Alice Schertle*

"I have always loved cats, and have usually lived with one. A few years ago I was watching my old calico, whose name was Baggage-Who-Drools, lapping from a pie pan of milk on my dark blue kitchen floor. There she was, it seemed drinking the moon; even the flecks of milk spattered onto the floor by her tongue looked like pinpoints of stars. That image grew into a fairly long narrative poem. In the process of tinkering with that one, trying and discarding various approaches, I suddenly wrote, 'In the beginning, when the cat could fly . . .' That opening made me realize that I was writing a feline account of the fall from grace in the Garden of Eden. I called it 'The Cat's Version,' and it became the first poem in my cat collection, *I Am The Cat.*"

For: The Egypt Game *by Zilpha Keatley Snyder*

"Books can have many different idea roots. The first root for me goes back to when I was in the fifth grade and my class studied Egyptian history. I was completely carried away by everything Egyptian. I went around being an Egyptian for weeks! I collected things that looked Egyptian. I wrote in hieroglyphics. I read everything I could find about Egypt.

"I think what really started the book was my interest in the imaginative games that kids play. As a child, I had games for everything. The setting for the story came from where I taught school in Berkeley. The area where April and Melanie lived is very much like the area where I taught. When I thought of using that setting, I got out a picture of one of my classes. Certain aspects of those very real children inspired my characters. The boy that inspired Marshal was quiet and self-contained, possessed a great deal of personal dignity, but seemed to need a certain amount of comforting stability. These characteristics, as I remember them in the boy who inspired Marshall, led me to create Security.

"The shortest, most influential root of the story came from my own daughter when she was in sixth grade. I told her about my Egyptian game and she and her friends started playing a game very much like the one in the book, but in our basement. They even mummified our parrakeet after it died by feline assassination. I used that in the story. Later, when my daughter was a teenager, she often threatened go through all of my books looking for good ideas she had given me—and charge me for them!"

For: **Staying Fit for Sarah Byrnes** *by Chris Crutcher*

"The event of the burning came first. Then I asked the question, *what if?* When I realized I didn't have enough of an insight to that character, I created Mobey to tell the story about her. I didn't have enough experience with that kind of trauma myself, to make sure I'd be on the money all the time if I were writing from her perspective."

For: **Faraway Home** *and* **Pulling the Lion's Tail** *by Jane Kurtz*

"I identify with the father in my book, *Faraway Home.* He is me as a parent, homesick for Ethiopia and at a loss as how to explain the country of my childhood to my own children. My parents lived in Ethiopia for twenty-three years, where they worked for the Presbyterian church, and I thought of it as home for all that time, even thought I knew I had another home in the U.S. where I would return some day. As with most third culture kids (as children who grow up as I did are sometimes called), I've spent a lifetime sorting out just where my home is. I was deeply attached to Maji and to my other homes in Ethiopia, but by the time I came back to Illinois for college, I was sure there was no way to talk about my childhood home with people here in the U.S.

"One day, many years later, my father told me an amusing anecdote about a family friend who emigrated from Ethiopia to the U.S. When he showed a photograph of himself as a schoolboy to his children, his son stared at the picture and then asked, 'Why did you take off your shoes to go to school?'

"The story stuck with me, and one day it struck me as a wonderful illustration of the gaps that loom between people who grew up in one country or region while their children are growing up in a different place—which is my story. I drew on my real memories of Ethiopia and the misconceptions that my own children and friends have had about my childhood to create the specific memories the father talks about. This book, and my third novel, *Jakarta Missing*, are in some ways, my most autobiographical pieces; my effort to capture what it's like to move back and forth between two very different places of the earth."

"*Pulling the Lion's Tail* came from a story I'd heard as a child in Ethiopia. I always heard it told as the story of a young wife who was afraid her husband didn't love her or as the story of a mother who had lost the love of her son. In typical folktale fashion, the story didn't explain *why*—it was simply told as a kind of fable to illustrate the importance of patience. I decided to create a character who was clearly impatient, (the kind of child I used to be) in the beginning and learns that 'much of what is good comes slowly.'

"I tried retelling from the point of view of a young bride, but the editor who became interested in the story thought young readers would have a hard time relating to it. When the editor and I were talking over what kind of relationship would push my character, Almaz, to brave the lion's den, the idea emerged of a stepmother.

"I called an Ethiopian friend and asked her to describe what it would be like for an Ethiopian child with a new stepmother, and when she described the great lengths to which most families would go in their desire to make sure the stepchild respected and honored the new mother, I knew I had found a true source of tension: a girl longing for love; a cautious stepmother, holding back because of shyness and the need to insist on respect; a grandfather who could send Almaz to gather some hair from the tail of a lion.

"Once I had the premise and the characters figured out, telling the story was fairly easy –just a matter of listening to the rhythms in my head of all the folktales I'd been told and read over many years."

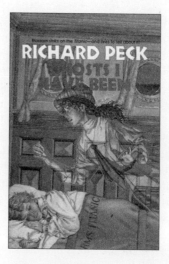

Featuring Richard Peck

Richard Peck has written more than thirty award-winning novels for young people, including *The Ghost Belonged to Me, Ghosts I have Been, A Long Way From Chicago*, the Edgar Allan Poe Award's *Are You in the House Alone?*, *Fair Weather*, and the Newbery Award-winning *A Year Down Yonder*. An Illinois native, he makes his home in New York City.

In your Blossom Culp stories, you've said that her character evolved from a combination of your female relative's voices. Many writers use character charts to develop their characters. Can you talk about how you developed Blossom?

"I can't talk about how I developed Blossom Culp, not from this distance. She was real for me from the beginning, and now she has assumed the role of someone I knew once and never forgot. Certainly her voice came from my great-aunts and much of her utter self-confidence. But somehow she seemed to spring to life and I'm not sure I can take much credit. I merely stepped aside and let her take over."

All of your books have a sense of immediacy, as though your very-real characters are talking to the reader, even when you use third person past, as in your Grandma Dowdel stories. How can writers aspire to develop the 'voice' in each of their books?

"Writing is a craft of listening. A writer doesn't develop his 'voice.' He—and she are apt to need fifty different voices for every book. I was born listening. I was not permissively reared. My word was not law at home. I listened carefully to my elders, trying to decode adulthood. I know of no child who does that now, or has to."

In Presenting Richard Peck *by Donald R. Gallo, you say you never rush through your first draft, but write your early chapters over and over. Does this revision process help you develop your plot? Do you ever outline your chapters?*

"Revision is everything, and I'm far more comfortable re-writing than writing. There is nothing more daunting than that blank page. I tinker at length—six times through the manuscript. Then when I come to the end, I throw out the first chapter without rereading it. Then I write the first chapter that actually anticipates the rest of the book. After all, the first chapter is the last chapter in disguise."

Your humor grows from your quirky characters. With Grandma Dowdel, the reader can't wait to see what she will do next. Were the anecdotes in those stories from your past? Did the situations come first, or did they come after you developed your characters?

"In my two novels about Grandma Dowdel, I rely heavily on other people's memories. These are not stories from my childhood. Significantly, they are set where my father grew up. I have country cousins to this day, and they are my sources for rural life and an agricultural community through the seasons of the year: fox trapping, etc. All fiction is based on research, and I make lavish use of other people's experience. I don't write what I know; I write what I can find out."

The reader sees Grandma's actions without any explanation. Then the reader is shown the reason why in the rest of the story. Can you talk about how writers can build anticipation and suspense in their books?

"You learn the pacing of anticipation and the construction of suspense by reading how other writers do it. Dame Agatha Christie can teach you much about the laying in of clues and the shaping of story even when you aren't writing a mystery. After all, every story needs to be a tale of suspense, to keep the pages turning."

In the 1980's, there was a movement to censor the Blossom Culp series. Can you talk about this? Was The Last Safe Place on Earth *censored too? Did you respond to the challenges?*

"My comic ghost stories did indeed find their ways onto a forbidden list. The movement to purge public schools of supernatural stories, *Hamlet*, Halloween decorations, and witchcraft is seen as the attempt of the religious right to assume political control of public schools. The censoring parents I have met in person, however, clearly have more personal agendas. They tend to be doctor's wives and executive's wives in northe rn, new-money suburbs looking for scapegoats at school for their failure to control children at home. The problem continues, but the true censorship in schools now is the set reading curriculum that forbids teachers from drawing up their own reading lists with their own students in mind. This is clearly the school administration's attempt to placate parents and to quench censorship in advance.

I combined a number of censorship issues in my novel, *The Last Safe Place on Earth*. I haven't heard that it has been challenged, but then I haven't heard that it has been much read. It's the kind of book that needs teaching, and we're finding fewer and fewer secondary-school teachers willing or able to adopt our books for the classroom."

9

Day In and Day Out

What's a writer's life like? Here are some of their words about working.

Playing for Profit

"Ninety percent of my writing is at a desk at a computer in a home office. I also design video games so I fit in the writing when I can or write all day."

David Lubar

A Word from the President (of SCBWI)

"I have to write at the Society of Children's Book Writers and Illustrators office. Sometimes I make notes at home, but the actual process happens at the office. Sometimes I've rented offices and it felt more professional."

Stephen Mooser

Not Banker's Hours

"I begin writing or illustrating around 9:30 a.m. and I work until my husband comes home about 7 p.m. Sometimes I also work at night or on the weekends. I tend to be a workaholic, but only because I love what I do!"

Joan Holub

The Black Hole

"I have an office, which is a mess. My husband calls it the black hole! Before my son was born, I worked from 8 a.m. until noon. I had a two hour lunch break to eat, make phone calls, run errands. Then I'd get back to work from 2 p.m. until 6 o'clock. Now, since I have a son, I work from 9 a.m. until noon each day. I don't have a day-to-day schedule in the summer when he's out of school. I just write when I can, which is tough. I have never been good at

writing fifteen minutes here and there. My advice would be to try and train yourself to write in snatches."
Lee Wardlaw

School Bell

"When my children were home, I wrote in my bedroom with the door open. The best time for me was during school hours. I'm still writing during school hours! I write in pencil first, then later I write on the computer. I appreciate the computer, since I'm not a good typist."
Marilyn Sachs

"When my kids were growing up, I paralleled my work schedule to be a parent. I worked around the school bus. I still do that now even though the kids are grown. The sound of a school bus makes me feel it's time for recess!"
Ginger Wadsworth

Dentistry and Deadlines

"I write just about every day. I wake up at five a.m. so I write from 5:30–6:00. Then I go to work as a dental assistant. When I come home, I write from 6:30 p.m. until I go to bed. I have to discipline myself. I'm off Friday mornings so I write then. I try to do a little bit on the weekends, but most of my writing is in the evenings."
Loretta Ichord

Long-Hand

"I try to write in the morning and then edit in the afternoon. I don't compose at the computer. I use a legal pad and pencil for the first draft. Later, the third draft is on a computer."
Joanna H. Kraus

Lunch Break?

"When my son grew up and moved out, I took over his room as my office. However, for twenty years it was also the Society of Children's Book Writers and Illustrators office! When Maxine and I worked in it at the same time, it was pretty busy. Finally we rented an office for Society of Children's Book Writers and Illustrators.

"It's a pretty big room and inundated with books. I have more books than many small libraries. They're on shelves, on piles on the floor. I'm a morning person, so I get up and have coffee and juice. I read the paper, do the crossword puzzle. I get to my desk at 6:45 a.m. but at 8 o'clock at night I'm gone! I work til 11:30 a.m. then I eat something. If my work is going well, I'll go back to it. If not, I don't. I learned years ago, not to push it. If I did, I'd throw away what I had written the next day anyway.

When my youngest went to school all day, I wouldn't stop for anything, not even to eat. Then, when I'd read what I wrote the day before, I'd find that my characters were eating or shopping for food all the time! So I realized my body was saying, '*You're hungry!*'"
Sue Alexander

Discipline
"I always say I don't have a schedule, I just meet deadlines."
Ruth Radlauer

Early Riser
"I always wrote in the morning. I got up at 4 a.m. and wrote until breakfast time."
Ed Radlauer

Rockin' Around the Clock
"I don't sit at a typewriter and compose. One of the features of my disability [dyslexia] is needing to experience movement while thinking. I was one of the kids on the playground who'd swing and swing to make it clear to me. Every room in my house has two or three rocking chairs. To me, it puts me in a place to think or visualize. Sometimes while listening to music—walkman ear phones—I literally leave my body. Into my internal life where the stories are! I could be thinking about a current event or things I've observed, then I'll flesh out the story. I'll rock and ruminate for days. Once I sit down to type it, I know every word. Then I have to end it and then there will be a lot of back and forths! My editor, Patty Gauch, knows my code. She knows what I mean."
Patricia Polacco

Concentration
"The best thing for me is to write for a long time, in one sitting, without interruption."
Bruce Balan

On a Roll
"Not having been able to quit my day job yet, I write evenings and weekends. I write for an hour each evening and two hours each weekend day or holiday. I take Friday nights off. When I am on a roll, working hard, I work much more than this. The problem is stopping—I need to quit by 10 PM so that I can watch TV for an hour and calm down enough to sleep."
Angelica Carpenter

Healthy Mind, Active Body
"I love to write in the mornings, first thing, but now I exercise first thing (or

else it doesn't get done). I work in a small office in my home—formerly the guest room—where I have my resources and supplies and stacks and stacks of books."
Larry Dane Brimner

Alarm Clock
"I do my best work in the morning. Either the magic comes or it doesn't. I wish I knew how to make the magic happen."
Mary Downing Hahn

The Nitty Gritty Process

Don't Panic Be Happy

"The length of my first draft is often only sixty-three pages. It's very terse—some scenes, some narration. First I panic—'I will NEVER make this long enough for a book.' Then I relax and go back to work, expanding and polishing."

Karen Cushman

Starting Fresh

"I free write with a pen. I start off writing in my bed. I doodle with words. Then, all of a sudden, something will click. Then I'll write four or five lines and I rush to the computer to flesh out the poem. I write when I'm the freshest, in the morning, the loveliest time of day. I slowly build a poem."

Gary Soto

Note This

"For a biographer, this is the research process. I take notes in chronological order on the computer. For each book, I start with 150-250 pages of notes. I duplicate some notes into separate files organized by topic. I give a source for each note. I use abbreviations and note them in the bibliography."

Angelica Carpenter

I Gotta Be Me

"My process used to bother me. Teachers are always telling their students to get their thoughts down on paper in rapid fire fashion. Revise later. I once took a university fiction-writing course where the instructor maintained that if you couldn't write ten pages a day, you weren't a real writer. I'd go home from that course, look at three hundred variations of my opening sentence, and become really discouraged.

The fact is, there is no right or wrong way to write. Each of us has a process, a method, and what works for one may not work at all for another. I've come to trust my process. I suppose that subconsciously I'm mentally sorting out the entire story as I physically work on the beginning."

Larry Dane Brimner

Tell a Book by Its Cover

"I personally believe that a project starts with a title. A short, snappy, hopefully lively title that embodies the spirit and mood of the book, as well as clues the reader in to the premise. When I was starting out, an editor I respected once told me that if she loved the title of the manuscript, she *wanted* to love the book.

"To me, a snazzy title is the face on the body of your work. If it's attractive, animated, *smiling*, then readers will be drawn to it. For example, I try to keep my titles relatively short and as alliterative as possible, because they're fun to say: *The Peanut Butter Poltergeist, Leap Frog Friday, H.O.W.L. High, Robot Romance, Racetrack Robbery.* Or I think in a joke-like or *pun*ny way to avoid a boring title. If I'm writing about snakes, I'd come up with something like *The Hiss Factor* or *Something Slithers in Mrs. Solomen's Class.* By creating a catchy title first, I usually can motivate myself to work up a solid plot and interesting characters to sustain a title.

"Right after I come up with the title, I then work on the second most important thing: an imaginary jacket of the book. I sit down and visualize what the cover of the book will look like, even to the point of writing book-jacket copy that depicts the main action of the story. This then serves as my inspiration and compass for whenever I lose sight of where I'm going with my plot or characters. By mentally envisioning the book jacket, I can get back on track with the direction of the storyline. In a sense, I'm eating "dessert" first by working on the title, then cover and blurb of the book, but it always manages to keep me going through the long, boring main meal of the actual writing!"

Ellen Leroe

Children Count

"Read! Pay attention to those books that children like best. Children's librarians are the best help there is. Then look at the form. There are kinds of stories that need to be chapter books, some easy readers, and other need to be picture books. You have to figure that out."

Sue Alexander

Picture This

"For me, the idea with the pictures comes first, and I continue to see pictures all the time I'm writing it down. For me, writing a book is like watching a play. Sometimes a story idea has been triggered by a real-life event and it's been woven

Everyone Needs a Joe Patino

"Starting in 1967, for a period of twenty years, I had a mentor. Joe Patino. Joe started working with me when our first few easy read high interest books were published. At that time, I was still principal of a large suburban elementary school. I put these newly published books in my office and let it be known to the fourth grade that these books would be available for 'check-out' during recess times. The result was instant interest.

"As each recess began, fourth grader Joe Patino led a group of boys charging into my office to 'check out those books.' As required, recess over, they brought the books back. It soon became apparent that Joe Patino's concept of author-illustrator was inoperative because frequently, when returning a book, Joe would hold it up, point to a picture and say, *"Hey, Mr. Radlauer, did you see that?"* Or a passage in a book, *"Look what it says here, pretty funny, huh?"* I never violated Joe's author non-information, but I did adopt him as my mentor-in-residence for the next twenty-five years. During this period, as I wrote and illustrated almost 200 books, Joe always remained a ten-year-old fourth grade lad, sat right by my side and made sure I wrote appropriately and used only pictures 'worth of being shown to me.' When I finished writing a page, I'd turn to Joe, get his comments, edit and go on. I suppose I should have, but I never did share any of my royalties with ten-year-old mentor Joe Patino."

Ed Radlauer

into completely unrelated imagery. That's fun—and why I always carry a small sketchbook with me. The simple book *Love and Kisses*, for example, came from seeing and sketching an unlikely cat nuzzling an obviously pleased dog."

Sarah Wilson

Who Needs It?

"For my nonfiction books, first I check library shelves and *Books in Print* and talk to librarians to make sure there is a need for my book. If my idea seems worth pursuing, I begin my research. That means collecting every bit of useful information I can get my hands on: I talk to experts, write letters, read library books and order more books and articles via interlibrary loan, and keep copious notes. I check the Web, though this can be time-consuming and information is not always reliable. For historical research, the Web isn't as useful or as much fun as poking around library shelves, where serendipity plays a part.

"As soon as I have a good idea of the material I have to work with, I begin to organize it. I make a tentative outline, roughly dividing the material into chapters with ideas about what each chapter will contain. I start with one loose leaf notebook, but very soon have so much stuff my office resembles a recycling center, so I must create temporary filing cabinets. For these, I use hanging folders and the brightly colored plastic 'milk crates' you find in stationery stores. Marking pens and lots of manila folders, in many colors, are essential!"
Kathy Pelta

Day at the Zoo

"Working with a photographer is an interactive process. I come up with an idea for a topic and I develop a basic list of questions along with a wish list of the pictures we need. If it's an animal, we need some standard photos: one of a male, a female, an eating photo, sleeping....I do enough research to know what the particular pictures are for that specific animal.

"Most of our animal books were researched and photographed in zoos or wildlife parks, where we had permission to work. We'd designate an intense week or two when we'd go to the zoo together and spend the day watching animals. Animals spend a lot of time sleeping, so we were always waiting for something to happen. When it does [happen], we have to be ready to watch and take pictures.

"My photographer's job is to get the photos. My job is to help him. I'm a second pair of eyes. While he's taking a picture of one thing, I can look for the next picture. We get better pictures that way. My personal observation of animals later plays a great role in my writing."
Caroline Arnold

Obsessions

"An idea (for a novel) starts and something jolts me to realize it would make a good book. *Blackwater* came when we were at Niagra Falls. A guide showed us a rock in the river and said teens swam there. Very often there were drowning deaths. I knew the idea wouldn't work as a picture book. It's a long, hard road, with a novel. I don't actually write anything down or make a synopsis. But I do think it all through as much as I can before I start. With a picture book, I know the story and the last line before I begin. With a novel, I know what the story and theme will be, and I know what the ending is...but I don't know the middle. Then I start writing.

"You have to live with it a long time. It really takes over your life. I have to BE the person in my novel. When I started, I didn't understand how obsessed you are

Fasten Your Seatbelts

"It took me a long time to realize I needed to figure out how I like to learn to do things rather than take for gospel what other authors might have told me about 'how it's done.' One can only learn so much from teachers—most lessons about process I've learned the hard way—by making mistakes and by persevering. In many respects, my writing process is like the bumpy road of life; I'm often slowed by dips and detours, but something inside compels me to keep on traveling; be it hope, joy, or the curiosity of what's going to happen next. I think it's probably that way for most other writers as well. We don't really know how we do what we do, or why. We just know we do it because we have to."

Susan Hart Lindquist

when you're doing a long book. It's the same with a picture book, but it's a shorter duration and not quite as intense."

Eve Bunting

Surf's Up
"When I begin a nonfiction project, the first place I go is to the Internet. I check for books that are available from online booksellers. I make a list for my librarian to order. I also make a list of books I want to buy. I read online articles and surf the Internet for ideas, important related topics, etc. Next, I read, read, read. After I've read several books, I outline the book I plan to write. Then I do more research with that plan in mind. As I research, I discover important questions that I have. About midway through the process, I call experts with those questions. If I can, I visit people or places I am writing about.

"Then I begin to write. As I write, the book changes, more questions arise; I keep gathering information. I ALWAYS end up with too much material. I edit the material I have from a kids' point of view. *What are they interested in? What do they need to know to understand the topic? What can they pick up later?* Then I edit for structure, timing flow, and readability. Last, I check facts a couple times more than I think I need to."

Suzanne Morgan Williams

The Finger or There Was a Crooked Man
"I type with one finger. I've done three hundred books with one finger. My finger is wrecked; it's curved! It's a horrible sacrifice for my art!"

R. L. Stine

11

Magical Inspiration

There's a zone writers occasionally find themselves inhabiting, a magical place where ideas flow so freely, that current time, place and situation dissolve, as writers truly *live inside* the scenes they're creating.

Musical Magic

"One day I happened to find an old piano book of mine, which I used when I was a teenager. I flipped through it, and sadly, discovered that the classical arrangements looked too difficult for me to play, since I hadn't practiced the piano regularly for years. But I felt a longing to try it. I sat at the piano. Carefully and slowly I played the first few notes.

"Suddenly, my fingers flew up and down the keyboard. They automatically knew where to go. It was a fast piece, but somehow I kept up with the pace. All at once, I heard lines of dialogue from my characters in the book that I was writing. The dialogue came from scenes I hadn't written yet."

Elizabeth Koehler-Pentacoff

Traffic Jam

"It usually happens when I don't expect it. I was stuck on *Thwonk*, and I sat in my chair, frustrated and the whole idea for my third book came to me. So I wrote it down and went back to *Thwonk*. It was like having too much traffic on the highway.

"I've learned to trust my subconscious. If I don't get something right away, I believe it's inside me, cooking somehow. It will get out. But I can't always control it. You can make yourself nuts. Sometimes it's important to stop writing and go do something else that feeds your creative soul. I need to do that more. I can drive myself pretty hard."

Joan Bauer

That Other Dimension

"That time certainly exists. But a writer writes anyway. Sometimes writers wait for that moment. When a book is good, you're in some other place. You aren't even aware you're typing. The words just flow. When this doesn't happen, some people think they have writer's block. I don't think that's writer's block. I write anyway. I just press on until the draft is done. Someone once said, *'How do I know what I think, until I see what I've said?'* Writing is often like that for me; I need to have a whole draft before I'm ready to re-shape it."

Kathryn Reiss

Alone Again Naturally

"I wouldn't be the artist today, if I hadn't had a lot of time to let my imagination run free. Solitude is very important. I go crazy if I don't get my solitude. It's like food. Doodling is healthy!"

Elisa Kleven

Cart that Laundry, Scrub the Stove

"I get inspiration when I'm folding laundry, cleaning the stove, or doing other simple tasks that let my mind wander. Sometimes the ideas come so fast I have to drop what I'm doing and dash for a pen or pencil to get my thoughts down as they come flying out."

Deborah Lee Rose

In the Belfry

"Ideas for books are flying around in my brain like bats, arguing to see which one gets to come out next."

Connie Goldsmith

Warm-up...Ready...Set...Go!

"When I'm driving on the freeway or around town, my mind can go into creative state. It also seems to happen at about four o'clock in the afternoon in my studio. From about four to six I seem to be in my most creative state. Sometimes it feels as it has taken me all day to warm up, and by late afternoon the juices are flowing."

Thacher Hurd

Do Re Me

"Inspiration often comes to me while driving, too. Also, when working out at the gym. I once read a book about creativity in which the author states that movement facilitates creative thinking. He pointed out that the ancient Greek philosophers often went on long walks through olive groves when working out a problem

Long walks in the wilderness are also pretty great, but I have to be alone for inspiration to strike.

"Some music also inspires me. Sometimes before I write I put on a certain song that I know moves me deeply to get me in the mood. I find music especially effective when my character is at an emotional point in her story. I figure I can read the previous five chapters to get back into that emotional mood, or I can listen to one song."
Debra Keller

"My best writing comes if I'm writing to music. I like light jazz or gypsy guitar, like The Gypsy Kings. It frees up my brain, relaxes me, opens up my creative subconscious, and helps put me in the meditative state to receive my muse. I usually write in a semi-hypnotic state, almost channeling ideas from somewhere in the universe. At least that's how it seems at the end of each writing period when I read what I wrote, and I have no idea where it came from. The ideas certainly weren't in my conscious mind when I started writing that day. That's why I can't use an outline—I don't know what I'm going to write till I do. That's why music is helpful. It helps get me into that meditative, hypnotic state."
Marisa Montes

Stoke that Fire
"Falling asleep, in the shower, driving. These are definitely good places, because you can get into a relaxed state where your mind is active. But often I'll have ideas floating around my mind and then something will hit me that makes one come into sharper focus. Sid Fleischman says that you need two sticks to make a fire. Friction, you know? Each story needs two sticks. Well, for a long time, I had an idea about a family in which memories are passed down to give power to younger family members, but I didn't really have a plot. Then one night, I was watching some silly TV show and someone said something like, 'They never tell you what it's like to be the child of a super hero.' And, because my favorite super hero is Spiderman, I made the powers in my family, spider powers. That's from my book, *Cobwebs in the Sky*."
Karen Romano Young

In Control
"The magic happens when I make it happen, when I finally force myself to sit in front of the computer and write. And write, and write, being willing to stick with something the ten or fifty drafts it needs before it takes shape. I often get a 'brilliant idea' in the middle of the night, when I can't fall back asleep, or when I am puttering around the house, letting my mind wander—but that's not the magic part, for me. An idea is only as good as what I make of it, through drafts."
Janet Wong

KITCHEN SINK FOR THE SOUL

"Art happens when you get yourself out of the way. Each writer, simply by writing, will learn to turn on the faucet and get out of the way. Whatever your process is, discover it, then honor it."

Kathleen Duey

Squeaky Clean

"Being wide awake on a summer night. The windows are open, it's quiet and serene. I create some of the best poems, actually, when I'm not trying to. I usually get up and write so that I won't forget the words or the lines in the morning. Another form of inspiration, for me, is taking a shower. Hot water and steam make me think clearer. I know I won't have to answer the phone or the door. No one asks you a question. I even keep a pad of paper and a pencil right outside the shower door, and sometimes I open the door quickly to jot down an idea so I won't forget.

"Notebooks. Journals. Just looking at those empty pages gives me the urge to fill them up with words and feelings. Jotting down favorite words that could be the start of a poem one day is something I like to do. I might write pages and pages in one of my many journals. I must have ten at least! Then again, I might not write in them for days.

"I really have trouble thinking too much about poetry when I'm around other people. I might get a snippet of an idea, but it's hard to let your mind go free and mingle around other words in the neighborhood. I sometimes write on planes and in hotel rooms, but I rarely finish a poem this way. I like to be in my surroundings; my writing room with shelves of books, my comfortable chair, my clocks, photographs, notes and postcards."

Rebecca Kai Dotlich

12

Serendipity

Remarkable coincidences often occur to writers during their creative processes. While writing my chapter book, *Louise the One and Only*, a real person served as the basis for the character of Mr. Shelby, the kindergarten teacher. Since I knew the book would be illustrated, I never described what he looked like. In fact, I didn't describe any of the characters, nor did I correspond with the illustrator, Bob Alley.

When I received the early illustrations via fax from my editor, I was surprised to see the real person, who Mr. Shelby was based on, staring back at me! The current picture the illustrator drew of the principal, Ms. Humphreys, looked exactly like the real-life principal of my son's elementary school. When I gave a talk to the school, the kids asked me if I had sent a picture of their principal to the illustrator, so he'd know what to draw! Bob Alley must be inside my brain. And it didn't stop there. He did the same thing again with a character in my book, *Wish Magic*.

A similar thing happened to Zilpha Keatley Snyder, for her book *The Runaways*. She says, "When I saw the artwork for the cover, I was shocked by its similarity to the kids I had been imagining. I felt like the illustrator must have been able to look inside my head! The characters were exactly like *I* pictured them."

When Susan Hart Lindquist wrote *Walking the Rim*, she imagined her son, Charlie, acting out the role of Rudy, the main character. When she received the book jacket in the mail, there he was, looking exactly like her son.

Gennifer Choldenko wrote about a fragile, elderly dog in *Notes from a Liar and her Dog*. She decided against having the dog die in the story, since she really didn't want to go through that experience on the page, nor make her readers. But while the book was printing, her *real* dog suddenly developed cancer and had to be put to sleep. Her real dog wasn't sick at all when she wrote the book. She wasn't even old. Says Gennifer, "It was like life trumped me. I didn't want to experience the fictional death, but instead I had to go through the real thing.

Little Toot

"Although it took seven years to write, sell and publish *The Beetle and Me: A Love Story*, which is about a girl who restores an old VW Beetle, the year it came out (1999) was the same in which the new Beetles were introduced by Volkswagen."

Karen Romano Young

Metaphors

"Serendipity frequently happens during my process. Starting with one of my early novel's, *The Law of Gravity*, I discovered a quote by Sir Isaac Newton '...I seem to have been like a boy playing on the seashore...' which tied in perfectly with my story of a girl who is working on a summer project of trying to defy gravity and who periodically writes to a classmate who is vacationing at the beach with a request for seashells that she can identify as an alternate project.

"When I was writing *Aldo Ice Cream*, an ad in my local newspaper gave me the idea of having Aldo take part in a dirty sneaker contest. And more recently, writing about Dossi Rabinowitz who in 1910 leaves New York City to spend two weeks in northern Vermont, I accidentally stumbled on the fact that the New York Public Library building that was being completed at that time and, which Dossi brags about, was constructed of Vermont marble."

Johanna Hurwitz

Timeliness

"The day after puzzling over a *Cobblestone Magazine* theme on the Buffalo Soldiers, I read an article in the *Los Angeles Times* about a film honoring the Buffalo Soldiers that would be showing at the Autry Museum of Western Heritage that weekend. Before that time, I had no idea who the Buffalo Soldiers were. Pulling my patient husband along for the ride, I saw the film and suddenly had tons of ideas for articles. It led me to meeting the editors of *Cobblestone* personally and launched my magazine writing career."

Alexis O'Neill

Not Exactly a Coincidence...but Lucky....

"After I wrote a humorous article about the writing life for the *San Francisco Examiner*, children's author Ellen Leroe read the piece and wrote me a fan letter. Upon receiving it, I wrote back, and a friendship developed. Today I consider her one to be one of my best friends. And it all happened by writing about writers."

Elizabeth Koehler-Pentacoff

"The most fortunate thing for me is having my children. The confluence of being a children's writer and having children is wonderful. Everything they say is research! The thing I like best about being a writer is living in the world *like* a writer. Taking notes. Observing. It's a nice perspective and a wonderful way to raise children. You hear them differently. You're not managing and patrolling, you're observing. And it turns out to be good parenting. You're curious as to what their next thought is.

"I love being around them and their friends. I listen to their conversations and feel connected to what I do. I reinterpret a child's experience. That's the kind of serendipity that is most important to me."

Lin Oliver

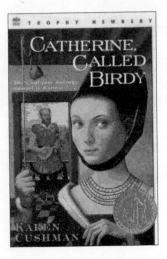

Featuring Karen Cushman

Karen Cushman has an M.A. in human behavior and another in museum studies. She served as assistant director of the Museum Studies Department at John F. Kennedy University in California. She is the author of several novels for children. Her first novel, *Catherine Called Birdy*, was a Newbery Honor Book. Her second book, *The Midwife's Apprentice*, won the Newbery Medal. (Not bad for a beginner, huh?) Her other books include *The Ballad of Lucy Whipple* and *Matilda Bone*.

From Catherine to Matilda, all of your characters tell their tale with a strong voice. What kind of questions do you ask yourself as your characters evolve?

"If I knew the answer to that, I'd have a lot less trouble when I sit down to write! I do ask myself, Would this character *really* do this or say something in this way? Often the answer is no, and I have to change the way they react. I ask myself, how is this character different from Catherine or Matilda? Do they face the same challenges? How are they different from each other? I often ask, what is it about the character's life that would *make* her act a certain way? These questions usually come after the first draft. In the first draft, I'm just frantic to get the story down.

"I don't think my characters exist outside of me nor do I talk to them in my head. But I do try to think of them as real people. For example, in my orphan train book, I put miners that Rodzina encounters on a train to Virginia City, Nevada. In 1882, silver mining collapsed. I thought, 'They wouldn't go there now. Everything is about to go bust.' Then I realized that the characters wouldn't know that yet.

They only know what happens to them up to 1881. I'm the only one who knows how it's going to turn out. These characters are outside of me."

You make your readers feel as though they're really in the gold mining camp with Lucy and in an apothecary in the Middle Ages with Matilda. How can aspiring writers choose details that will make them feel as though they're really in the setting?

"I do a lot of research—more than I need. I like the process of doing research, for I start to feel like I'm really in the apothecary shop. I close my eyes and try to describe it. I find details that appeal to the various senses. *How does light hit something? What can you hear? What are the smells?* Smells are important in a mining camp—pine trees, flowers, garbage heaps, unwashed miners. I brainstorm on the senses in a setting. I tell students, 'Close your eyes and imagine a tent in a mining camp. How can you tell you are *not* in twentieth century California?"

What has been your most challenging creative problem and how did you solve it?

"Matilda was challenging. I wanted her to be a different character from all of these independent, feisty young women I had written about. I wanted her to be less self aware. I wanted her to feel superior and removed, but also vulnerable. I wanted her to grow. I rewrote the book many times. I didn't want her to be too snotty or too short with Peg. And I wanted her to be difficult, but not unlikeable."

On that note, I noticed you had a credit of 'Associate Producer' for the TV movie of Lucy Whipple. *Can you tell us about that experience?*

"Glenn Close and Jena Malone were wonderful. And I thought they did a good job with the sets and costumes and details of life. When I saw the sets in person, I was impressed by the care they took to make the town look real. I know Glen Close worked very hard to keep things authentic.

"I wasn't crazy about the script. I was supposed to have script approval. They kept saying, 'We want your vision.' In reality, I got a call saying, *'We're almost through filming and when would you like to visit the set for a couple of days?'* I did get a copy of the script at that point, but there was no way for me to change anything then!

"They added characters and took out things from my book. I thought Lucy's relationship with the escaped slave was distorted in the movie. In the book, I made her realize that she treated him like a pet and be sorry for that. That wasn't dealt with in the movie. They added the character who killed himself. I assume it was to show how difficult life was, but that was what my whole book was about. And I wasn't sold on Lucy learning all those law books.

"I read a quote from Ann Tyler that helped me a lot through the experience. She said that once she sells something to TV or the movies, she no longer thinks of it as her book. It becomes *their* movie, and she lets go of it."

Do you have any advice to give about researching historical fiction?

"Start collecting all sorts of books at used bookstores that are in some way related to your interests. Books cannot only jump-start an idea, but once you need to know something, there's a good chance you'll already have a source. For example, I bought a book for five dollars called *The Universal Self Instructor*, published in 1883. I didn't know when I'd ever use it but it looked so interesting, a general reference guide to language, transportation, homemaking, farming, manufacturing, Shakespeare, food, phrenology! And lo and behold, I set Rodzina in 1881 and the book has been invaluable to me. And for five dollars.

"The public library is invaluable, too. Librarians are knowledgeable and helpful. I found lots of old books in the public library. I started out doing research at university libraries, but their books didn't tell me what I needed to know, not who was king but *Where did people go to the bathroom? When did they have bathtubs in houses? When did they have gas lighting?*

"I also recommend using non-book sources: photographs, songs, and objects. When I was in England, we were on a tour of a castle, and down in the dungeon, there were swords and other implements of torture. They let us lift a heavy, black sword and it gave me a different idea of what a mediaeval fight was like. Looking at the moisture on the walls, feeling the damp and the cold, helped me place myself in the Middle Ages. Objects and historic houses can give you a sense of what it was like to live in another time or place."

13

Rejection

Have you received a rejection from an editor recently? If you have, you're not alone. Rejection is frequently a part of nearly any writer's life. Here are encouraging words to read, and reread again, when you receive one of your manilla envelopes back in your mail box.

Bull's-eye

"Don't be discouraged. If you like writing, stick with it. Get over the rejections. I throw darts through my rejection letters! Then I feel better and get on with it."

Loretta Ichord

Game of Chance

"I've always looked as submitting a manuscript as entering the lottery. Each time you send a story out, it's like you're buying a ticket. You can reuse those tickets—something you can't do in a regular lottery. When I was starting out it also helped for me to regard my writing as a hobby. People spend a lot of money on hobbies. All I had to spend was postage. So I wasn't out too much and I wouldn't be disappointed if it took me too long to get published."

Suzanne Williams

Go, Girl

"Give yourself permission to pout. It's a loss. You go through a mourning process but you send the manuscript right back out. What usually happens to me is that grief turns into a fight—renewed determination."

Linda Joy Singleton

Movin' On
"I don't let it get to me. I move onto the next thing."
Katie Davis

Here's to Good Health
"Katherine Paterson said, *'We write to learn.'* That makes rejection more acceptable. I think I would write regardless whether or not I got published. When we write, we go through that learning process. People who write tend to be healthier. They've done studies with people with cancer. They have better recovery rates. Writing is good for you!"
Cynthia Chin-Lee

FOR CRYIN' OUT LOUD

"What do I do when I get a rejection? Cry! Then I don't let the sun set on a rejected manuscript. I send it out immediately. Another editor might think it's wonderful. After several rejections, I take another look and see if revision might be called for."

Ruth Radlauer

Make Lemonade
"I see rejection as an opportunity to revamp a story, or have the story go in a different direction. Sometimes it means the editor already has one on a particular topic. You often don't know how close you've come to publishing. The writer has no idea about hierarchal observances. Which is too bad. I almost wish they were called reply cards. You know, here's the *real* reason your manuscript didn't make it."
Patricia Polacco

Laundry Day
"Sometimes, I've wondered why writers don't have calluses from handling all of our rejection letters. I've read of one author who strings a clothes-line across the stage during school visits, then uses clothes pins to hang up his rejection slips. That's such a great idea. Collect them as personal medals for commitment and perseverance.

"Rejections always sting, no matter how kindly they're written. Humor helps me, but so does having several different manuscripts in circulation at the same time—like fishing lines. I also have a large rejection collection. Even the worst and meanest letters are kept, on the chance that a particular work *might* sell, and sometimes

THANKFUL TRICKS OF THE TRADE

"Be appreciative if you get a personal rejection letter. Write the editor and tell her you appreciated the critique.

"Twenty years ago, I took a class on how to write for children. The teacher, an author, held up a manuscript of mine as an example of everything that could go wrong in a manuscript! It absolutely humiliated me. I had sent it out to a publisher before this. I was devastated and never would have sent it out again. Lucky for me, the publisher bought it! That book is still in print. The point is, you have to be careful. It's important for writers to learn not to buy into everything people tell you, good or bad, about your manuscript. You must learn to recognize useful feedback that will help you revise. That's the trick to making it as a writer.

"I had a book that was rejected more than forty times and it was published with great success. I keep my rejection letters and then later I read these letters plus some of my good reviews to other aspiring writers so they can see the full range of comments I've received on each book. It's always an eye opener."

Ellen Jackson

does, to another editor who will really love it. I also try to sit down with a manuscript as soon as it's returned and decide whether or not to rework it. If so, I'll type another draft ASAP and mail it out to the next publisher."

Sarah Wilson

Playing Games

"There isn't much feedback with illustration submissions. Most of the time they don't respond at all, unless it's to send everything back. Rejection is part of the game, and if you're serious, you shouldn't take it to heart. The whole publishing process is so subjective. Getting rejected doesn't mean your work isn't worthy, just that it doesn't appeal to that particular person. Impress your friends with your big white binder of rejection letters. Works for me!"

Eve Aldridge

A Good Read Aloud

"I don't mind rejections. I like them as they get more and more personal.

Closer and closer to being published. Obviously I don't like them as much as accep
tances! But rejections are a form of feedback. Every book has to go through a cer
tain number of rejections. The first thing I do when I get a rejection letter, is I rerea
the story. Then I say to myself, is it really good enough to be published? If it is, I sen
it out again. Rejection letters are fun to read when the book finally gets published!

Bruce Balan

Believe It or Not

"I sent *Ghost Cadet* to Brenda Bowen at Holt because she had said in th
Society of Children's Book Writers and Illustrators' bulletin that she was intereste
in American history with strong family connections. They held it for two year
because they lost it! Finally, I got a phone call that she had just read it that weeken
and wanted to buy it. She said the manuscript was everything I said it was in m
cover letter. Have faith in your manuscript. Hedge your bets by rereading you
manuscript, if it comes back, and revising it if you think you can improve it. I thin
that's a very important part of coping. It helps you feel like you have a better chanc
too. But if you reread it and still think it's the best writing you have in you, the
keep looking for the right editor."

Elaine Marie Alphin

Out of Order

"Know that you're going to get discouraged. Keep sending your manuscrip
out and write something else. Don't wait. Soon after my first book was publishe
the publisher bought the other two I had written before the first book sold."

Kathryn Reiss

A Winner Never Quits

"You haven't failed until you quit. If you don't quit, you'll reach success som
where down the line. Hard work and persistence do pay off."

Wendelin Van Draanen

Lucky Number

"Succeeding in this business is completely all persistence. The second tim
Well Wished got rejected, I was devastated. Then my husband read the rejection ar
he said, "They liked it!" If you get any kind of personal rejection, you are mil
ahead of the game. Keep revising. *Well Wished* was rejected twenty-two times."

Franny Billingsley

Love Affair

"Unfortunately, artists are skin-thinned by nature. You have to believe in you
self. Author Tillie Olson once said something to the effect that publishers are runni

a business and you are practicing an art. Another quote I keep up in my studio is by author George Ella Lyon. 'Work is its own cure. You must love your work more than you like being loved.'"

Elisa Kleven

Loony-Tunes

"Why are writers crazy enough to keep going after so much rejection? I guess we figure we're going to write anyway, so we may as well send out what we write just to see if it's publishable."

Debra Keller

I Swear . . .

"When I get a rejection letter, I'm irritated at first and say to myself, 'Damn! Why can't they see how *good* this is?' Then in a few days I look at the letter again to see what I can learn from it."

Connie Goldsmith

Chris Crutcher

staying fat
for sarah byrnes

Featuring Chris Crutcher

Chris Crutcher is the award-winning author of many novels for young adults, such as *Whale Talk*, *Ironman*, *Staying Fat for Sarah Byrnes*, *Running Loose* and *Athletic Shorts: 6 Short Stories*. He graduated from Eastern Washington University, and became a teacher and director of an alternative school. He's been a child and family therapist for the past twenty years in addition to his work as an author.

How do you begin writing a novel?

"Usually I start with some character or a composite of characters or some specific attributes that I need my character to have for the plot. My characters develop after I put them in a situation. When I get in the middle of the book, I go back and do quite a bit of editing in the early chapters."

Do you outline your plot before you begin the actual writing?

"I'll start with a main idea or an event. I don't know how that event will get resolved. Part of the fun of writing the story is finding that out! I usually start to figure out the ending around chapter eight."

Writers may have strong beginnings and endings for their fiction, but often get bogged down in those 'murky middles'. Does this ever happen to you?

"It happens all the time. The trick is, don't let them scare you. If I get stuck in the middle, it means I haven't thought out what happens. For me, the best way to think a story through is to go running. Or I talk with other people. Sometimes you can talk through your plot problems."

How do you know if you're writing a middle grade or a young adult?

"I don't think about the audience at all. I write the story and if I've done something that gives my editor chills, I'll talk about it. If it doesn't hurt the story, I'm willing to make changes. The older your reader is, the better you're able to take on meatier scenes. Young adults want to know, *who am I and how do I fit in the universe?* When I give talks to middle school, the emphasis is more on action. In high school, the emphasis is on ideas."

Can you discuss your opinions and experiences about censorship?

"Being censored almost makes me as proud of my books as being on a best books list! When the censor starts to take information from kids, they take themselves out of the list of people to turn to. If I have a twelve-year-old daughter and I protect her from reading a book, she may agree with me. But when she's fourteen or fifteen, she'll run into the stuff that offends me, and I won't be the person she'll talk to. If she gets pregnant, I'd be out of the loop.

"I was in Texas when *Athletic Shorts: Six Short Stories* came out. I was at a dinner at a teacher's house and someone asked me what the first story in the book was about. I said, 'It's about a kid with two sets of gay parents.' The room got quiet, so I changed the subject.

"The next day, I got up at five in the morning and went to Denny's. I'm thinking, this is the first time no one knows where I am. Then the waitress says, 'Telephone call for Chris.' I pick up the phone and a woman who had been at the dinner the night before had tailed me. She said, 'When you talk to the students, will you be mentioning homosexuality?' I said, 'I don't think so.' She said, 'Thank goodness. Here in Tyler, we don't mind the rape and incest so much. But not homosexuality.' Here I was going to talk about swimming!

"Another place near Houston, Texas, a guy ran for the school board. He had nothing but quotes from my book on his flyer. At the top of the flyer, it said, 'This man has been in our schools! If I'm elected, he'll never *set foot* in our schools.' The focus was bad language, because I included the word 'God.'

"I had been to one school where they asked me not to say the word 'asshole,' since it had been in my book, *Iron Man*. So when I talked to the students, I said, 'I can't tell you what the word is, but it rhymes with gas hole!' They loved it! It freed a teacher to say the word when he read the book to his classes."

Research

What sources do authors use when they want to find information about a topic? Where do they find information? How do they organize their research? How do they know when to stop researching and start writing?

Statistics
"I make a three ring binder for my research. I read through it over and o
again so it becomes a part of me. I probably use ten percent or less of what I fir
but it's the other ninety percent that makes me secure in place and time."
Karen Cushman

Here's the Scoop
"The Internet has made my life easier. First, when I decided to write a bc
about the history of ice cream, I went to the library and saw what was availal
Next, I typed in 'ice cream' to all the search engines. I connected with so ma
fabulous organizations and people! I did have to triple check the facts, though. Y
can't trust everything you read on the Internet. But there is a wealth of materia
your disposal. I found pictures online through the Library of Congress, museu
and historical societies. They would email the photos as an attached file to
publishers. I linked up to one gentleman's personal web site. He was a doctor lis
in the Guinness Book of World Records as having the largest collection of anti
ice cream freezers. He had done years of research, so he gave me names and nu
bers of other people I could talk to. I interviewed one eighty-year-old man w
writes a newsletter for a national ice cream retailers association. He worked a
soda jerk in the 1930's. Without the Internet I wouldn't have stumbled on th
fabulous, informative people. And it would have taken me much longer to resea
and write the book.

"While researching the book, I did a lot of traveling. I toured two ice cream factories and a dairy farm; interviewed industry taste testers; took scoops lessons from the former soda jerk; made ice cream, cones and fudge sauces in my own kitchen; and tasted every brand of ice cream I could get my spoon into, gaining six pounds in the process. The Internet is great for research, but cyber ice cream just doesn't taste the same!

"When the book came out, I threw an ice cream social to celebrate. I found a caterer who brought in a real soda fountain from the 1920's. He and his two daughters came dressed in soda jerk garb. They spent three hours making tasty fountain treats I'd never heard of. A delicious time was had by all!"

Lee Wardlaw

AHEAD OF TIME

"When I have verified a fact at least three times, from good solid sources, I can stop the research. I'm very careful about research from the Internet, although the History Channel web site and college web sites are pretty good. I try to back everything up with book research as well.

"When I wrote *Covered Wagons, Bumpy Trails*, I had a verse about the colonials seeing a daffodil hill. But through research, I found out that daffodils were planted *after* they came, so I changed the flowers to violets. Then I realized the pioneers came to California in the fall, and violets don't grow in the fall, so I changed it again—to poppies.

"The smallest things like that can make a big difference in your story. If you base your story in history, it's very important to portray that history as accurately as possible. When children read it, they will believe it because it's in a book. They'll remember it and it will be a fact all their lives."

Verla Kay

Take Time

"When I wrote *December Tale* I spent more time researching Joan of Arc than I did writing the book. They have wonderful records of her trial, which I read over and over. I over-did it. Same thing with *Ghost in the Family*. I got hung up on the history of the Spanish presence in the presidio."

Marilyn Sachs

Too Much To Tally

"If you're going to interview someone, do your research! I didn't and it was a lesson I wouldn't forget. In 1988, I was asked to interview Eve Bunting and write up a short article about her, which would serve to announce her as a speaker at our annual Asilomar conference. I was a new children's writer then, and I hadn't yet heard of Eve. I called her, and after we had spoken a few minutes, I asked, 'Could you give me a list of your books for my article?' 'Which ones?' she said. 'My most recent?' I replied, 'All, of course.' *Of course!*

And she replied, 'But I have 116 books!'

I'll never forget that number. As of January 1988, Eve Bunting had published 116 books!"

Marisa Montes

Never Stop

"I search libraries, science museums and I buy a lot of books. The California Academy of Science has been very helpful. The Sea Educational Association in Woodshole, Massachusetts, was very cooperative with good information about the Sargasso Sea. I went to Korea for background material for *The Korean Cinderella* and to the Galapagos Islands for *Galapagos Means Tortoises. When should you stop researching?* I never really stop until the book is with the publisher. I keep referring to my resources and trying to get more information as long as I am still writing and illustrating."

Ruth Heller

Silver Screen

"I do interviews and travel to areas I'm writing about. I go to the library and do historical research for details. One novel of mine is set in 1939. I talked to older people who lived then. Research can be fun. I have an excuse to watch movies of that era for historical detail!"

Cynthia Chin-Lee

Accordian to Her . . .

"To organize my research, I have a big accordion file for each book. I copy all of my sources and clip things together. When I send the manuscript, I include all of my research. Then my editor has a copy. That saves time."

Ellen Jackson

Playing Detective

"I enjoy research because it's a lot like solving a mystery. I love a good mystery. There's information about your topic out there; the mystery is in finding where it is and how you're going to get to it."

Larry Dan Brimner

Travel Agent

"I'm a hands-on research person. Make history alive by going to the place where it happened, and when possible, holding things related to your subject, or that belonged to the people you're writing about. In England, I held Richard III's military strategy book and his prayer book. I'm a big believer in primary sources. The next best thing is going to the library. Use interlibrary loans to get the book you need, even if you live in a small town. I use online sources to plan my trips more than to do original research."

Elaine Marie Alphin

Expert Advice

"My library has an interlibrary loan service. They can order books from any other library on the service. Through interlibrary loan, you have the resources of numerous university and metropolitan libraries available to you. Don't be afraid to pick up the phone and call an "expert." Most people are thrilled to help you present the topics they love to children. This is fun. I've talked with folks from Chinese medical doctors to Appalachian quilters."

Suzanne Morgan Williams

Play a Hand

"I use old-fashioned index cards, with subjects noted in the upper right corner and a number for the source in the upper left. Elsewhere, I have an index card with a list of sources. My goal is to be able to put all the cards in the order that I want to write the story. The trick is identifying the rubrics. They change as I do more research."

Ann Manheimer

The Write Research

"I used three-by-five cards for years to organize my research, before I finally woke up to the fact that they didn't work well for me. I was always losing them. Now I use spiral-bound notebooks and keep all my research notes in one place. I number the pages of the notebook and leave the first few pages blank for a table of contents so that I can find notes from a particular source or on a particular subject without leafing through the entire notebook. I'm still experimenting with ways to make my table of contents more helpful.

"I usually am not done researching before I begin writing. I've done the lion's share, but generally a moment comes when the characters are ready to speak and can't be held back anymore, so I begin even though I know I'll have to keep looking things up as I go along. The truth is, I rarely know what it is I'm going to need to know until I find out what's going to happen in the book—and at least some of that must be found out by writing it."

Katherine Sturtevant

Count Down

"I keep a loose leaf notebook. I number the books I use in a bibliography. When I take notes, I place the book number and page by the note. That way, I can verify information and make decisions about conflicting or questionable facts by returning to the source. I cut and paste this information, including the book number and source, under different headings. Then I'm ready to write."

Tekla White

Horses and Foxes and Bears Oh My

"Bob [his brother, author Robert San Souci] goes to the Bancroft Library [a California history library] and does a tremendous amount of research for his folktales. He saves visual references for the illustrator. When I work with him, this gives me a starting point. I spend lots of time doing my own research. My wife is a librarian and her speciality is research. When Bob was working on *Mulan*, she helped out with the research.

"When I work on my wildlife books, I go to wildlife refuges and zoos. When I did *Ice Bear and Little Fox*, I went to Alaska and I photographed the landscape, then went to the San Diego Zoo to research the polar bear and arctic fox.

"I'm working on a book about wild mustangs. I felt like I wasn't a good enough photographer to get good shots of the horses running in a herd, so I paid for the rights to use professional photographs."

Daniel San Souci

Dig for Treasure

"A good librarian is invaluable. So is the Internet and email. Dig as close to the source—original material—as you can get."

Tricia Gardella

Get Organized

"I looked at the bibliographies and suggested readings lists from other nonfiction books. I contacted the archives of newspapers and got copies of stories written over 100 years ago, for my book, *Lost in Death Valley*. I visited Death Valley and spent half a day with the museum curator. When you begin reading the same information over and over again, you know you've finished your research and it's time to start writing.

"I ended up withe two boxes of photocopied research. I didn't organize my material very well, and when the editor needed certain information, it took me hours to find what I needed. In some cases, I had to go back to the library and search for the source of a quote. The material for my second nonfiction book was much more organized."

Connie Goldsmith

Research for a Play

"My play, *Sunday Gold*, was commissioned. Funded by a theater, a museum and other sources, I was to create a one-hour school tour play on North Carolina history that would require no more than six actors. I could choose any subject. It was a bit like giving a child a piece of paper and saying, 'Draw whenever you like.' Initially tempting, the project became more frustrating as my topic did not leap out, bow and present itself.

"To get to know some of the history, I studied the classic text, *North Carolina Through Four Centuries*. But I wanted to write a play about a woman, and women were woefully absent. After much discussion, all parties finally agreed on the same topic: the North Carolina Gold Rush.

"For two intense weeks, the Museum staff guided me and gained access for me at the North Carolina Museum of History, state archives, university libraries and the Reed Gold Mine. At Reed Gold Mine, I went down the mine shaft, panned for gold, and examined nineteenth century mining artifacts.

"At Gold Hill, the old mining town and ultimately the setting for the play, I conducted interviews with the historical society and elderly residents who remember tales of the early days. I searched the cemeteries for names, took photographs, and jotted down sounds and images. I collected books, newspapers, magazines and journal articles; I photocopied visuals, theses, and a dissertation to examine later. I started separate files, e.g. General Research, Reed Gold Mine, Gold Hill, Characters.

"But so far, all I had was a lot of notes: information on the dimensions of mining equipment, minting coins, how the essay office operated, but nary a woman's name or human interest story. Finally, one hot, humid fall day, while plowing through a nineteenth century Wages Earned list, just when I was about to give up, I saw a woman's name and found out that young girls had been employed to operate the rockers. I began to ask questions about these rocker girls. There wasn't a lot of information, but an idea was jelling.

"Someone had earned her first pair of shoes working at the mine. CLICK.

"At the Gold Hill Museum, there was a pair of women's handmade leather boots. CLICK.

"Immersing myself in the archives, I found that one-half the labor force had been hired-out slaves and that in the 1840's, the issue of free education was up for a vote. DOUBLE CLICK.

"Though originally, I'd planned to write a play on the impact of gold on those who discovered the precious ore and those who didn't, I began to change my mind. Characters jumped out. Barefoot Lizzie who wants the gorgeous red boots she sees in the window and longs for schooling that her pa doesn't deem necessary, and Annie who wants nothing more and nothing less than her freedom. Through their friendship and acts of courage, they find out, not all the gold is in the ground."

Joanna H. Kraus

Enquiring Minds Want to Know....

"I read the newspapers of the period so I begin to feel I'm in the era. I have old encyclopedias. The first one I bought was a 1906 edition. I wanted to know what Milwaukee was like for Golda Meir. I looked up Milwaukee, and the description created Milwaukee for me. I have a 1906, 1911, 1943. It's a wonderful way to look up things!

"There are bound volumes of newspaper articles, front pages of the *New York Times*. It is better to read the way it was recorded then, than to read the way historians describe it now. You get the excitement that was there at the time.

"When I researched Joe Louis, I read the *New York Times* and other mainstream newspapers. Louis was described as 'something sinister and perhaps not quite human.' 'Out of the African jungle, like a panther on a hunt!' That was the mainstream press! The images show the sentiments of the time. I could have said they were prejudiced, but this is more vivid.

"I did eight books on the Holocaust and often used details, descriptions, and quotes from witnesses and survivors. My book, *We Remember the Holocaust*, is filled with quotes and photographs from survivors.

"It took me over five years to interview the people for *We Remember the Holocaust*. During the interviews, I had to continually focus the survivors to get the heart of what happened. The tension was painful for them. I was shaken. They were shaken. I taped some of the interviews and for some I took notes. I always sent the quotes to the people I quoted to look over. What was telling also, was after the book was written, I went to the Yad Vasheum Jerusalem Holocaust archives. The first day, after searching for photographs for my book, I ate in their cafeteria, and later came home with an upset stomach. I thought it was the cafeteria food. The next time, I brought my own lunch, and I was *still* sick. Then I realized it wasn't the food, it was the pictures."

David Adler

Digging up Facts with Caroline Arnold

Caroline Arnold has written over 100 books for children, specializing in nonfiction, many of them on scientific topics. She studied art at Grinnell College and the University of Iowa. Her titles include *Stories in Stone, City of the Gods, The Ancient Cliff Dwellers of Mesa Verde*, and *Watch Out for Sharks!*

"I often get ideas for new books when I do research for another book. I'll come across a tidbit or small fact and I want to find out more. In a book of mine about Mesa Verde National Park, there's a one page spread on petroglyphs, or rock art. I'm a member of the National History Museum in Los Angeles, and they offered a field trip to a petroglyph site in the Mojave Desert. It's the richest site in the nation, but it's on government land, so the access is limited.

"So my photographer and I went on this field trip. I knew it would be a good topic for a book. On that particular trip I took some of my own photos. Those are my personal research. If they end up in a book, it's nice, but they're like tourist photographs; when I get home it helps me remember what I saw. Then I can do enough research to write a proposal.

"To research a potential project, I go to the library and check *Books In Print*. I also check Amazon.com. If there are too many books on the subject already, there may not be enough room for yours. If you don't find anything on your topic, ask yourself, is there enough interest to merit a whole book? That question may be hard to answer. One way to get feedback [about ideas] is to have contact with children or schools. If the topic is used in schools for reports and reading to supplement the curricula, there's a likely market for it. If it doesn't have a curricula tie, it's probably going to be a tough sell.

"If your idea is too focused and too narrow, write a magazine article. If it's a whole book, it must have a broad, general application. However, the subject can be an event or person if that event or person illustrates a larger idea.

"There is a tendency nowadays for people to think they can find everything on the Internet. The Internet is actually an invaluable resource. But it's not *all* there. Anything you find on the Internet must be double checked. Anybody can put something on the Internet. At the library, the facts that you find in books, magazines and encyclopedias, have already been edited and fact-checked.

"Don't be afraid to ask reference librarians to help you. They'll know where to find resources that don't pop up when you do your catalog search. The one thing I don't like about the computer catalog systems that have replaced card files in libraries, is they're not very forgiving. If you misspell by one letter, or don't come up with the right search word, you won't find anything. In the old card catalogues, you would find cards just before your topic and after.

"For resources that don't come up on your search, you have to be more creative. Use a search and come up with the call numbers of the books that might be helpful. Then go to the call number bookshelves and browse. There will be a lot of books there, whose title won't be your subject. But those books might have information about your topic if you check the table of contents.

"For instance, when I researched a book about El Nino [inspired by the El Nino weather pattern in California of that previous year], there were no books on it in the library. I was researching it before anyone knew what the topic meant! At the time, it was only written about in science journals. A librarian suggested a specific book to me, that was about current events. That book had a whole section on recent weather and had the information I needed. Now you can find information on this subject everywhere.

"Similarly, when I find I'm in the midst of researching a topic, I talk about it to people I know. It's amazing what people say. *Did you see an article on such and such?* People that you know—who are not necessarily experts on the topic—can sometimes give you little bits of special information that you might not uncover by yourself.

"When you research your topic, contact the experts. Ask your expert to recommend any reading or other resources to you."

First Drafts/Revision

From Start to Finish

"I think everybody writes their own way. I write the story from beginning to end. I don't move on until most of the major problems are solved. I might still rewrite the story ten times, but I don't leave a major problem. Sid Fleischman once said he never leaves his writing with a problem at the end of the day. It's always an easy place, so he can get started the next day."

Stephen Mooser

Dem Bones

"A lot of the story occurs during rewrite. I tend to write bare bones the first time through, and then do a great deal of rewriting. My favorite time of writing is when I've reached THE END, am well acquainted with my story, and start an extensive rewrite. I print the manuscript, and then go through it in hard copy, making notes in the margins. Then I start over, adding and subtracting as I go."

Zilpha Keatley Snyder

Worth the Wait

"In my critique group, we read our manuscripts aloud to polish them before submitting. Sometimes it's hard to wait on sending out a manuscript I love. But it's a mistake to send something out before it's ready."

Joan Holub

Be True to You

"Somebody said writing is rewriting. I don't show it to a lot of people—they'll get you all mixed up. Show it to one or two people you trust. Be careful. They might muddy the waters with *their* own voice. It's *your* voice."

Marilyn Sachs

IT'S THE REAL THING

"The real writing for me happens in revision. I actually enjoy revision. I get the burst of creative pleasure from writing the first draft, but I get the craftsman satisfaction from the revision."

David Lubar

First Drafts

"Read Anne Lamott's book *Bird by Bird*. The first draft doesn't have to be good. It's supposed to be terrible! It's for finding out what the book is about, what you think about it, and just what you want to say."

Karen Cushman

"To paraphrase Anne Lamott's famous advice, allow yourself to write a 'poopy' first draft—but get it down! Then settle in to the wonder and beauty of the rewrite."

Mary Pearson

Go Crazy

"I free-write about how angry I am. Do momentum writing about what's not working in your manuscript. Identify the one thing you love and expand on that. Highlight the things that don't work. Say *why* you don't like it. Use your yellow marker and take out the stuff you hate. Write forty drafts. Address the part that makes you nuts!"

Deborah Norse Lattimore

Best Book Ever

"Kids have asked me, 'How does it feel to get corrected?' I *love* getting corrected. It means the person (who corrects me) loves my work enough to help me and they want to help my book be a better book."

Katie Davis

Know that Knob

"My license plate used to be REWRYTE. To me, the hard part is getting something down. So I write anything. I don't care if it makes any sense or if I have cliches or misspellings or stupid plot ideas. Then the fun starts! I think it's important to have a strong critical eye, but you have to make sure your critical self has an on/off switch. Turn it '*off*' while you're writing. Turn it '*on*' while you're reading what you've written."

Gennifer Choldenko

Let it All Hang Out

"One thing I heard John Irving say on public radio, he said, '*I'm not much of a writer, but I'm a hell of a rewriter.*' I don't care if what you write is embarrassing. Let it go off in all directions!"

Chris Crutcher

Chase Those Worries Away

"Expect your first draft to be pretty crappy. That's okay. Nancy Farmer is in my writer's group and she told me to be patient. She said, 'Take your time.' She wrote in Africa before she came to the U.S. so a lot of her 'instant success' was because she had written years before [she became published]. I have a full-time job and a family, so I have to be more patient with myself."

Cynthia Chin-Lee

No Balking Allowed

"I have never balked at being told to rewrite. My editor, Patty Gauch, has written forty-two books herself. I respect her."

Patricia Polacco

Type and Type Again

"I often rekey poetry. I like that process. With a new book of adult poems I've finished, I had to retype the book because I lost it in the computer. But I wasn't troubled. To redo the poems is a measure of patience. In my prose, the story will be skeletal. Then I'll add more phrases and sentences. Each scene gets bigger and bigger."

Gary Soto

Been There, Done Yet?

"I never send anything off until I can't think of any way to make it better. If I can think of something to change that will make the story stronger, I know I'm not done yet. That means I may write ten revisions until I'm satisfied."

Kathryn Reiss

Depth Patrol

"My usual reaction to a long letter of revision is *Ack! This is too hard. I can't do this. Wasn't my story brilliant the way it was?* Since the answer was obviously 'no,' I've found that the best approach is to immediately put your subconscious to work solving the problems raised by the editor. Moodle the points for a day or two, then sit down and tackle the comments one by one. What you discover is that the 'problems' that seem major, can be fixed or adjusted by nuance—by adding a word, phrase, sentence, or paragraph—or by deleting one of those. Often a piece does not require major rework, but merely the process of layering, that peeling of the onion, that gives the story more depth.

"Rewriting is difficult work, but the only solution is to stay with it. If you disagree with some of the recommended changes, discuss them with the editor. Often revisions will go back and forth several times until both parties feel that the story is where it needs to be. The hardest experience is being close to an offer, (of a book contract), then getting a near miss rejection."

Dian Curtis Regan

Time and Time Again

"I usually type my fiction directly into the computer. When I write *Cam Jansen*, if I finish the first chapter I'll rewrite the first chapter, then go on to the second. Then I rewrite the first AND second chapters. I rewrite continually.

"I rewrote my book *B. Franklin, Printer* many times. I sent it to my editor, and she said she loved it. But by the time she got back to me, I had rewritten it ten more times! It's hard for me to let go. I enjoy the rewriting process. Knowing I'm going to rewrite makes the first draft so much easier. It's a liberating thing.

"Do an outline for your book and then wait a month. Then, write the book and wait another month. Rewrite the book. Wait a month. It becomes a better book!"

David Adler

Biggest Creative Problem They've Ever Faced

"The toughest book I've written was *Hope Was Here*, which won a Newbery Honor Medal. It's nice to know that your problem children can go out into the world and make you proud. It's a story that grapples with so many things—honor in politics, cancer, the importance of caring about community, what's it like to learn to trust again when you've been burned so many times. The plot was getting bogged down, the humor wasn't coming. I had a list by my computer of careers I could go into in case this book didn't work! My editor, Nancy Paulsen, was so deft on how she worked with me. She showed me how to cut the political speeches and show the power of the people behind them by what they did. I learned the show, don't tell rule so powerfully as a writer in the working and reworking of this story. I had to strip away layers and layers. I had to write a campaign that didn't have any political speeches. I had to do it all through the characters.

"I saw afresh how we writers can bring so much of ourselves to our stories. Sometimes we need to step back from that a bit. As a woman in my forties, I have some real political issues. I came to this book politically jaded and it hurt the writing initially because I was putting my issues on my sixteen-year-old character. So I started asking myself, what kind of a candidate would kids rally to? And I came up with G.T. Stoop, not a trendy guy, but a honest, true one. I think, ultimately, kids are looking for honest people. They can tell the fakers a mile off. I also asked, what is

the unique message about honor and politics that a teenager could deliver? I had a lot of tunnels to dig, but I'm glad I had an editor who was not pushing me on time."
Joan Bauer

"While working on a book of poems for the forthcoming book, *100th Day of School*, I originally submitted fifty-two poems. The book was accepted with the suggestion that I write sixty-eight more. That way, the editor could eliminate twenty of them, leaving a collection of 100 poems. I thought I'd already conjured up all the ideas I had about 100, but I was able to tap regions of my imagination where I'd never even dared to venture before."
Betsy Franco

"I have to balance my time between writing and other activities like booksignings and speaking engagements. I am still learning that balancing act, but again, what I find to be the most helpful is to set goals for my writing—a combination of daily word counts and 'due dates' for the manuscript. That way I manage to keep some writing balance."
Mary Pearson

Elements of Fiction
and Nonfiction Characters

Revelation
"I'm learning to involve more of the whole fabric of the narrative in revealing character. I've also learned the aspects of prose that I've tended to slight are the most important ones for me to learn to polish."
David Lubar

Getting to Know You
"I like to take my character for walks. Pretty soon I am the character."
Deborah Norse Lattimore

Obsessive Compulsive?
"Give your character an obsession. Elevate it to a level of compulsion."
Franny Billingsley

What If...
"One way to develop complex, realistic characters is to 'write outside the frame.' If you're writing a novel, spend some time writing pages that you know will never be part of the book. Put your character in various situations and see how he or she behaves. *How would she react if her house had burned down and all of her possessions were gone? What if her best friend won a contest she'd been hoping to win herself? If the person she resented most in the world suddenly gave her a present?* Since these situations don't have to appear in your book, there's an endless list of them. You can put your character in scenes with her parents, siblings, or friends

until you feel you have a good handle on how she would behave under a variety of conditions."

Katherine Sturtevant

Character Portrait

"I often draw people to get to know my characters. It was interesting, with my book, *Outside In*, to draw the kids. The book has many scenes where the kids in the neighborhood are together, and when I drew them I discovered things about them: who'd be sitting next to who, who'd be leaning on someone's shoulder or looking at someone else, (exchanging glances or making googly eyes) or leaving plenty of space between them. In the story some of the kids build little elf houses and the furniture that goes inside. I began drawing the furniture and imagining which kid would build each piece. It showed a lot about age, creativity, patience, and other things about them. The furniture drawings are going to be in the book!"

Karen Romano Young

Psychic Connection

"In my own personal growth as a writer, I am learning to delve deeper into my characters' psyches to find those universal truths that make readers see themselves in another person's story."

Dian Curtis Regan

Bring to Life

"My main characters are often based on people I know. Cam [from the *Cam Jansen* mystery series] is based on a classmate of mine with a photographic memory. Now, after more than twenty Cam books, the character exists on her own in my mind. I no longer think of my classmate, I think of Cam.

"Additionally, when I pick a setting the setting becomes a character in my book. *What else is happening there? Who else is there?* Including this information keeps my story from being too linear.

"With Cam, I tried to create a strong enough character so that even if the reader figures out the mystery, he'll want to keep reading. The character becomes a familiar friend."

David Adler

Bits and Pieces

"Minor characters are one of the things I have the most fun with in my books. One of the most useful writing assignments I've ever been given was to write a series of one-paragraph sketches, each designed to reveal as much as possible about a character. It relates to a private game I've played since childhood. Wherever I go, I'm always studying people—thinking about their clothes, their hair, their scars and moles and tattoos, the way they walk, what they're carrying, the expressions on their faces, what they're having for lunch. When I go to someone's house for a visit, I can't help looking to see what kinds of objects they've surrounded themselves with. *What kinds of books do they own. What kinds of pictures do they have on their walls? Are there interesting smells? Are there pets? Are things neat, cluttered, tidy, dusty?* The object of this game is to create a story to go with the few bits of information I've collected about a person.

"The man who sold me my new car was bald, tattooed, and looked as if he lifted weights and ate nails for breakfast. He wore no wedding ring. But he was friendly and likeable, and had a picture on his desk of himself with his arm around a ten-year-old boy, both of them grinning ear-to-ear, in front of an antique motorcycle. On the wall of his office was a small, hand-lettered piece of paper that said, 'One day at a time.' I went home feeling as if I'd known him all my life.

"Of course I didn't really know him at all. *I just felt as if I did.* That's the key. A few carefully, chosen, unusual details about a minor character can make the reader feel as if they know everything about him or her. With Madam Isis, the fortune teller in *The Power of Un*, it's her velvet robes, the scarab tattoos on her fingers, and her rough, foreign voice."

Nancy Etchemendy

Overnight Guests

"Characters just sort of come in my house and live for awhile. They come through the door and open the refrigerator! It's a good thing I live alone. It's all about what the characters will or will not do. I don't have to worry, *would this character do this thing?* I know what will happen and what they will do and won't do. I don't have any control over them."

Angela Johnson

Avoid Clichés

"First I ask myself, what is the general story premise and what kind of traits in my protagonist and other characters will offer interesting questions, problems, themes, and situations for that story? I start with a couple characteristics related to plot; as I play with plot, more character traits emerge, and vice-versa. I also toss in elements that just come to mind and feel like a good fit. Sometimes I'll go back late in the writing process and add character traits as opportunities reveal themselves. For example, in *The Sacrifice*, while writing the major escape scene near the end of the book, I realized that I could heighten its suspense and significance if I went back and added a certain trait to the protagonist's horse, Bull. Although a horse, he served as a character.

"I also used a detailed checklist of open-ended questions for each major character, to stimulate ideas. For example: Talents? Religious beliefs? Relationship to family members? Weaknesses? Worst fear? What does his/her room look like? Etc. Some questions will not spark anything for a particular character, others will. I find that an excellent final question for any character checklist is, In what way does this character *avoid* being a stereotype? This forces you to dig for more depth and quirks to make your character more original."

Diane Matcheck

Step Back in Time

"Characters intrigue me more than plot. The plot grows out of my characters. I put characters in situations and see how they will respond. I do a lot of research. Do a yard of research and you'll use two inches. But this will give you a real feel of the time. I looked at women's magazines from the 1930's and '40's on microfiche. *What were their recipes? Their issues?* It gave me a feeling for the women. For the childbirth scene, I read the various superstitions black women had. A lot of research gives you a feel for the character and will help make your characters real."

Karen English

Howdy Stranger

"My main characters have to be complete strangers to me when we meet— with no obvious parts of anyone I know, and mostly no parts of me. Once I get to know them well as independent individuals, it's safe to let these parts seep in.

"The first question I ask myself is: *'Will this character be interesting enough? Interesting enough not to bore me to death after we've spent a month or a year together?'* What I mean by 'interesting,' is a personal thing –sort of like choosing close friends. I need to figure out whether my character and I will be having the same conversations every time we speak, or whether we will lead each other into exciting places—lead me somewhere I've never been?"

Susan Hart Lindquist

Voice

The Big Picture

"I think it's easier to get a character voice in first person, and harder for third person. I'm conscious of mood, tone, and theme and the big picture intent behind it. *Is the story intended to feel formal or casual? Tense?* Then my word choice will start flowing in that direction. Ask yourself, *what is your intent of the scene?* One editor told me, 'Voice is like pornography. I can't define it, but I'll know it when I see it.'"

Diane Matcheck

Write Right

"Worrying about voice is like wondering what you look like without the left-right mirror reversal. Forget about it. Spend all your time getting your characters right. And write and write and write and write...then one day you'll realize your voice has found you."

Gennifer Choldenko

You'll Run Into It

"I used to be a runner. There's a runner's high, when you run past being tired. That happens with writers. When I'm writing a book, halfway or two thirds of the way through my first draft, the characters begin to tell me where the story is going. The voices 'click in.'"

Joan Bauer

Talk to Your Characters

"I don't make charts. Instead I carry on numerous conversations with my characters. In time, I learn much about them that might never be included in a story, such as their favorite food, TV program, game, etc. Part of my daily routine is taking an early morning walk of a couple of miles. I don't wear a headset and listen to music as some people do. Instead, I'm working out my story plots and 'talking' with my characters."

Johanna Hurwitz

Honesty the Best Policy

"I think it's easy to confuse voice with style and tone. These days, in contemporary fiction, we usually mean the 'voice' of the character, rather than the 'voice' of the author. Traditionally it's been the other way around. Perhaps that's why there's such a fascination with it today—because it's added something exciting to the writer's toolbox that allows him/her to create a deep intimacy between the character and reader. But it has no rules, and for that reason, among others, it's hard to advise anyone on how to 'create a strong voice' beyond allowing a character to have opinions and a sense of humor, setting him/her free to react to the world, and above all, encouraging him/her to speak honestly."

Susan Hart Lindquist

18

Setting

Show Don't Tell

"I recommend handling setting as you would a character. Choose a setting that you're interested in. Remember, you'll be spending a lot of time in this setting and you'll enjoy and probably do a better job of writing it if you choose a setting you know or want to know and care about.

"Focus on specific characteristics according to what will further your plot, mood theme. Ask yourself: *what place, time, weather, etc would be logical and interesting, but not already done to death; present challenging obstacles or plot twists; add atmosphere; resonate with your theme?*

"Show your setting in action rather than just describing it. Ask yourself what would a character really notice in this scene. Leave out everything else. *How might the character interact with the setting? How could the setting advance or set back the plot?* For example, if your character is running from the law in Arizona, he would not pay much attention to the state's natural beauty, but would probably be on the lookout for potential hiding places and alternative roads, a different mode of transportation, etc. Something in the environment may trigger a memory, perhaps a previous trip through the desert under happier circumstances. He may also turn on the radio to see if there's any news about this case, have to stop for gas/food/water at some point and try not to be noticed, etc."

Diane Matcheck

Character Reactions

"Present setting from the inside out. Make your character *react* to it if you can. Don't waste it—make it work for you. Above all, have a reason for mentioning something."

Susan Hart Lindquist

19

Dialogue

Writing good dialogue is one tough endeavor. A sense of reality is the goal, and for this, it is important that the author knows his or her characters well and writes true to how each character would speak.

"First, people have to listen to the way children talk. Very often I see authors write children's dialogue as they *should* speak, not as they *do* speak. Listen to the interrupted speech. No one speaks in perfect sentences. The ear comes into play here. Notice the difference how kids are and how you want them to be."
Marilyn Sachs

"Write lots of it."
David Lubar

"Listen to people talking to get ideas for new phrasing or vocabulary. Take notes. Robert Louis Stevenson had two journals with him: one for his own compositions and one for taking notes of other's conversations."
Angelica Carpenter

"When you're trying to write dialogue from a historical period, look at materials from that time—court transcripts and letters are especially good—and jot down phrases and expressions that you can use in dialogue. Also, notice the structure of the sentences. Sometimes changing the word order of a sentence or getting rid of a contraction will give you the flavor of a certain time period."
Katherine Sturtevant

Plot

Say It with Post-Its

"One of the best sources of help I've ever found in strong plotting was a book called *Screenplay: The Foundations of Screenwriting* by Syd Field. Although it's a manual on crafting successful screenplays, it can also be used just as effectively for creating well-constructed plots in just about any genre or age level of children's books. Syd Field uses a three-act structure for plotting that's effective in setting up your children's story, introducing the characters, bringing in the conflict, and then wrapping everything up in a satisfying finale.

"When I use the three-act structure for my own plotting, I make it more fun by separating a large worksheet into three portions, calling them Acts one, two, and three, then doodling ideas and action on Post-its that I can move around the different sections on the page. This way I feel freer to explore different avenues, knowing I can easily change where they belong in my storyline, or just take them out if they don't work."

    Ellen Leroe

Rehearsals Equal Rough Drafts

"Writing is like a ballet performance. What the audience sees is an end product. You're not seeing the times the performers stumble, or the hours and hours of practice. It's the same thing with books."

    Suzanne Williams

Stew About It

"I think about a story idea, take notes and let it simmer in my head for a few days or weeks. Then I jump right in and write the first chapters. I make a rough outline and jot down ideas. I know where it's going. But I leave a lot of room in my outline for sudden inspiration. In #5 *The Killer*, I created another complete murder mystery that I hadn't intended. But it made sense. I plot my beginning, middle and ending as a progression of action."

Linda Joy Singleton

A Stitch in Time

"We have to take a thread and keep it going. I used to make outlines which I don't do anymore. But I think I have to get back to it. An outline can show how the story develops. You don't need to use great detail, though, because you don't want to limit yourself. There's something in our brains we don't know we have. It's a magic time when the story comes to life. Suddenly the character is no longer a character but a person who wants to say what he or she wants to say."

Marilyn Sachs

Pacing

"If you are stuck, go back and read everything you write several times. Refresh your memory. You get a sense of your characters again. *What is your goal? What are your characters doing? Where did they come from and where do they have to go?* Spend some time thinking. Good books have some kind of musical structure. When you're doing a novel, it's a mistake to follow a quiet chapter with another quiet chapter. When people talk about books being too quiet—a book can be about emotion and not be quiet. If one chapter is more dramatic, then the next chapter can be more quiet. Learn to weave information and don't hit a reader over the head with it immediately."

Marilyn Singer

Pleasant Scents

"I outline and then I don't stick to the outline. As new possibilities emerge, I outline again. If I follow the first outline, the book stinks. If I don't outline at all, the book stinks. The key is to find the nice-smelling ground between."

Gennifer Choldenko

Plan Ahead

"I figure it out ahead of time. Characters and plot are inexplicitly bound together. Plot develops character; character develops plot. I move the story forward in interesting directions by asking a lot of plot questions. *What does the protagonist want? How can things get worse? What else can the protagonist try? What could go wrong with that?* The pre-writing stuff is delightful to do!"

Elaine Marie Alphin

What Is this about?

"I have a notebook and I keep revising summaries for myself. This is what the story is about. This is what happened in the past. Then I get a better idea which becomes version B. Then there's a version C . . ."

Kathryn Reiss

Helpful Hints

"I think plot is the easiest to master. It has basic principles unlike character or prose which is much more complex. *Making a Good Script* Great by Linda Seger was recommended to me by Paul Zindel at a conference and really helped me to understand the structure of plot. I also found that the first few chapters of *20 Master Plots* by Ronald B. Tobias helped me to understand the synergy of plot and character and how they work together to create story.

"Early on I used to use story maps and graphic organizers to help me address and grasp parts of the plot and also character. I think they can be very useful. At this point, I have internalized those things so I don't actually have to write it out anymore, but sometimes I will still jot down scenes on index cards or post-it notes and rearrange or delete as necessary. Even if I am winging it as I go and just going where my character takes me, I still find it helpful to jot down flashes of inspiration that are dropped in my lap that I may want to use later."

Mary Pearson

Just Say Write

"Sometimes I'll list things, but that's the most I ever do, and generally I just wing it. Revision often involves tracing one thread through the whole story and strengthening it or checking on continuity, logic, etc."

Karen Romano Young

Shh...Don't Tell

"True confession: I've never understood all the angst, articles, and online discussions about how difficult it is to plot a novel. I'm not implying that it's easy, but I am saying that for me, it's possible to get the basic story and the rhythm down in the first go-round. I've never had to throw out large sections of a book—yet, although I have had to condense many beginnings. I think it's common for writers to *write themselves into the story*, then go back and keep only what the reader needs to know. A good book about structuring a novel is *The Writer's Journey* by Christopher Vogler."

Dian Curtis Regan

Take Heart

"I don't handle plot too much until it's time to revise. That's when I begin searching for the heart of the story, it's arteries and veins and nerves—those things that work together to make it come alive and move."

Susan Hart Lindquist

Dominoes

"I can't work from an outline. If I have an idea for a novel, I mull it over while I'm writing something else. I have to let it grow in my subconscious. Once I'm committed to start the novel, I brainstorm ideas and create a loose outline—a series of possible scenes—in my journal document, on my computer.

"I only know my main character and maybe a few other characters. I expect to meet other characters along the way. I also know what the story is about, and I usually, although not always, have an ending. If I don't have an ending, it often comes to me by the time I've written half of the book. At least I have an *idea* of the ending, though not the specifics on how it will happen.

"I always create my plot from a 'what-if' technique. *What if this happens? What if that happens next?* This creates a tightly plotted story. A tightly plotted story is made up of a series of scenes, each of which is causally connected to the other. If you take out any causally connected scene, it leaves a gap in the storyline and the reader wonders how the writer got from here to there. In a loosely plotted story, you can take out a scene and not affect the rest of the plot. A well-plotted story is tightly plotted. It should have the domino effect: the dominoes are all lined up and when you push the first domino, the rest fall until you get to the last one. If you take out one of the scenes, [dominoes] the story abruptly stops."

Marisa Montes

All Clear for Take-Off

"I don't tend to start with plot. I start with character and emotion. As I get to know my characters they will determine where the story will go. Plot can take over; character can be one-dimensional. I put characters in a kooky setting and see what happens. Also, I've learned that when you get to the end of the book, you have to rework the beginning. The seeds of the end of the book need to be in the beginning. When you're in the second or third draft, these things start to happen. Writing novels is very cognitive. You ask yourself, *does that make sense? Where are the holes in my story, in my characters' lives?*

"Being a writer is a little like being an air traffic controller. You have all of these planes on the screen and you have to focus and not take your eyes off of them! They're all in your sphere. If the phone rings, that can break the focus for me."

Joan Bauer

Ha! Professor, You Were Wrong!

"Sometimes I start with a character. Sometimes I have an idea for a plot but I never outline. I had a terrible time in college when one of my English professors insisted that everyone write an outline before they wrote their essay. 'It will be too boring that way,' I insisted and he predicted that I would get a failing grade if I didn't produce a satisfactory outline. Well, he was wrong. I wrote a good paper and I wasn't bored because I did it my way. And that means I know where I'm beginning and I know where I want to end up. How I get there is an adventure, for me as well as it will be in the future for my readers. Sometimes I get lost. Sometimes I waste time. But I always reach the end. And I've learned not to panic when it seems I've written myself into a dead end. A solution always is waiting for me to discover it."

Johanna Hurwitz

Plot in Six Easy Steps

"You can get great practical understanding of plot from reading up on how to write suspense; all the elements are the same for a non-suspense book, but plot is exaggerated in suspense so it's easier to see the pieces at work.

"My general conception of a traditional plot is this: 1. Create a character your reader will care about. 2. Give him a significant problem, which creates a question in the reader's mind. *Will the character succeed?* 3. Have the character try to solve the problem in various ways that only make matters worse. 4. As you go, plant lesser but relevant questions to pique reader curiosity. 5. Never answer a question without having at least one other question still dangling...6....until the end. When is the end? It's when the main story question is answered."

Diane Matcheck

Follow Your Character

"I deal with plot less than with character. When the grain of a book is coming up, I will write the entire novel on a character, or a title. My books are so character driven, the book writes itself around the character. I write in a circular way; nonlinear."

Angela Johnson

Another Style

"I write in a linear fashion. I like to outline, for I want to know where I'm going. I write an outline for the book, but not the chapters."

Karen English

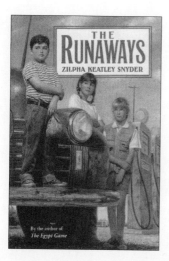

Featuring
Zilpha Keatley Snyder

Zilpha Keatley Snyder is a three-time Newbery Honor winner, for *The Egypt Game*, *The Headless Cupid*, and *Witches of Worm*. Her other award-winning novels are *The Gypsy Game*, *Cat Running*, *The Famous Stanley Kidnaping Case* and *Fool's Gold*.

"The first thing I do, is make character outlines. I give the characters names, although they may change later. Then I write down everything I know about their personalities. I discover their strengths and weaknesses, what they hate and love, what their attitudes are toward their families and schools, as well as their general appearance. Plot ideas sometimes arise out of that character list.

"For my book *The Runaways*, when I saw the artwork for the cover, I was shocked by its similarity to the kids I had been imagining. I felt like the illustrator must have been able to look inside my head! The characters were exactly like *I* pictured them.

"Next I do a plot page. I sometimes tell kids it's like writing the book report before the book is written. It's a shoestring plot line, and it gives me an ending to head for. If I don't do that, I often find my characters in situations that I am unable to resolve in any logical and convincing way.

"I need to know where I am going. Sometimes that takes a lot of work. Once in awhile a theme is the starting point. Then I wonder, *what can happen that will lead my character to embody and illustrate that theme?* But, for me, themes generally arise later in the process, after I have done considerable work on the characters and plot."

Suspense

Ticking Clock

"I think it's important to set a time element. If the bad guys are due into town at sunset, if Friday is the day of the school play—that's the easiest way to build tension. It's also helpful for writers to study good mystery and suspense movies. Those people are masters at that."

Stephen Mooser

Eye of the Beholder

"I create suspense by trying to put myself in the reader's place then asking myself what would be suspenseful to me."

Karen English

Try These Tips

"Increase suspense in your fiction by taking risks and by allowing your characters to do the same. Of course, you can put your character in danger, but the smaller potential losses—the losses of the heart—are the one's I find make me care most as a reader.

"Offer hope, then pull the rug. Making the reader care enough to worry about what's going to happen next—then making them wait to find out what that is.

"One technique is to build a question into every page—even the smallest subliminal worry or wonder can make a reader want to turn the page. Raise the stakes. As a writer, I try to ask myself, 'What's at stake here?' at the end of every page. Piling on details, focusing general to specific, shortening sentences."

Susan Hart Lindquist

Reader Reaction

"One technique to increase suspense is called 'moment-by-moment.' Slip into the character's skin and feel every emotion, no matter how subtle, for a short period of time, such as one to two minutes—the period during which the tension or suspense needs to be heightened. In your first draft of the scene, write sensations such as heart beats, prickling scalp, sweaty palms, etc. Include smells and sounds the character could hear during that span of time. Then read it over and pick the most powerful emotions and sensations to keep.

"Another technique is to slow down time from the main character's point of view. As if a film is in slow motion, or as if a character is moving underwater. Use this slow-motion pace at a moment of high tension. It should be used sparingly; no more than once or twice in the entire book.

"The difference between 'moment-by-moment' and 'slow-motion' is subtle. In moment-by-moment, you're describing what's going on inside the character. In slow-motion, you're describing what is going on outside the character from the character's point of view in a heightened emotional state.

"You can combine them, by weaving in commonplace sights, sounds, smells or recurring scary thoughts in the main character's head. A short line or two in between the scary parts draws out the tension, contrasts the creepy with the normal, giving the scene an almost surreal feeling. It's also a good way to bring tension to a scene that would otherwise be a normal, every-day scene.

"For example, the main character is having dinner with a friend, the salad is being served, the smells of steak and potatoes fill the air, the normal sounds of cars passing and birds singing can be heard, and all the while she's hearing her ex-boyfriend's words in her head. *If you leave me, I'll kill you,* but she continues eating her salad, trying to control her trembling hand. A book I've read recently that does this really well is *Sleeping with the Enemy* by Nancy Price. It's an adult thriller about an abusive husband stalking his wife.

"In my book, *Something Wicked's in Those Woods,* I infused the story with atmosphere. The setting was the aunt's rustic, redwood house nestled in the woods of Northern California, which are dense with ancient oaks and tall pines. Very eerie and dark. Whenever possible, I would weave in descriptions of the twisted branches and ghoulish forms of the oaks. The main character, Javi, had just arrived from Puerto Rico, where he had spent all his life in the warmth and sun of the tropical island. His mood was affected by the imposing ancient oaks, the cold fog, and the dark, rustic house."

Marisa Montes

Create Tension

"Suspense is a function of the tension created by well-developed characters the reader can identify with. In other words, the writer must present her characters in such a way that readers will increasingly care what happens to them. I don't mean the reader has to like all the characters. The reader only has to care. For example, say the pivotal character is a fanatical extremist with a bomb strapped to his chest, which he plans to detonate on a city bus. How could anyone like such a person? Still, readers will care what happens to him, because if he dies, it will affect the people on the bus and all their loved ones. So the first rule of good suspense is to people your story with characters the reader can identify with and come to care about in some way. If you can lead the reader to care about every character, even the bad guys, so much the better.

"In a suspense plot, timing is everything. Particularly in children's books, which are often read aloud a chapter at a time. I try to end chapters in the midst of action scenes or dialogue scenes in which some pivotal fact is about to be revealed. These are the areas where the suspense is usually greatest. I also try to provide interludes, usually in the central portions of chapters, during which the pace slows a bit to give readers a chance to catch their breath. Variety, even in pacing, always adds interest and increases the reader's ability and desire to keep reading.

"For an exercise, try picking up copies of several best-selling novels. Authors such as Danielle Steel, Stephen King. In children's books, *Harry Potter and the Sorcerer's Stone*. Write a synopsis of each plot, then go back over the synopsis to pick out points that heightened the suspense for you. What you're looking for are places where your reaction, as a reader, is '*Oh no! What will happen next? I can't stand not knowing!*' When you find a place like that, study it to see if you can figure out how the writer made it happen, and why it happened where it did."

Nancy Etchemendy

Cranking Up Suspense
"My best advice is to write, to read, to rewrite, to persevere, to rewrite again, and did I mention rewrite? Actually, I could go on for hours about different ways of increasing suspense and tension in a story. I'll try to give you a few ideas on that.

"Set up multiple mysteries. Every story is a mystery, regardless of the genre. Example: The opening two lines of *The Dark Side of Nowhere*: 'Ethan died of a burst appendix. That's what we were told.' Here, the mysteries are already piling up. Who is Ethan? Why is he important? Does that second line imply that this was a lie? If you can keep posing questions in the reader's mind, that's what keeps the page turning. They *have* to know the answers. And those answers had better be satisfying.

"Keep the reader active. Writing a strong story means challenging the reader to keep on thinking. Don't be so quick to tell the reader what's going on. Drop hints, leave clues, let them discover the unfolding story for themselves.

"Keep an eye on rhythm. Stories have a natural rhythm to them; the pace quickens, the pace slows, there's a moment of humor, then a sobering moment. If you keep the pace moving too fast, it becomes numbing. Too slow, and it's dull.

"Catch the reader off guard. Just as they're being lulled into what we expect will be a soft, tender moment, the bottom drops out, and the action picks up, or perhaps it's just a moment of heartfelt poignancy when we least expect it.

"Make us care about your characters. Tension and suspense only works if we care about what's going to happen. One of my favorite **exercises** is to pick a mundane location, and then try to describe it as thoroughly as possible, using all five senses. You'll find there's no such thing as a mundane location, if you describe it effectively."

Neal Shusterman

SPOOKY MUSIC = SUSPENSE

"Any build up of suspense depends on adequate foreshadowing which means a lot of preliminary plotting. I don't know how anyone can foreshadow adequately if they don't plot ahead. Foreshadowing gives hints that *warn* the reader—and builds the suspense.

"I like to tell kids, it's like the music in a film. You know, when the music suddenly goes spooky and ominous, and you prepare for something scary or awful to happen. You're ready, and you'll react. In writing, you have to build suspense with words instead of music.

"I try to give just enough clues to intrigue, but not enough to give away the secrets of the story. Sometimes that requires a great deal of rewriting."

Zylpha Keatley Snyder

Shh...Don't Tell Yet

"Tell as little as you have to tell at any given point to get your story going. Later you can do some foreshadowing that will highlight the things that will happen next. The element of surprise is always possible.

"In *Running Loose*, Louis talked about his girlfriend all the time. But he doesn't say she died until late in the story. This shock works well because it really brings the nature of his trauma home.

"In *Staying Fat for Sarah Brynes*, I told as little about Virgil as I could, because Moby will find this out. Then it all escalates. At the point someone else knows about this, Virgil will get pretty ornery. With first person, you have your character narrative, so the reader knows only what the character knows. It's pretty legitimate to leak things out. In third person, there is a conscious choice in what I tell and don't tell."

Chris Crutcher

Picture Books

So you think writing or illustrating a picture book is simple?

Meaningful Metaphor
"I've always enjoyed *Owl Moon* by Jane Yolen, but until my five-year-old son verbalized his thoughts about the book, I didn't know how much the book meant to him.

"One day, on a long car trip, he requested the tape of *Owl Moon*. As I looked for it, he stared out the window.

"'You know, Mom,' he said thoughtfully. 'The snow *is* whiter than the milk in a cereal bowl.'

"It had been months since we had read *Owl Moon*, but that image had stayed with him. Good writing is like that."
Elizabeth Koehler-Pentacoff

Let Nature Take its Course
"Find a story that actually fits a short mode. A lot of people try to fit a story into the picture book format. If you read the best ones, you'll see they couldn't be anything else."
Gennifer Choldenko

Better Than Good
"You need an exceptionally good idea and work exceptionally hard at it."
Stephen Mooser

Picture Book Envy
"We picture book writers are dying to have a middle grade novel out there. Middle grade writers are all dying to do a picture book!"
Suzanne Williams

Picture This

"You can't write a picture book without thinking visually. Every sentence, every phrase, has to bring up a visual picture. Read the new picture books that are out today and as you read them, block everything out but the words. Ask yourself, *does this bring a visual picture to my* mind?

"I'll go through with a pencil on my manuscript and number the pictures. Then I look to see how far apart they are. Pictures must be evenly spaced. There should be at least fifteen or sixteen pictures. I try for a minimum of sixteen and a maximum of twenty-two. If I have too many, I have too much going on and it needs to be simplified. If I have too many words and not enough pictures, I have to cut or change some words and get more visuals. Instead of Johnny was mad, Johnny threw his truck on the floor and stomped on it. *That* is visual.

Verla Kay

Your Assignment

"Read as many as you can. Study the really good picture books, the enduring ones. Look at any of Kevin Henkes' books. Look at Susan Meddaugh's *Martha Speaks*. Read the story of *Cinderella's Rat. Olivia* is a perfect picture book. She's a great charmer. Look at any one of Peggy Rathmann's. She's brilliant."

Katie Davis

To Be or Not To Be

"Understand what a picture book is and what it is not. I learned about picture books by going to the library and asking the children's librarian to show me the favorites of kids. I took them home. The books that were written by one person and illustrated by another. I typed out the text, which taught me immediately a bunch of things. It taught me how short they were. It taught me what to put in and what to leave out. It made me understand what the illustrator's role was. And what I had to do to give the illustrator what to illustrate without directly telling him. The content has to come from within everyone. What is wonderful content for me, isn't necessarily [wonderful] for someone else.

"My favorite picture books include *Don't Fidget a Feather* by Erica Silverman, all of Charlotte Zolotow's books and Jane Yolen's tales."

Sue Alexander

Visual Clues

"Keep the language simple. Think visually. What can be represented visually you won't need to describe. The surprising thing about them [picture books] is there is so little interaction with the artist. The publishers are protective of the illustrators."

Cynthia Chin-Lee

What's New?

"Familiarize yourself with what's already out there. I volunteer at a library and read all the new books I can get my hands on. I ask myself, *why did they publish this book?* That makes me think like an editor."

Ellen Jackson

Feelings

"A good picture book has artwork that reinforces the *tone* and *emotion* of the words. It has page-turning pacing that fits the story, and characters or ideas that invite you to come back for another visit."

Nancy Barnet

WEIGHT OF WORDS

"When you're writing a 500 word picture book, every word is 1/500th of the story. When you're writing a 40,000 word middle grade, a single word is not nearly as important."

Bruce Balan

Lose It Over a Celebrity (or Tomorrow I'll be a Hollywood Movie Star)

"If I hear about one more celebrity writing a picture book, or any other children's book for that matter, between sessions in the make-up chair, I think I'll puke! I was at lunch the other day with some other writers when it was announced that a pop star of the month had just signed to write a young adult novel. One of my colleagues announced, 'And I think next week I shall become a rock-and-roll legend.' People think that writing for children and young adults is easy because the books are shorter than many of those for adults. The words 'easy' and 'short,' however, are not synonyms.

"The secret to picture books, if there is one, is to tap into the spirit of child-hood, to look at the world through a child's eyes and see that world in all its wonder and mystery."

Larry Dane Brimner

Creative Unconscious

"My picture book ideas come from different ways. Sometimes I get a strong image first. As far as picture book rules, there aren't any. In general, there should be a balance of pictures and text. The pictures should extend the stories and hold surprise. Subplots through the pictures are nice.

"In the book I illustrated, *Abuela* by Arthur Dorros, it's about a grandma and a little girl flying over New York City. My editor thought I'd enjoy it because of the flying character. Grandma takes an imaginary flying journey. Unconsciously, I gave both the little girl and the grandmother, clothing with a sky motif. They both wear sky blue skirts, and Grandma's skirt has stars in it. I went through the whole text without realizing I had done this!"
Elisa Kleven

Dummy Up

"Learn to dummy your manuscript. Create a blank book of thirty-two pages. Allow four or five pages for front matter—end pages, title, copyright, etc. Then cut your manuscript into sentences and put them on the blank pages the way you think an illustrator would break up the text. This is the best way to tell if you have enough changing pictures, good page turns (the right hand page is the tension page), a balanced text—not too much on a page—and the right length for a picture book."
Stephanie Jacob Gordon

Collaboration

"When you work with an illustrator, keep in mind that he or she will probably have very good ideas for the book that you did not even think of. An illustration may suggest necessary changes or additions to your original manuscript—so keep an open mind. Don't be surprised if you never meet or have direct contact with your illustrator. Your editor will most likely be the vital go-between who ensures that the text and pictures complement each other."
Deborah Lee Rose

Read Read Read!

"Picture books need to pack so much of a story into so few words. Anyone who wants to write picture books should have read at least 500 picture books that have been published in the last five years, including, of course, all the Caldecott winners and Honor books, and American Library Association Notables."
Debbie Duncan

Slide Show

"When I teach writing picture books at conferences, I always tell would-be writers, first of all, keep it short. Since it needs to be so very visual, think of your story in terms of slides, because there is a space between each picture. Slides move forward and move the story along, so you'll have a moving picture of what your book shall be. It works for me."
Eve Bunting

How Is Yours Different?

"Picture books are much harder than they look. They have to be unique, somehow. That's where knowing Spanish works for me. I've sold some without Spanish, but it was much harder and required many more rewrites. A fresh idea, a lovable character, an exciting plot, a great title, a memorable ending, and good rhymes contribute to the ones I've sold."

Susan Middleton Elya

How To

"For me, the story comes first, but it's based on things I already know I want to draw. After I have the story, I draw dozens and dozens of sketches in black and white. If the publisher has already bought the story, I'll make a thumbnail quarter-size dummy to send to my editor. I don't have to submit any finishes, since the editor already knows me. The editors go through the manuscript and dummy to see if it's paginated. Pagination is the way the text has been divided up and placed on the pages. Authors don't get to decide how a book is paginated. That's an illustrator's job. If you're both the author and illustrator, you have to decide. That explains books where there is six or seven lines on one page and another page has only one line. It may have kept the pacing of the book or increased the appeal of the pacing. Paginating is all about pacing. You won't just divide the text up equally. Illustrators have a good instinct for pagination.

"After they accept the pagination, then I do a dummy that is half-size. I work out any changes and critiques. I run it by the art director, but the illustrator has the last word. Then the art director blows up the drawings up to 200 percent and creates the text mechanicals where the illustrators says where the text goes. I don't choose the typeface, however. I leave that to the designer. They're experts in that. I'm not a graphic designer. Some art directors want certain margins. Some beginning illustrators will put the type too close to the edge or the gutter. [Center fold]. The gutter is a very important place that you should try to stay away from.

"Then the publishers send me back large xeroxes with the type in place. I do a finished sketch and transfer it onto a nice piece of paper."

Ashley Wolff

"I've Always Wanted to Write a Picture Book..."

"It's always two women, well coiffed, clean and more put together than I am. I look like I've just fallen out of a hammock! One woman said, 'I've always wanted to write a picture book but I don't have the time.' *Is that it? Lack of time?* I should go out and be a mathematician! My mother is an accountant, so if she stops that, she could write one too? There are those few people, because children's books are so accessible, when they read it they think they're easy to write. But there's an art to it.

"If that happens, it's better to smile. If they tell you the cute things their grand-children said, there's nothing else to do but be gracious. They are pure of heart. Most people are kind. I rarely run into the mean ones. The mean ones save themselves for adult literature. I've seen adults yell at authors of adult works. If they use a character many times and then the author kills the character, people will almost attack them!"
Angela Johnson

Keep It Short
"Picture book manuscripts are short. Five and a half double-spaced pages is a very, very long manuscript for a picture book. Manuscripts that long are only for the oldest range of readers. A five and a half page manuscript is way too long for a picture book for two to four year olds.

"Take one of your favorite picture books and type it out. Compare the number of pages and the number of lines in a paragraph with your own manuscript. Or count the number of words in a couple of your favorite picture books and compare those numbers with the number of words in your own manuscript."
JoAnne Stewart Wetzel

Interactive Reading
"Read them with a child in your lap! I'm always amazed by which details a child zeros in on versus what I might have thought was interesting. This is most illuminating, and something I always think about when I'm writing. One thing I've done that has been helpful for me, is to read the text of the book I'm working on to a child and then ask them to draw a picture of the story. Children sometimes see something totally different than what I'm imagining, or they see a quirky detail I hadn't imagined."
Maureen Boyd Biro

What Are You Trying to Say?
"Understanding this genre, which is a wonderful mixture of poetry, movement, fun and theme, comes from reading them with care and attention, reading aloud, and caring deeply about language. For me, the theme is also critical. I spend so much time writing and re-writing that I want to deal with an important theme in each book."
Caryn Yacowitz

Real Live Kids!
"I try to keep a clear idea of what real children are like. They aren't some fragile, idealized creatures needing to be pampered with precious thoughts. They're wild, dirty, bloody, funny, frightened, willing, loving. They need a good hug and a book that they enjoy reading over and over."
Tedd Arnold

Take Time

"Do a very precise picture book (black and white) dummy. Then put it aside. Go back and look at it later. Your *first* idea is not necessarily your *best* idea. When I schedule my books, I allow time so I can put each book aside and work on something else for awhile. When I look at that project again, I sometimes rework the illustrations to improve the book."

Daniel San Souci

ANYTHING GOES

"A best-selling picture book has a magic all its own that can't be taught or distilled into a formula. I used to think that at the very least, to compete in this tough market, a picture book that tells a story (one that isn't nonfiction or a concept book) should have conflict and a plot. That is, it shouldn't be a slice of life or simply a funny series of events. But I've seen many plotless stories that have been published since 1999. They seem to be a mixture of concept book and story book.

"I think what sells depends on the publishing house and the editor. Some houses love whimsy and sweet bedtime books, others won't touch them. Some love wacky, edgy books that push the envelope, some want funny and others want folktales. The only constant seems to be that the book should call you back to read it over and over."

Marisa Montes

Picture Book Peeve

"I still want to know why picture books are filed by the author's name. Yes, I understand it's always been done that way and would disturb the natural laws of the universe if changed. If anything, an author and illustrator should receive *equal* credit.

"Of course, I'm biased and feel that the illustrator should actually get more credit, as I don't think it's commonly understood how much the illustrator brings to the table. If you think of the story as a skeleton, the illustrator gives it flesh, dresses it, puts it somewhere and breathes life into it. A whole world is created and filled with things that are not in the text at all, but that fully round out the story. The illustrator has written a parallel story in pictures, but too often that goes unnoticed or credited to the author—especially in reviews.

"Often the whole review is spent retelling the story, and then at the very end, almost as an after thought, the reviewer might throw in a few words—if that—

commenting on the illustrations. Drives me nuts. And yes, my picture books at home are all filed by illustrator!"
Eve Aldridge

Miniature Novel

"I don't think people realize that many picture books, especially the good ones, are really novels with fully developed characters. Think of *Lyle Crocodile.* That's a novel. *Curious George* is a novel. Of course, books for the really young are less novels than illustrators' vehicles."
David Adler

Picture This

"I don't really know how people who aren't illustrators write picture books. I know that some writers do seem to have an innate ability to make stories that need pictures to complete them. I know when I try to write a story coming from the picture-making perspective, I wind up making pictures in comic book fashion. I plot the thing out drawing pictures and then I add the words and take out the pictures that aren't needed.

"You have to think visually. It must be difficult to write picture books, as editors don't like the author and illustrator talking about their projects. I can understand that. The illustrator finds out too much about the background of the story. It's best if the illustrator can approach the text just as the reader will approach it."
R.W. Alley

Nuts and Bolts:

- Condense. Use few words –but don't sacrifice the beauty of language, the effectiveness of the well-chosen word.
- Launch right in. The first sentence begins with action. No long openings—the editor will delete them anyway.
- Remember the illustrator, but don't do the illustrating. Provide variety, action, illustratable scenes that change. Create images and characters that will illustrate well. But don't describe them so completely that there's no room left for an illustrator's creativity.
- Don't try picture books because you expect them to be easy. It doesn't follow that because it takes up less space on the page, or fewer pages, it will necessarily take less time to think about it, develop it, change and polish it.
- Benjamin Franklin, who didn't write picture books that I know of, said, 'I don't have time to be brief.'"
Alice Schertle

A Short Guide to Writing Picture Books by Thacher Hurd

Thacher Hurd was only sixteen when he collaborated with his mother, Edith Hurd, on *Little Dog Dreaming*, illustrated by his father, Clement Hurd. Thacher attended the California College of Arts and Crafts where he later taught writing and illustrating for children. His books include *Mama Don't Allow, Art Dog, Santa Mouse and the Ratdeer, Little Mouse's Big Valentine* and *Mystery on the Docks*.

"People forget there's a structure to a children's picture book. First of all, you have an idea. Everyone has ideas. But some people don't realize that's the first of many steps! How is this idea going to come to life? A good idea is to make a dummy, even though you're not an illustrator. Lay out the text and the pages to see if it has a beginning, middle and end. And most importantly for a picture book, to see how the pages turn.

"If you really want to understand how children's books work, read Dr. Seuss. *How The Grinch Stole Christmas* is, to my mind, a perfectly constructed picture book. His books are incredible crafted, and he always knows just where the story is going. Don't get lost in your story. He makes it look so easy, but people don't realize that he worked on those texts for six months or a year.

"Really look to see if your book has any suspense to it. All good children's books have suspense, no matter if it's a mystery or something else. What's going to happen? Pretend you're three years old, looking at this big picture and then turning the page. Each new page is an opportunity for the illustrator to surprise the child. Suspense and surprise are really crucial in a children's book. Children will only read a story over and over if the book is interesting enough and the author is skillful enough to make it seem new each time.

"It's a good idea to read your story out loud to yourself. Pacing is really important, and its easier to hear the pacing when you are reading out loud. Then read it aloud to someone else, not necessarily kids. You can work up to kids. They're ruthless!

"Make a dummy, a mockup of the book. Feel how the pace goes as you turn the pages. Imagine the pages as measures in music. Each page turn is a measure. See what the rhythm is like. Count the rhythms as if it were a poem. It's like micro-managing the text. Count the beats in each sentence, even if it's prose. You're looking to really open your ears up to what each line's rhythm is. I think good writers do that unconsciously.

"Every story has a problem that needs to be solved, but a common mistake people make is to start the story, 'Little so and so wanted a bicycle. (or a cat, a dog or whatever)' The reader immediately feels no need to read the rest of the story, because the situation is so tightly set up that the reader knows for certain that 'little so and so' is going to get what he wants. Think about deeper, more indefinable longings: home, adventure, love, companionship. Then present these longings indirectly or obliquely. *Sailor Dog* starts with him wanting to go to sea, and he gets to the sea right away, but then there is much more in the way of adventure still to happen. The obvious one can be resolved, but the character wants something in a more emotional way. If the character only wants a specific object, that's a mistake. That's not really important in life. You want a deeper sense. That's why *Where the Wild Things Are*, by Maurice Sendak, keeps being read by children; it's about more basic issues, such as anger."

Time for Play

"Picture book ideas may come from word combinations, like aardvark angels, that make me want to draw pictures. The more I draw them, the more familiar they become, until they have their own story. Other ideas come from songs that I want to slip my own vocabulary into and ads and photos in magazines generate ideas too. I keep an idea file and give myself an hour each morning to *play with the ideas* that are the most appealing.

"Then I try to put my finger on *why* that idea is appealing to me. I usually find it is linked to some of my own experiences. For me, writing and illustrating are very similar processes; sometimes the words come first, sometimes the images. First drafts of a story are just like first sketches of a picture. No one expects you to say it just right the first time, so start your writing with word sketches, phrases you like, a scene, and fill in. If you know the ending of your story, start there and move backwards.

"The illustrator in me is picturing the medium—pencil, paint, pastel—that I can best use to match the pictures in my head. The writer has to listen for the story's voice. *Does it need narration, dialogue written in prose? Or does it bounce along better with alliteration and wordplay?*

"Even if you are not an illustrator, make a small paper model of the book;

twenty-four to thirty-two pages, and see if you have a story that can lend itself to illustrations. Some very good stories are turned down because they do not lend themselves to enough scene changes. A well-told story often lends itself to magazines or can become an anthology submission."

Teri Sloat

Word Pictures

"Your words must count. Are your words painting images an illustrator (or an editor, for that matter) can 'see?' Enough images to fill a thirty-two-page picture book?"

Tricia Gardella

Poetic High Wire

"A good picture book has a balance between illustration and text. Text shouldn't overpower the illustration. It's good, too, to learn how to get to the point. Don't meander with your words. Having a poetic sense helps. To me, picture books are small poems."

Bernard Waber

Dreams Can Come True

"If you love picture books, and if you dream of creating picture books, you can make it happen. Let your heart go forward in the genre. Read stories like you have never heard another story before. Buy the books that you can't live without. Take them home and map out the text. Go over journey after journey, until you can set out on your own. Then again...let your heart go forward, and write stories like you have never heard a story before."

Margaret O'Hair

What Pictures Do You Have in Mind?

"Choose a subject where you can picture quaint or enchanting illustrations. Keep possible illustrations in mind when you write the words."

Jacque Hall

The Basics

"*Some helpful things I've learned about picture books:*
- Avoid telling the reader your theme.
- Create an interesting character and tell her/his story in as few words as possible.
- Stay in your main character's viewpoint.
- Let your main character find creative solutions to her/his problems.
- Show, don't tell! Use action and dialogue to show your story.
- Write from your heart. If you love your book, others will too."

SuAnn Kiser

Wide Audience Appeal

"The best picture books are not written just for children. The book must appeal to several audiences, from agents, editors, and art directors, to librarians, booksellers, and grandparents. But the second most important audience, after kids, is the parents. These are the poor folks who will be asked to read favorite books over and over again, so a fun, well-written book is a godsend to them."

Kevin Kiser

EACH AND EVERY

"You can't pull a fast one and get away with it. In a picture book, every word, every single word, must be the perfect word. It can't be almost right or close, it must be exact. Every word must sing, even when you're writing in prose. In a book for adults, every scene must move the story. But for children, every single *word* must move the story or get out of the way."

Linda Kay Weber

Lots of Steps

"Sing songs. Learn and recite nursery rhymes. Take a class in how to write poetry. Read as many picture books as you can. Have your antennae up for poetic elements in prose. Remember your childhood with clarity and objectivity and write down what you loved and what you feared. Make drafts of one or more stories. Then workshop your stories with other children's writers and keep revising until your story sings. Then submit it to publishers until a brilliantly perceptive editor recognizes your talent and offers you a contract."

Alexis O'Neill

Featuring
Rosemary Wells

Rosemary Wells attended Boston Museum School and began her career at Macmillan, working as a book designer. Max, Nora, and Morris are a few of her unforgettable and endearing characters. She's written and illustrated more than sixty award-winning books for children, including *Noisy Nora*, *Max and Ruby*, *My Very First Mother Goose*, *Here Comes Mother Goose*, *Felix*, *Yoko's Paper Cranes* and *Bunny Party*.

Max's First Word, published in 1979, became the first board book. What are some important differences in writing board verses picture books? Could you relate some writing advice to those interested in this genre?

"It's all in the length. A perfect story has a beginning, middle and end. A board book has ten pages. It's the most perfect of precis writing; the most condensed kind of writing. It's the most disciplined medium I know. But advice is so general and writers are so individual. The only thing I can tell young writers is keep it short and keep it funny."

Characters are the real compelling reason people read books. Your characters are all fully developed and endearing. How do you develop characters?

"It's almost impossible to say. People say there is a process but I don't think there is. It's as individual and random as the creation of a string quartet."

Since our best writing appears to come from our unconscious self, how can we unlock those powers that we have within us?

"You sit at a desk and allow it to come to you. It's a gift."

What were your favorite books in your childhood?
"I loved all Robert Lawson, particularly *Mr. Revere and I*. I read all Dr. Doolittle, Beatrix Potter, Francis Burnett. I loved *Nancy Drew*. Now we have too many children's books. Then we didn't have enough; we read them all and then we started them all over again."

What inspires your illustrations?

"I never use photographs. It just comes. I'm a great student of early twentieth century commercial illustration. I study trademarks, posters and advertisements from the early 1920's."

What mediums do you use?

"I use a number of mediums: watercolor, gouche, pastel, pen and ink. Really good thick paper and sable brushes. Even rubber stamps, which I have made. The entire thing is a curious combination of being unbelievably well-disciplined—I work all the time. I'm at my desk at 7:30 a.m. The rest is all whim and fancy."

Any last thoughts about picture books?

"Remember one thing. Good children's literature has to be written to stand up to 500 readings aloud. It has to be short and sweet, good and to the point and *about kids*. Not about some sweet *idea* about kids.

"How I go about writing a book has, alas, almost nothing to do with the process of a beginner. I live the professional life of a well-established artist and writer.

"What comes to mind so often in interviews, is what Joe DiMaggio said when he'd visit the sand lots. Young boys would say, *'What's the secret of your success, Joe?'* He'd answer, *'Hit home runs.'*

"Somehow that gets lost all the time. People think there's a key. That if you know the right somebody it's going to work. Whether it's a baseball player or a guitarist or an artist, you succeed if you have the gift. You can't acquire the gift. If you don't have the gift, know that you have other gifts and do those."

Tips from Rosemary Wells for Aspiring Children's Authors
- Don't read your manuscript at your local school and tell your publisher the kids loved it. This is not a real test of anything. The kids would love it if you read them the phone book.
- If you send your manuscript with a SASE, you will get a reply. If you don't,

you won't. It will be thrown away. Sorry, but that's a face of publishers' small staffing.

- Never start a book with the sentence: 'Suzi was bored.'
- Don't ever think this is easy. Because the voice for writing for children is rare. In any generation, there are a few handfuls of people who can really do this, and no more. There are lots of novelists, but very few, really top-notch picture book authors.
- Do not flaunt how many times your manuscript has been turned down and compare it to *Kon Tiki* (thirteen turn downs) and *Mary Poppins* (seventeen rejections). If you get three 'turn downs' put your manuscript in a drawer.
- It's almost impossible to make a living at this. So keep your day job.
- Do not go to a publisher with an illustrator you select. They hate this. The publisher should see your *story*. It's for the publisher to determine who will illustrate the book.
- If you should be so lucky to get an offer from a publisher, and an accepted manuscript, do not take the contract to a real estate lawyer or your Uncle Joe who went to law school. Do not argue with your publisher over your first contract. Just get yourself a publisher. There is plenty of time to argue when you get to be a big name, and you're worth something monetarily to your publisher. Get your foot in the door and try to learn about the publishing business.
- Remember, the publisher is making an investment in you. If a publisher asks you to revise, REVISE. It's not about the book you want it to be, it's about what *they* want to publish. I listen to my editor every single time because my editor is the third eye I never have. Editors want these books to succeed and be good.
- Don't be proud. It's not about your ego. Don't act like a prima dona when no one knows your name.
- Be prepared to wait forever for answers. For new people trying out this field, the bad news is, there are fifty envelopes on top of yours every morning. The world thinks it can write for children, because they believe it's easy. The good news is this: If you're good, publishers are looking for you and you will be discovered and published.

For Art's Sake

Perfect Fit

"Art directors can't always tell you why your artwork is mass market or trade, but they do know where your style fits in the marketplace. I work in various different art styles, some of which work better for mass market and others for trade. *Cinderdog* and the *Wicked Stepcat* is painted in a more trade-looking style. Some people seem to pop out of school with their art style already defined and perfected. I envy them. It has taken me ten years to develop a style I'm comfortable with and that is somewhat unique."

Joan Holub

From All Around

"My illustrations come from my imagination, from photographs or from the actual objects—flowers, animals, etc."

Ruth Heller

You Can Do It!

"The story inspires the art. I didn't have a lot of confidence in my art work. I kept expecting them to say, 'You can't do that!' Now I feel better. I figure if they're willing to spend $100,000 to make a picture book, they must know something. Most creative people have their insecurities about their work. I'm told that somehow I'm able to create a feeling with very few lines. With a simple drawing, I can create a lot of emotion. I have ideas for other books that I want to make more skewed and wacky."

Katie Davis

Depth by Details

"I use photographs. Any artists who say they don't are lying! It's a way of capturing the essence of someone. Something as simple as how your skin wrinkles over your knuckles. It helps to have the model. Generally, my stories are reality-based. But sometimes I make up a person. Then that person has to look the same in every illustration."

Patricia Polacco

"I've used both models and photographs, but the photographs are more to remind me what someone or something looks like, not the pose or composition. I have the most fun drawing and painting animals."

Sarah Wilson

The Power of Nature...and Deadlines

"What inspires me is a desire to communicate some emotion to a larger audience. I'm also inspired by the way morning light transforms a drop of dew into a glistening diamond, or the way shadows change color through the course of a day. Not to be discounted is the inspiration that comes with a looming deadline!"

Nancy Barnet

Laugh the Day Away
"Humor often fuels my imagination and gives my illustrations their spark. I ask myself *what would make this funny?* I enjoy laughing while I work."

Eve Aldridge

Love It or Leave It
"In art school, I drew very realistically. In my illustrations now, I don't generally draw from life or pictures, but I try to draw on inner inspirations. I take reference photos but use them in weird ways. For me it is important to be as spontaneous as I can be. Ask yourself as you work: Am I enjoying it? Am I engrossed? That's what really shows."

Thacher Hurd

Did You Know...
"Illustrations used to be pre-separated artwork. If you look at pictures from books years ago, you'll see that they are limited in color. Colors are layers of red, yellow and blue mixed to create greens, oranges and browns. The illustrators had to

create black and white copies of their art work. Each copy would have one color on it. There would be a yellow version, a blue version, a red version. When they were all printed together they'd overlap and create the color. It was tons of work! But everyone had to do that back then.

"Today, they use laser separation. It's a process where the art work is wrapped around a big cylinder—a drum. Basically the drum spins around and a last pulls out the separate colors. This caused a huge surge in children's picture books in the 1980's. It caused a Renaissance."

Ashley Wolff

Words Plus Funny Illustrator

"The manuscript inspires my illustration. And for me, the funnier the better. If I can, I add humor in the illustrations to further enliven a text. I use watercolors and colored pencils."

Tedd Arnold

Art a la Mode (or What Foods these Morsels Be)

"I'm like a wild chef. I reach for this and that. My main media are watercolors and pen and ink. I also use coloring pencils, crayons, and dyes—if I want intense colors. More recently, for *The Mouse That Snored*, I used oil pastels with watercolors, which for me, was experimental. I advise using good paper.

"Immerse yourself in art. Frequent museums, galleries, and bookstores. Try to draw your own voice into a story which will make it unique. It takes time to find your own voice. Struggling artists and writers should trust their own instincts. Don't judge yourselves harshly as you work. Don't censor yourself."

Bernard Waber

Worth a Thousand Words

"Studying other children's books helps me solve problems. Going to art museums and galleries is inspirational. Although I don't like to use models, occasionally I need someone to pose. I use a Polaroid for this."

Paul Brewer

On Illustrating Others' Work

"I think I work a little harder. I feel accountable. I think the process can stretch me as an artist. But basically, it's more satisfying to illustrate my own stories, because it all comes out of my soul."

Elisa Kleven

"One useful bit of advice that doesn't always happen, is for the illustrator to read the text over and over. Doodle as you read but don't be too quick to commit to how you'll approach things. I usually sketch out the characters first. Then I work out the setting and scenery. When these seem good, that is when I think I've got the mood and tone right, I'll start dealing with the instances described by the plot. In many ways the plot is actually the least important part of illustrating. However, be careful; mistakes in plot details are usually the first thing readers notice and it can ruin the whole book for them.

"As an example of all this, in the book, *Wish Magic*, the main characters stuns her friends by flying. I tried showing her in a variety of standard superman flying positions before coming to the idea that I shouldn't show her, I should *be* her. In the final drawing, the reader is looking through our heroine's eyes, seeing the faces of her amazed friends far below.

"Finally, challenge yourself. This is the best reason for illustrators to try writing. You can come up with texts that no editor would have picked for you."

R.W. Alley

To Bookstore, to Bookstore, to Read a Fine Book

"The most valuable piece of advice is to know your competition—go to children's bookstores and spend some time looking at what other artists do and how they do it. Looking at other people's work will help you decide what technique you would choose in creating your own style—it will come naturally."

Paul Brewer

Art and Writing

"My training in art, my interest in science, and my love for reading and literature, all depend on keen powers of observation. There's an element of organization in the creative process that occurs, whether you're creating art or writing literature. You have to have a beginning, middle and an end and have something that ties them together.

Art also carries over into my books. On many of my books, I've worked with a photographer or been the photo researcher, where I am responsible for finding the photos to illustrate the book. In all of those projects, I'm actually laying out the book. Knowing what pictures are going to be in the book helps me know what to write."

Caroline Arnold

Mediums

What Works Best

"I used acrylics, gouache, watercolor, and oil paints in *Cinderdog* and the *Wicked Stepcat*. I use whatever medium works best for a given book. I've used pencil outline, ink outline, and no outline in different books. I even used cut-paper on the cover of *Vincent Van Gogh: Sunflowers and Swirly Stars*."

Joan Holub

Tools of the Trade

"A lot of us illustrators trace. Tracing is a good thing to learn how things are connected to other things. There was a picture I had to draw with a girl on a swing, but it was the view from under the swing. It looked like her knee was coming out of her forehead! Then I took a picture of Ruby, my four-year-old, swinging, and I traced it. It came out great. I hear Jerry Pinkney say he hires models to wear costumes he's rented. He develops the pictures and traces them and does his art from there. I thought that was called cheating. Now I know it's just a tool—a diving board."

Katie Davis

Art Salvation

"If I had my druthers, I'd rather use pencil and no color. 2B and 6B—soft leads. Then I use Pentell markers—an acetone marker—good for instant color. Sometimes I'll paint over it with acrylic paint. I'm a painter and sculptor independent of children's works. Painting in my adult life is the dark side—the things I fear. The paintings start as pencil drawing but could be seven feet by nine feet, with reality based things in them but rearranged so it will mean something different to you because of the life you lived.

"There would have been no Patricia Polacco if it had not been for art. The art presented to me in schools and home saved me. I'm afraid that we'll see less and less of that. The inner cities are losing money for these things and they're the ones that need it the most. All over the country, art, music and drama are being dropped from school curriculums!"

Patricia Polacco

Got Money?

"Watercolors—tubes, gouche, art store paint-sets; acrylics; technical pens; pens, brushes and colored inks; soft-lead pencils with sharp points; colored pencils; pastels; crayons and lots of markers. Buy the best quality you can afford. That goes for paper, too, even if it's only one sheet at a time, and talk with clerks in art stores for updates on supplies and suggestions. I've learned that I have to be careful with dark colors. Sometimes, I run light washes first, then build up color gradually."

Sarah Wilson

Surprising Outcomes

"I mostly use pencil and watercolor. Pencil is the easiest thing to control and I like how it glides around the page with the right paper. Conversely, I enjoy the unexpected results that come from watercolor and also its ability to give light color."

Eve Aldridge

Graphic Arts

"My primary medium is colored pencil, but I've also enjoyed working in pastel. Pastel dust does create a health concern for me, so I'm trying to come up with a satisfactory digital version of the medium."

Nancy Barnet

"Usually I use watercolor wash, brush and ink. Recently I did a board book on the computer by integrating photos and drawings in ink. I drew in ink on paper and then scanned it into the computer and manipulated the colors, sizes, etc."

Thacher Hurd

The Feel of It

"The world is full of texture. Although I admire good painting and draftsmanship, I've always been tactile and I'd miss the texture elements of collages. There's a playful element of collage that I like. I made a picture using paper doilies for snowflakes. I like to use fabric too. Collage is like making a quilt; it makes it very personal to me."

Elisa Kleven

A Different Look

"I started out doing linoleum block prints. They're not done in a traditional print-making way. I make only one block, like a giant rubber stamp, and print it with black ink. I paint the print with watercolor. Each one is slightly different. I will print five or six copies of the same picture. When I start painting I may decide I don't like the sky on this one, or the flesh tones on that one, so I'll throw it away and start fresh on a new print. This helps explain to skeptics why I bother to do prints. It's labor intensive. But I like the look of it. I don't know how to produce a print without carving light out of dark. It's my way of seeing and stylizing it."

Ashley Wolff

Highlights

"I paint watercolor. Lately, I use a little bit of prisma color pencils to highlight my paintings."

Dan San Souci

Color My World

"My most comfortable medium is colored pencil with a water color wash underneath. I can put layer on layer of color and change colors gradually, and I like the soft look. But I have been working with acrylics and oil pastels to brighten my work up a bit, so it can be seen on a shelf of bright books. Now I'm using Caran d'Ache watercolor crayons. They're amazing! Even though the background of the book I am doing is in colored pencil, the foreground will be with the watercolor crayons."

Teri Sloat

Favorite Mediums

"Pen and ink with some watercolor is my favorite medium to work in and look at. I gain some variation by using different papers and by sometimes using a pencil line instead of an ink line to give a softer look."

R.W. Alley

"Watercolor, colored pencil, pen and ink."

Paul Brewer

llustrative Advice

Artist's Agent

"The best advice I ever got regarding illustration was to get an agent. I signed with a great illustration agent, who kept me busy enough to pay my bills while I improved my illustration techniques. The worst advice I ever got was when someone told me that artists don't make good writers. I knew that was wrong. Rather than giving up on a writing career, I became all the more determined to succeed as both an author and illustrator."

Joan Holub

Start with a Good Drawing

"Most of the color you see in my books comes from colored pencils layered over watercolor or felt pen. The drawing is done first in pencil and then in ink. If the drawing is not good, the color, no matter how beautiful, will not make it a good illustration."

Ruth Heller

In the Groove?

"Illustration is very different from fine art when you illustrate for children. Always draw to the outside of the page—don't go toward the gutter, the part where the book will be folded. Learn to draw to the outside of the book. Draw usually with the story progressing from left to right. If there's running, go to the right. Unless there's a passage where they turn and run the other way. You're restricted on patterns and colors, because the laser camera will misinterpret. Dayglow can translate as black, unless you mix an opaque white with it. There are many technical considerations that aren't involved with a painter and a canvas."

Patricia Polacco

Memory Joggers

"Use a lot of reference material. I often hear kids and adults say they can't draw. They measure their ability by how well they can realistically reproduce something out of their head. One of the problems I have with art presentations and drawing by request, is that I can't draw either. I don't have the visual memory to make a cow look like a cow without a picture of a cow in front of me to refer to.

"Without that, we're talking horse/cat/bear morph. This doesn't mean that I am realistically rendering the cow to make it look like the photograph. I just need help remembering how the hipbone attaches to the leg bone and whether cows have horns and lips. Even if you have a highly stylized illustration style, having reference material can be very helpful."

Eve Aldridge

Lean Toward Emotion

"Don't let technique become the driving force behind an illustration. Technique is often trend-driven and changeable, whereas the passion behind a piece of art is what makes it come alive and communicate some idea or emotion that will have a lasting impact on the audience."

Nancy Barnet

Calling All Pack Rats

"Start collecting things. Become a pack rat! I keep patterns, origami paper, catalogs, newspaper. Look at the great collage artists like Leo Leoni, Jack Ezra Keats, and Eric Carle."

Elisa Kleven

Have Spirit

"Make your drawings fit the spirit of the book. Let people feel the spirit of the book in the pictures."

Thacher Hurd

Opportunity Knocks

"My favorite reference is the *National Geographic Book of Animals*, a two volume set. My reference books tend to be books of photographs. I have a clipping file that consists of five drawers packed full of photographs. In my top drawer, I have categories for Africa, accessories, antelope, apes, American Indians, alligators, etc. I use models too. But first, I look through my own clipping files.

"For illustrators, there is an oportunity to walk into any art director's office. Present your work in person. Seeing me and my art work, having my personality projected along side of my art, got me a job. My first book, *A Year of Birds*, came about when I met Donna Brooks. She told me to write something about the little

girl in my pictures. I wrote a calendar book and sent her the sketches. So I've neve
been through any rejection.

"Illustrators don't have to go to New York with a story thought out. Go i
with your samples of illustrations and a publisher might come up with something i
the public domain for you, or you might work out something on the spot, like wha
happened to me. It's difficult to sell an editor on your own story. On your first time
be content to illustrate someone else's story."

Ashley Wolff

What's Your Style?

"One piece of advice for aspiring illustrators is to remember that techniqu
and style are joined at the hip. I often see the work of illustrators who are unsure o
their personal style and it shows in their technique and vice-versa. I find myse
repeatedly saying to them, 'Whatever you do, whatever you feel their style to b
whatever your level of competence, you must master it!' For example, if you can
draw realistically, maybe you can achieve a folk-art look or a cartoon style.

"Here's an example I see a lot with beginners: they use ink on watercolor ar
their style is to have a clean black outline around every form, like a coloring boo
No problem. But they find themselves drawing trees and haven't decided what the
style is for drawing leaves, so their clean black outlining becomes impressionisti
leafy scribbles—they've just mixed two different styles of line drawing and the illu
tration typically looks stylistically unresolved. An illustrator must know their ow
style/technique completely and know how it is applied to everything they attem
to render.

"One of my weaknesses has always been achieving good smooth watercol
washes. Instead, I work around it. First, I intentionally dapple my paintings wi
sepia underpainting so that later I don't get too caught up in creating perfe
sweeps of color. Then with colored pencils, I scribble on top of the watercolors
add more color and texture, with the auxiliary benefit of being able to obscure n
less than perfect wash technique. That's just one way that technique effects sty
and vice-versa."

Tedd Arnold

Random but Purposeful

"I work on pictures randomly, not from page one to page thirty-two for tv
reasons. While I always start with a scene that I think is strong, my best pictures i
the book come after working on about half the book. By then I am comfortable wi
the medium I'm using, the design, the character's faces, etc. By the very end of t
book I'm running out of steam, and I don't want the last pages to be a disappoin
ment, so I mix them up."

Teri Sloat

ART AND WRITING

"My training in art, my interest in science, and my love for reading and literature, all depend on keen powers of observation. There's an element of organization in the creative process that occurs, whether you're creating art or writing literature. You have to have a beginning, middle and an end and have something that ties them together.

Art also carries over into my books. On many of my books, I've worked with a photographer or been the photo researcher, where I am responsible for finding the photos to illustrate the book. In all of those projects, I'm actually laying out the book. Knowing what pictures are going to be in the book helps me know what to write."

Caroline Arnold

Fear Not

"Don't be afraid to throw away a lot of paint and/or paper on a single concept or drawing. Sometimes work goes easily, sometimes not. Keep going until you're really happy with what you've done.

"Take a portfolio to New York, if you can, for an experience of the field and to meet art directors and editors. Society of Children's Book Writers and Illustrators has a lot of helpful information on ways to do this. Also, take along a resume, an illustrator's card with a sample of your work and if possible, one or more thirty-two-page dummies of your own picture books.

"If you can't go to New York, mail packets of illustration copies to different publishers with SASE's. When I started, I sent out fifteen packets of ten illustration copies to different editors and art directors. Out of those fifteen, I had two bites. One of them turned into a book. The other turned into an illustration job."

Sarah Wilson

Practice Makes Perfect

"My advice is try not to make the picture perfect the first time. Do lots of sketching until you feel comfortable with what you're doing. If you expect to be perfect the first time, you'll block the creative stuff. It's a proven fact among we art types, that things that at first seem like mistakes, will quickly turn into inspiration.

R.W. Alley

To Bookstore, to Bookstore, to Read a Fine Book

"The most valuable piece of advice is to know your competition—go to children's bookstores and spend some time looking at what other artists do and how they do it. Looking at other people's work will help you decide what technique you would choose in creating your own style—it will come naturally."

Paul Brewer

Featuring Doug Cushman

Doug Cushman has illustrated over eighty children's books, writing about a dozen of them, including the Aunt Eater and Inspector Hopper easy reader series. Some of his other books are *Hello Red Fox, Flora and the Tiger* and *From Head to Toe*. As a teenager, as he made comic books about his teachers, selling them to his schoolmates for a nickel a piece.

What comes first when you begin a project?

"I usually start with a character, sketched out in one or five or six sketch books scattered around the studio (and my various travel bags). I like to think my books are character driven; everything begins and ends with a strong character. A setting may set off an idea for a book as well. In many books, the setting is really the main character. (Think of the Mississippi River in *Huckleberry Finn*.) In *Inspector Hopper*, Hopper was the first character I developed. (I loved his long legs and goofy fedora in my first sketches.) But as I worked up the bug-sized setting, more and more ideas appeared. The insect world has many, many varied creatures. The hard part was to pick and choose the best ones."

Does being an illustrator help your process?

"Many decisions are visual, which ones would be the most fun to draw? I'm an artist first. I like to see things. One of the funniest drawings I think I've done in a book is one where Aunt Eater is hugging her sister Eliza. There are these two round little characters hugging with their long noses arching off in opposite directions. It's a hoot."

So how do you write an easy reader?

"Lillian Hoban once said that writing an easy reader is like giving someone directions to your house. It's a 'first you do this, then you turn here, then you turn there, and finally you arrive at my house' thinking process. It's linear. No flashbacks, no pausing for reflections. It's all action and dialogue. I like to say that I write what I can't draw. For instance, why would I write, 'Aunt Eater watched the red sun set behind the purple hills as she pondered her latest mystery' when I can draw a red, setting sun, purple hills and Aunt Eater thinking? Then all I would need to write is, 'This is a real mystery,' said Aunt Eater."

What has inspired your Aunt Eater series?

"Many books come from my own love of reading. I love mysteries. Agatha Christie's Miss Marple was an inspiration for Aunt Eater. And I love terrible puns! At that point in my career, I was sick to death of drawing cute little bunnies and bears and mice. I wanted to do an odd creature. An anteater fit the bill. I sometimes outsmart myself, however. As I was working up the dummy for the first Aunt Eater, my editor pointed to a drawing and said, 'Can you make Aunt Eater happier in this picture?' *I thought, how do you make someone without a mouth smile?"*

How will a writer know if their book fits a reading level?

"I've had many discussions with my editor about reading levels. I don't believe in them. It's purely for marketing in my opinion. A good book is a good book no matter what reading level is attached. I've had so many parents say, 'Oh this is a level two book. My child is a level three.' I can almost hear the 'nayah, nayah, nayah' in their voices! Their child is missing out on some great literature. I'm not just talking about my own work either. I don't bother with reading levels when I'm writing. I just try to write a good, entertaining story. The best judge is to look and study what's been done. Anything by Arnold Lobel, James Marshall, or Lillian Hoban for example. Study the rhythm of the language. And the pacing. Most authors are clueless regarding pacing in a picture book and easy reader. It's hard to explain. Study the masters."

What's your favorite easy reader that you've written?

"I don't have a favorite easy reader that I wrote. They all work on different levels for me. Aunt Eater has done very well for me and kids seem to like her. The first *Aunt Eater, Aunt Eater Loves a Mystery*, has a warm place in my heart because she started it all. *Inspector Hopper* is new. There's more that can be done with him I think."

How do you submit your easy readers?

"After twenty years I still submit a full blown dummy, text, sketches, and everything. It's more work, but it's the best way for the editor to understand what I am trying to do. I set the pace, the pictures and words in the dummy. Each element must play off of the other, work together like an orchestra, or better, a trio or quartet. One element is not more important than the other. If an author thinks her words are so damned important, why bother having pictures in the first place. The same with the artist. Too many books are out there with beautiful pictures and no story, no real story, just a thinly realized plot to hang a bunch of gallery paintings together. That's not book making. It's vanity."

What are some specifics regarding format?

"I always submit my *I Can Read* manuscripts in the short line format, double spaced, the whole works. My manuscripts are usually twelve to fourteen pages in length. I break up the story in chapters, so I might end a chapter on one page and start another one on the next page. Thus one manuscript page may have only three or four lines.

The basic format of the *ICR* is thirteen lines per page, thirty-six characters per line (including spaces and punctuation). The separations are usually between clauses, but if one reads a few *ICRs* you'll get the idea. *ICRs* are usually sixty-four pages but there are some with forty-eight. My manuscripts usually run about fourteen pages or less for a sixty-four page book. Anything beyond that is too much. There are forty-eight and thirty-two page formats now. As my editor says, 'Just write a good story. We'll go from there.'"

Here's a Genre, There's a Genre

Adventure

"I prefer writing middle grade humorous adventure stories with a crazy twist. It's what I liked reading growing up. I feel passionate about getting boys to read. The kind of stories I write are short with humor and adventure appeal to them. It will get them to pick up other books along the way."
Stephen Mooser

Science Fiction

"The biggest, most important thing to remember about writing science fiction is that you have to get the science right.

"You're probably thinking, oh sure, how am I supposed to get time travel or teleportation or faster-than-light spaceships right? Those things aren't real. We can't do them. We can't even fly men to Mars yet, let alone fly them all over the galaxy. How can a writer possibly get the science right when dealing with things that aren't real yet? The answer is extrapolation. Good science fiction writers begin with established science facts and carry on from there, never straying from what ought to be possible given what we already know to be true of the physical world.

"As far as we know, time travel, teleportation, and faster-than-light travel ought to be possible. There is spirited debate about all of these, but none of them have been proven impossible so far. We can therefore use them as a jumping-off place for exploring the ramifications of these technologies, even though they are still imaginary. If time travel might be possible, what are some of the problems that would crop up, given what we do know to be true of physics, logic, and mathematics? If we tried to colonize Mars, what technological obstacles would we have to over-come, given what we know to be true about conditions on Mars?

"Another thing to remember is that a good story of any kind has a backbone of cause and effect that hinges on known rules. In a mainstream story, the reader comes to the book knowing the rules, because they are the rules of everyday life. In science fiction or fantasy, the writer must often educate the reader as she goes, either be-cause the reader must be assumed to be ignorant of the science to some degree, or because the writer has had to create a set of rules for an utterly unfamiliar situation. I've had fellow writers express a sort of envy when I tell them I write science fiction and fantasy. 'It must be incredibly freeing,' is a statement I've heard often. 'You can just make it all up. Anything could happen. You don't have to follow any rules.' When really, the opposite is true. You not only have to follow all the rules about the known world; you must also imagine coherent sets of rules to govern what happens in unknown worlds.

"Last but not least, all of the literary qualities that are vital to any good story are also vital in good science fiction. Settings must be fully imagined, dia-log must ring true, and the plot must flow naturally, drawn along on the tension created by well-developed characters the reader can identify with. Which is some-thing of a trick if you're writing about an intelligent, purple encephlalopod, but it can be done."

Nancy Etchemendy

Fantasy

Play by the Rules

"My first editor, Jean Karl, told me that one of the most important rules about writing fantasy, is that fantasy must have a solid and *limited* base. The reader has to understand what underlies, the magic, where it came from and why, and just how much it might be able to do. Perhaps an ancient curse or tradition? You can't let the reader develop the expectation that, at any moment, an unlimited and unsolicited magic will suddenly swoop in and save the protagonist from danger—or there will be no suspense."

Zilpha Keatley Snyder

"In any form of fantasy, make sure you know all the rules of magic, whatever that magic may be, before you get too far into the book. The first draft of *The Unruly Witch* was total crap because I hadn't worked out the magic—its limitations and aspects."

David Lubar

Journey to Your Fantasy

"I borrow from our real world and accumulate a wealth of vivid and authenticating detail that convinces the reader he or she is there. You have to have elements that seem real and organized. The setting convinces them it's really there. It's not always easy to do in fantasy. Some people say, '*Oh, let's throw a dragon in here.*' But (your setting) really needs to address the needs of the story.

"Think about whether your fantasy connects with the emotional journey of your character. I think I did it in *The Folk Keeper* but I didn't do it in *Well Wished*. That's why I think *Well Wished* isn't as resonant as *The Folk Keeper*. For example, Corinna's story is really a story about identity. She starts out by being confident of being a folk keeper. Over the course of the book, she changes. As a fantasy writer, I am able to use my fantastical elements and take what is otherwise symbolic, and translate it into a literal plot element. If you're writing about identity, in a realistic book, you have to address it abstractly. In my book, Corinna is actually finding her skin. The fantastical elements are kind of inexplicably connected to the character's journey. Fantasy elements shouldn't be arbitrary. Character, plot and fantastical elements all connect with the character's growth or emotional journey."

Franny Billingsley

Cast a Spell

"Most of my books are set firmly in contemporary times with very twenty-first century characters until I add a fantasy element, therefore I call them contemporary fantasies. Example: Rilla is an average home-schooler, living in a bed and breakfast until the day she goes out to fetch the mail and finds a package that changes her life. This is from the *Monster of the Month Club* quartet. Humor set-up: trying to hide the monthly monsters and take care of them without anyone finding out.

"*Princess Nevermore* is my only high fantasy story, and even then, three-fourths of the book is set in contemporary times. Although this novel is not meant to be a funny book, it does have humorous scenes when the medieval princess encounters modern technology for the first time.

"Read the type of fantasy stories you're interested in writing. Authors of newer fantasies include J.K. Rowling, Garth Nix, Phillip Pullman, and Tamara Price. Older favorites are C.S. Lewis, Lloyd Alexander, Jane Yolen and E.L. Konigsburg. Jane Fitz-Randolf says, 'Poor fantasy is easy to write. Good fantasy is not.' Read the above authors to see how high the bar is set.

"Inventing a fictitious world may sound exciting, but in truth, there's a lot of hard work involved. Look how well J.K. Rowling developed details in the fictitious world at Hogwarts School of Witchcraft and Wizardry. We know what Harry Potter wears, what he eats, where he shops, where he spends his summers, what's beneath his bed, and how he receives his mail. And it's all very believable.

"A good fantasy writing exercise is to use the question, '*what if*' and use it as a launching pad. For example...*what if* the back wall of the classroom suddenly falls away and instead of looking out at the soccer field or the parking lot, a lush forest

TEN THINGS A CHILDREN'S BOOK AUTHOR HATES TO HEAR

Not long ago, I was hired to speak at a writer's conference as the token children's book author. When I stepped into the spotlight, ready for my introduction to the 300 participants, the conference coordinator—a writer of adult non-fiction—announced: "Lee has published even more books than I have. But then, hers are so much shorter than mine."

Jealousy? Perhaps. Ignorance? Definitely. Over the years, I've learned that most people, even writers for other markets, are clueless about what it takes to write and sell a children's book.

Sometimes I find these people exasperating. Sometimes amusing. Sometimes they're just an annoying pain in the...pen. I often long to take them under my literary wing and give them a thorough education. But mostly I just sigh, and add their unenlightened comments to my growing list of Things a Children's Book Author Hates to Hear:

1. "Are you published?" (In the days when my answer was 'no,' this question served as a painful reminder of my file cabinet stuffed with rejection letters. Twenty-three sales later, the question still pokes at my insecurities, reminding me that we're only as good as our next book.)
2. "Have you written anything I would've heard of? (Usually asked by someone who hasn't read a children's book since before the invention of dirt.)

Continued on the next page...

grows right up to the school. A path disappears into the trees. I will ask a student's name, then say, 'Erica (or whoever) rises from her desk, steps onto the path, and disappears into the forest. What happens next?"
Dian Curtis Regan

Folktales

"The challenges of re-telling a folktale are finding various sources for the tale in order to get a variety of details, staying true to the language of folk story and,

3. "How many books do you write in a day?" (Puh-leeze. Don't make me laugh.)
4. "When are you and your spouse going to retire on your royalties?" (I said, don't make me laugh. I'm going to bust a rib here.)
5. "When are you going to grow up and write real books?" (My husband usually has to restrain me from ripping out this questioner's liver.)
6. "I've always wanted to write a children's book...if I could only find the time." (Once professed to me by an Ear, Nose and Throat surgeon, as if he considered dabbling in children's fiction between tonsillectomies.)
7. "Your latest book is too good for kids." (Actually uttered to me by a clerk in a bookstore!)
8. "How much do you have to pay the publishing companies to publish your book? (Utter shock when they learn the companies pay me.)
9. "I'd love to read your next book. Would you send me a free autographed copy?" (Asked of me by at least forty-two people at my twentieth high school reunion.)
10. "I've written a picture book about a skunk who can't smell. It's 125 pages long and, even though I'm not an artist, I did my own illustrations. Would you be willing to read it and tell me what you think? And then introduce me to your agent?" (Uh, maybe I could take a rain check on that. Besides, don't you think it's about time you grew up and wrote real books?)

Lee Wardlaw

Lee Wardlaw is the award-winning author of more than twenty books for children, all of which are too good for grown-ups.

most important, retaining the original theme of the story in ones own re-telling of the tale. I chose incidents from the original tale that forward the plot to retain that same theme. One reason I believe folktales are folktale—that is, stories that have endured from generation to generation—is that embedded in them are very powerful themes and archetypes. Think of *Little Red Riding Hood* as an example.

"Read lots of folktales, find multiple sources for the ones you'd like to use, pay attention to language in the versions you have read, and be able to voice the theme so you can pass that along in your re-telling or adaptation of the story."

Caryn Yacowitz

"I actually find it a delicious process to re-tell a folktale from Ethiopia, because the plot is already there and I can fill the story with my own characters and with details that I love from Ethiopian life. When I had my first retelling published in 1994, editors were still looking for folktales. Now most of my editors tell me that it's an 'over published' genre, so I've found other ways of weaving traditional stories into my work. For instance, I did a retelling of a Somalia folktale as one chapter in *Jakarta Missing*."
Jane Kurtz

"Remember that the culture a story is from is its backdrop, its setting, and not the story. You still need a story with a universal theme—love, pride, fear, jealousy, —that everyone can relate to."
Teri Sloat

"Probably the biggest problem in retelling folktales for picture books is that folktales generally lack a theme, while picture books require one. So you have to dig deep into the story and try to draw out a meaning of your own, then use that as your focus.

"The first thing I do when retelling a story, is to find as many older, authoritative versions as possible. For example, for my retelling *Lady White Snake: A Tale From Chines Opera*, I gathered thirteen distinct versions of the legend, in print and on video. Next I research the background through books and the Web. For Lady White Snake, that research led me to explore Chinese opera, the city of Hanzhou and it's West Lake (today and historically), Chinese mythology, Chinese herbal medicine, Chinese festivals, and China's sacred mountains. This was probably my most-researched story!

"After that, I take it all inside and wait for the alchemical transformation that melds everything into a unified, powerful story—hopefully."
Aaron Shepard

Historical Fiction

Do Your Homework
"My 'Dear America' books are historical fiction. So is *Runaway Home*. The facts are accurate, but I created characters and put them in the context of a historical event. I research my historical fiction almost as long and hard as I do nonfiction."
Patricia McKissack

Backdrop for a Star
"When you're writing historical fiction, one thing you need to consider from

the start is whether your period will be a kind of background to personal events, or whether the historic events of the time will actually provoke plot developments. In *At the Sign of the Star*, I chose the quietest years of an unquiet period because I wanted the period to be mainly background. I could have set my story at the time of a plague, the Great Fire of London, a threat of invasion, or a persecution of Catholics—all of these things happened within a few years of my story. But I wanted to concentrate on the step-family problem, and I didn't want it to be overwhelmed by more dramatic events. In my next novel, which will be set at the time of World War II, there will be greater interplay between historical events and the problems of my character."

Katherine Sturtevant

"I try to place myself in the time and period. The research is essential, but even more important is the main character. I have to be that character, walk with him or her, and present the story from the character's point of view. I read, revise and reread out loud what I have written until the character has his or her act put together. I want to be sure that young readers can identify with the character in spite of the differences in time and place."

Tekla White

Acting Lessons

"I have written more than thirty historical novels. I undertake it like an actor. I rent and wear the clothes, I make candles, I read the primary source until I am goofy with details. I read about the era, about the place, the people. I read about world events they would have noticed, been impacted by. I find novels being read then, newspapers from the place and time the storey is set. I travel to see the venue whenever I can. I find people to interview, experts in the area I am exploring. I do whatever it takes to imagine myself inside the protagonist's skin. The day I can do that, I begin the book. Best advice for beginners: Don't include narrative information just because you find it interesting. Use only the thoughts and concerns logical to the characters.

"An example: I knew for months that there were no left or right shoes before the mid 1800's but couldn't find a way to point it out to the reader that wouldn't feel completely false and machinated. Then I read a primary source that mentioned a girl carefully switching her shoes each morning to ensure even wear on the soles. So I gave my character a pair of shoes she loved and wanted to take good care of and described her doing just that."

Kathleen Duey

A Good Defense

"I recommend going to as many primary sources as possible so you can make an informed judgement about what information is reliable, pick up interesting tidbits to add texture, and discover plot ideas. University libraries and presses are great sources of information on arcane subjects. Record details on all your sources and which source each piece of information derives from; you'll be amazed how often you need to go back to check on something, even as late as the copyediting stage, if your publisher is fastidious, and even after publication, if you are called upon to defend your research. This occurred with my first book. Also track all librarians, subject experts, and others who assist you; they'll appreciate an acknowledgment and/or copy of the printed work."

Diane Matcheck

The Other Way Around

"At the beginning of a project, have a feeling for the period and the situation, then just go ahead and tell the story. Do the big research—the digging, the exploring, the note-taking—*after* the story's been written. For me, research has become a job of revision.

"The way I organize my research is centered around what I *need*, not what I *know*. I have two basic organization tools—Post It Notes and a loose-leaf binder with tabs. I keep track of what I need on post its attached to my manuscript—different colors for different needs. I take research notes on binder paper according to topics separated by tabs. I list bibliographical material on individually numbered cards, and put the corresponding number in the margin of my notes."

Susan Hart Lindquist

Humor

Not Even Trying

"I have a loose wire in my brain! When I get in trouble, I wisecrack. I didn't start out *trying* to be funny. I just found it as I wrote along. Early in my career, I wrote three teen occult thrillers for a packaging company. Every one of them had more humor than I planned. It's the way my brain works. It's a gift; it's there and I try to take advantage of it."

Bruce Coville

She Who Laughs

"If I try to make someone else laugh, the humor comes out formulaic. I don't know what anyone else will think is funny. I only know what *I* think is funny."

Gennifer Choldenko

Movies about Underwear?

"Read a lot of humor to see how other people put together situations. Go to the movies. There are shortcuts and tips to follow. If you take the movie, "Kindergarten Cop," you can see how that was pitched. Arnold Schwarzenegger in kindergarten. It's a fish out of water story. Take characters and put them into situations where they don't belong. Gourmet chef judges a junk food contest. Keep in mind who you are writing for. Take Dav Pilkey's *Captain Underpants*. An editor once said, if you just mention the word underpants, kids will start laughing. If you're aware of this, you're ahead of the game."

Stephen Mooser

Eye of the Beholder

"Have a sharp eye. Be observant. Humor is part of everything—even tragedy."
Marilyn Sachs

Good Humor Man

"Good humor is just the other side of tragedy. It's comedy when it happens to someone else and tragedy when it happens to you!

"Any time you try to break down humor, it dissipates in the air. I live in a world where tragedy is an every day part of life. Humor is real healing. I've used it as a therapist.

"I use my life more than anybody. A lot of the fat jokes in *Sarah Byrnes* came from my life. I'm the runt of the litter. I learned to count calories."
Chris Crutcher

Who Laughs When?

"Find out what your audience considers funny; this differs with the age of the child. Think bigger than life. Have fun with words!"
Judith Ross Enderle

Have Fun Reading Funny

"Read humor. Read David Sedaris. Read Dave Barry."
Debra Keller

Funny is as Funny Does

"Most publisher guidelines express an interest in humor. One editor told me that anyone can write a sad book, but few can write funny ones. Editors are always looking for humorous voices, but it must be said that humor is very subjective. What's funny to one person may not be to another, yet readers generally agree on topics that are sad or serious.

"I think it's impossible to instruct someone on the art of writing humor. It all has to do with a writer's voice, or style. You either write with a slightly off-centered way of looking at the world, or you don't.

"Another editor once said to me, 'I like the way your mind works,' which brings me back to the point that it's all a matter of voice."
Dian Curtis Regan

Funny You Should Think of That

"I think it's important to have humor with depth. It gives your character multiple layers. My first drafts aren't particularly funny. I'm getting the serious underpinnings down. Have your characters grapple with real issues. It's only when I know who my characters are and how they view the world, that I can come up with humor for them. One-liners are fine, but they don't define the depth of the heart. Don't write a joke, write an important thought in an off-beat way."
Joan Bauer

WHAT MAKES A GOOD SHORT STORY?

"Same things that make a good book. Some short stories are plot driven—you have a 'gimmick,' a one-joke premise, so you know that the whole story revolves around that premise. Other stories have a central theme, that might have a bit more depth, but not quite enough to fill up a book. Others are character studies; slices of life that are calling out to be told, but not requesting to be made into an entire volume. Usually the idea, itself, will tell you whether it wants to be a novel or a short story. The trick is listening!"

Neal Shusterman

Have an Attitude

"Humor is an attitude. I try to find humor in my life. If you can't laugh at a flat tire or a flooded basement, it's much harder to get through the week. When I write, I try to avoid easy laughs like toilet humor. That seems like cheating to me."
Johanna Hurwitz

Honesty the Best Policy?

"I think kids are the most honest, funny, unselfconsciously charming people on the planet. I suppose a great deal of what we think of as humor has to do with completely honest viewpoints, maybe because they're so unusual that they give us a little jolt of delight when we come across them. The older we get, the less honest we become. We learn to be diplomatic or tactful, or just plain duplicitous as we gain experience with the world. But completely honest viewpoints are something most children have naturally. Often, if you just present a kid's situation as accurately and honestly as possible, it comes out funny with no effort at all, simply because every kid's theories about the world are unique and refreshing.

"Having said that, there are a few things kids always seem to find funny. Bodily fluids are a big one! Poo, snot, and barf are pretty sure-fire paths to major laughs if you can stand to write about them. So are interactions with the opposite sex, younger siblings and animals."

Nancy Etchemendy

It's All in Good Fun

"If writers or artists are playful, it will permeate their books. I come from a family that likes to laugh a lot! That's where it begins."

Bernard Waber

Don't Worry, Be Funny

"I have no specific advice or formula, but I think there is a nerve connection between anxiety, fear, embarrassment and humor."

David Greenberg

Mysteries

Favorite Mysteries

"My favorite children's mystery books include one of the best, *View From the Cherry Tree* by Willo Davis Roberts. I also love Ellen Raskin's *The Westing Game* and Leo Garfield's *Smith*. *Cherry Tree* for its suspense, *Game* for its wit and inventiveness, *Smith* for its Dickensian twists and turns and fiendish cleverness."

Mary Downing Hahn

Important to a Mystery Story:

"Pacing, fair clues and timing....You don't want to give away too much—that's no fun for the reader. But you don't want to make it an unfair puzzle either, where the reader couldn't possibly have figured out who the culprit was."

Wendelin Van Draanen

"Interesting, likable characters involved in a dangerous situation, suspense, atmosphere, a few twists, and a satisfactory conclusion are important elements in a mystery. The characters and the mystery come first. Setting and the working out of plot come next."

Mary Downing Hahn

"For me there needs to be rising tension throughout, and worry for the character. Either that the character is in danger, or that the character will be affected by the outcome of the mystery. That's why I never liked Nancy Drew. She was completing the pieces of a puzzle, but she didn't change and grow. A character must change."
Katherine Reiss

"The mystery influences my plotting. I've read a lot of mysteries and I've picked up the rhythm of when red herrings and clues should be plotted."
Linda Joy Singleton

"In creating a ghost story, it's important the ghost be a fully developed character. Quirky. Complex. Believable. Because he's the driving force in the book, his motivations must be strong and clear. There must be a resolution to the ghost situation as well as the living character's story problem."
Elaine Marie Alphin

Starting a Mystery

"For me, what's often come first is the title. That becomes a mystery to *me*. Like, who are the Sisters of Mercy, and what are they doing in my brain? When structuring a mystery, I've got to know whodunit from the get-go. I can't decide in the last stages of the book. I have to build a cast of characters who have some beef or negative history with the victim. I get to know their histories and base their actions on what's gone on before the story begins.

"My mission is to get kids to think about the directions they're taking. I'd like them to take some proactive steps to make sure they wind up in the place they want to go."
Wendelin Van Draanen

"Whether or not they are mysteries, I write all my books the same way—making them up as I go along. In the second draft, I make sure the story hangs together and sounds credible. My ideas for suspense come while I'm writing; I'm not consciously aware of technique."
Mary Downing Hahn

"Most of the time I have a book seething in my mind. I call them books of my heart. I *have* to write them, no matter what. I've done six of those, where I write the whole manuscript and send it to my agent or editor. Other times I've been asked to write books. For instance, I was asked out of the blue to write a trilogy about a ghost in a dollhouse. The characters and plot were left up to me, but I was paid for the three books before I'd written a thing. Now I'm working on books in *The American Girl* line of *History Mysteries*. The publisher wants an inviting mystery set in the past, solved by good independent, creative thinking girls. Historians are on their staff to make sure everything is accurate. The plot and characters are entirely my own, but the publisher must approve an extensive, chapter by chapter outline before offering a contract. I wrote a thirty-page outline for a 150-page book. I found I didn't have to stick exactly to the outline once I was actually writing the book. I could play with it."

Katherine Reiss

"For me, I have to construct the plot—the mystery. I outline so I have a general map to follow. That gives me guidance with lots of room to tell the story, develop the characters, throw in surprises, clues and red herrings. Then I write the opening line. Once that's down, the story just seems to flow. I'm a firm believer in strong opening lines—they're the catalysts for the rest of the mystery.

"I start with a unique idea, such as a woman who's found on top of a grave instead of in the grave, or a woman waking up on the embalming table just before she's stuck with that trocar, or a man who's accused of killing his mother but can't defend himself due to overlooked deafness. Then I think up a batch of suspects— who's likely to be involved in this story—relatives, police, best friends. I give each one a secret that could be the motive for the murder—but only one is strong enough to kill for. I add clues along the way, often mixed in with ordinary descriptions or information, to disguise them, then add a few red herrings if they're needed."

Penny Warner

"First, I pick a setting. Once I have that, I make a list of things that can happen in that setting. From that list, something emerges. For one *Cam Jansen* mystery, the setting is a department store. I wrote all the things you can do in a department store. 'Returning things' popped out of the list. Then I think, if I had a criminal mind, *how can I use that?*

"Once I have the crime, I find what the clues will be. *What clue could there be that Cam could describe?* In Cam's situation, it has to be a visual clue, because she has a photographic memory. It has to be something she sees and the reader can be made aware of. I won't let Cam have an advantage over the reader. The older Cam readers are easier; I can bury the clues with descriptions and detail. In the younger Cam readers, it's harder, because I can't have that many details."

David Adler

Building Suspense in a Mystery

"Multi-plot lines help not to have a sagging middle to a book. There's so much going on and trying to tie them together makes for a lot of possibilities for movement. When you're a kid, you like things fast-paced. I like cliffhangers. If there's a cliff, I'd start the next chapter. You finish the book before you realize it. I work

MAKE IT COUNT

"Raise the stakes as you write. First, the protagonist needs to have a good strong reason to solve the crime. Otherwise, turn it over to the police and let them do their job. Second, she needs to be hunted while she's doing the hunting—so she's in danger. She also has to have something emotional at stake –she'll lose her reputation, she'll lose her family, whatever. Then crank it up as the story progresses until the climax, where she nearly loses her life. Paint yourself into a corner— then try to get out."

Penny Warner

those into my writing because I liked them as a kid. It's a good tool to continue through the book.

"Put lengthy, flowery descriptions in shorter and fewer blocks so the kids will get it and you won't lose them. Humor is another key. I didn't like stories that made me depressed. I try to keep things hopeful."
Wendelin Van Draanen

"You have to have a number of elements that are unrelated. But by the end of the story they're woven tightly together. That way, the reader has a feeling of satisfaction and can see how the character has changed through solving the mystery. The weirdness is accounted for. Don't leave the reader hanging."
Katherine Reiss

Employ Red Herrings
"You gotta have them! It's not fair to mislead the reader, but it's fair to toss out clues. Back when I was a kid, I didn't like it when I felt cheated at the end of the book. You can get cheated in a mystery in two ways: cheated if you know who did it too fast or who did it could not possibly be discerned by the reader because the author didn't give enough. There's fine line between giving too much and too little. Red herrings are fun to keep the reader guessing until half a chapter before the denouement. I want the reader to find out who did it *just before*."
Wendelin Van Draanen

"Most of my books are not mysteries, so I've never used red herrings. But what I dislike about red herrings is the artificiality of it all. In a good mystery 'why' is always more important than 'who.'"
Mary Downing Hahn

"I have things appear to be red herrings, but they turn out to be important after all—sort of reverse red herrings. It's another way of building clues."
Katherine Reiss

"I don't think there's a formula for red herrings, but you need a few to keep the story puzzling. I don't like to set up really false clues that would make the reader angry about being misled, but I do give each character a reason to have committed the murder. The red herrings should be explained at the end of the story—and they must be logical and fair. Often red herrings take shape in the form of personality— the mean old landlady, the gruff alcoholic, etc. But this is an illusion meant to misguide the reader. Look at the physical evidence, not the personalities, for true clues."
Penny Warner

Good Writing Exercise for Aspiring Mystery Writers:
"Learn how to incorporate suspense in your stories. It doesn't have to lead to terror; it needs to lead to anticipation that something will happen. Write one minute in your character's life, but take ten minutes to write about it. Stretch out the moment for the reader. Like waiting for the phone to ring. What is she thinking? Why is this important? What is going to happen that hasn't happened yet? When the minute is up, then there is a sense of satisfaction by the reader. Just like movies use music to create a mood. When it finally happens, there is a release."
Katherine Reiss

"Start with character. The story is what happens to that character and how she changes over time as a result. The protagonist should be offered choices, and those choices will lead her to solve the mystery—but not without some physical and emotional jeopardy along the way, of course."
Penny Warner

Horror

Everyday Events
"The best horror springs from the mundane. If you drop a character into a completely terrifying world where everything is horror, you have no story. But if you put a character in a totally normal world, where *one* thing is wrong, you have unlimited potential."
David Lubar

Nonfiction

What's Out There?

"Does the topic get you excited? Don't worry that the topic is too difficult. Most subjects can be simplified to kids' level. Do you think about child development when you choose your topic? Gardening can be presented to preschoolers. A child needs more experience to understand the Vietnam War.

"It helps to know the school curriculum at different grade levels. This will help see your book to potential publishers (teachers and librarians will be interested) and it will give you clues about the age group your subject matches.

"Look at the work already available. If yours will be the only book on diving for underwater treasure, it may mean a ready made market is waiting for your work. On the other hand, if there are no books on underwater treasure, it may mean no market exists. You have to decide which is right. Can you find information on underwater diving? Is there a way your book will be different from the three books already in print?"

Suzanne Morgan Williams

Six-and-a-Half All Over Again

"I took a class from Caroline Arnold. She said, 'What's your attitude? What's the emotional quality?' An editor once said to me, 'I'm six and a half and I'm going to listen to you read your work aloud.' Make nonfiction suspenseful."

Deborah Norse Lattimore

Story

"Human anecdotes bring nonfiction alive."

Susan Hart Lindquist

Get Smart

"I ask myself, what subject might I be in a good position to cover? When I wrote a proposal on astronomy, I interviewed a scientific establishment. Because I had that special expertise, a publisher took the book."

Ellen Jackson

Wow 'em

"I try to find interesting ways to present information. For example, a guessing game or '*wow*' kind of facts to keep the reader interested. Sidebars, captions, and bulleted facts can break the text into shorter sections for young readers or draw a reluctant reader into the text."

Tekla White

Stash It and Slant It

"When I hear an idea I think will be good, I stash it in my head for a couple of months. If I still think it's good then, I can feel pretty confident in proceeding. One caveat is that people who don't read a lot don't seem to have a good sense of a good idea. Many people tell me, 'You should write a whale book.' I think, 'Hello, there are ten gazillion whale books out there.' Of course, I just DID have a whale book published (*A Whale Biologist at Work*), but that's because I found a unique slant on the subject."

Sneed B. Collard III

I Wonder . . .

"What is exciting, fun, or intriguing about your subject? What fills you with wonder? Focus your book or article around that. You'll do a lot of research; you'll learn a lot of fascinating stuff, but you'll have to leave it out if it doesn't fit your focus. You can always save it for another project."

Elaine Marie Alphin

Gotta Love It

"Don't write about anything that you aren't or can't become passionate about. Ask yourself, what makes this fabulous? Writing for children isn't about giving them every fact about a subject. They have years to learn. Non-fiction for children should make them curious. Give kids credit for wanting to know why things are. *Why* is always a more interesting question than *when* or *what*. Kids want to know how things work. They like to be amazed! Give them details. It's more real and impressive to know an eagle spots a fish from a mile away, than to know eagles have keen eyes."

Suzanne Morgan Williams

Make Your Nonfiction Compelling! But how?

"Include information that will either make them laugh or have them want to

find out more on the subject. Including projects, like recipes, is also a fun, hands-on approach for learning about history, as is including facts that will make them squirm and appreciate modern times."
Loretta Ichord

Quirky but True

"Search for quirky details that will intrigue children. Make analogies that ring true to them. Use the real words of real people whenever possible to add to the sense of time and place. Today's best nonfiction books for children are filled with photos, illustrations, graphics, and sidebars to help the book come alive."
Connie Goldsmith

What's Not Mentioned?

"I always begin any nonfiction book by reading as many children's books about my topic as I can. Doing so gives me a clear understanding of my topic, but more importantly, it acquaints me with what already exists. My goal, then, in doing my research in more technical adult resources, is to find information that was missing in these other books.

"For example, that Pluto is the smallest and most distant planet in the recognized solar system is common to every book about the planets. What *wasn't* commonly mentioned was the controversy surrounding its planet status. As soon as I ran across this division in scientific thought, I knew I had material I was going to simplify and include in my own Pluto book. Essentially, I look for the odd bit of information or the heretofore untold story."
Larry Dane Brimner

Lure 'em In

"When I begin a nonfiction project, I go to the library, bookstore, used bookstores, and online bookstores, plus Internet sites on my subject. I e-mail and phone experts in the field. Then I write a detailed outline on my subject. Next, I create a file of time periods in order by chapter and attack each chapter one at a time. I stay with the chapter until I'm satisfied that I have made the information interesting and enticing for young readers by giving them plenty of fascinating details and a connection to their own daily lives. I also travel to study my subjects up close."
Loretta Ichord

Urp and Slurp and Ick and Sick

"Make nonfiction interesting by finding interesting people doing interesting things. Obscure facts! Gross statistics! Use the shock factor to get their attention."
Susan Taylor Brown

Be in Touch

"Talk with kids and try to see the world from their point of view; look at programs for young people on PBS; talk with librarians and teachers; try to remember what interested *you* when you were a child, find out what books kids like and read them yourself."

Kathy Pelta

Don't Forget Fiction

"The battle has already been fought and won with many children because they are naturally drawn to nonfiction books or to your topic. To attract others, you have to rely on many of the devices that fiction writers use: characterization, dramatization, mystery, dialogue, development of theme."

Larry Dane Brimner

Storytelling 101

"Look for the story. Stories are about change. Change, like facts, can teach lessons. It can help to ask yourself the usual fiction questions: What did the major characters learn while overcoming the obstacles in the story being told, and how did they learn it? Then work backwards, so that every single event recounted contributes to that lesson. All the aspects of good fiction storytelling—a problem, interesting characters, increasing tension, and a crisis resulting in change—apply. And including these things in your nonfiction story helps avoid moralizing."

Ann Manheimer

Be Real

" 'Tell a good story,' is the best advice I have to offer anyone writing nonfiction. Weave the facts into the action. Someone once said, good fiction should read like nonfiction, and good nonfiction should read like fiction. Ideally we want young readers to say after reading one of our titles is, 'What a good story!'

"I'm often asked, 'How do you develop good story when the facts are set and you can't embellish anything?' Find as much action as you can and surround your character with action, put your person in a time and place. For example, if they are born in Chicago 1939, then show your reader what Chicago looked like then; how were the people dressed?, etc.

"I don't create dialogue or conversations in nonfiction unless it is a direct quote. I'm afraid it might be confusing to a young reader who might get the impression that it is real. I always make a note of where the dialogue/conversation can be documented. That's the key word: *documentation*."

Patricia McKissack

INGREDIENTS FOR A WINNING NONFICTION BOOK PROPOSAL

"In many ways, the proposal has to be like the opening paragraph of the book. It has to tell what the book is going to be about, including a few interesting facts and features that pull the reader in and make you want to know more. How will it fit the curriculum? What's the competition?"

Caroline Arnold

"• A query letter that is short and to the point.
• A beginning sentence that will capture an editor's interest and attention.
• A brief explanation of why *you* are the one who should write this book, how much research you have done and how much more you intend to do, why there is a need for this book and how the material will fit into school curricula.
• Brief mention of your writing history (other books or articles, awards) and...
• the SASE."

Kathy Pelta

Biography

"Robert Louis Stevenson said, 'In biography, you have your little handful of facts, little bits of a puzzle, and you sit and think and fit them together this way and that."
Angelica Carpenter

"I think I choose to write biographies because I'm a real snoop. I love to read letters and diaries and that's what you are supposed to do when you write about people's lives!"
Beverly Gherman

"Children need positive role models and I would rather that they read about Rachel Carson than a rock star or a television personality."
Ginger Wadsworth

"In biographies for young readers, I try to include two types of details. One, are those that are crucial to history. The second, are the details that for me define the subject. In an early reader, there's no way I can tell everything. When the reader closes the book, he needs to know the person. I like to use quotes, so the subject can speak rather than me speaking for him."
David Adler

How do you choose your subjects?

"I choose my subject in two ways. I only write about people I admire, so that eliminates a lot of famous people. And I tend to want to write about people who have done something special on behalf of Mother Earth. John Muir and Rachel Carson are two examples.

"I do research at my local library and/or the Internet. If there are too many books out on a potential subject, I won't write the initial proposal or continue my research. It isn't a good idea for the publisher, or for me. For instance, there are many wonderful children's books out on Eleanor Roosevelt and I will continue to admire her, but I will probably never write a book about her."

Ginger Wadsworth

"I usually select someone who intrigues me and has unanswered questions. Why did Georgia O'Keeffe paint skulls? Why wouldn't E.B White talk in front of groups? Why are today's students still interested in Norman Rockwell? I have many projects that I couldn't sell because editors were not familiar with the person or felt they would not be commercial. 'Write an article, but don't think about a full biography,' is what I've been told."

Beverly Gherman

"I think it is easier to write about a subject you can admire, but you must also find one whose life will sell."

Angelica Carpenter

One biographer recommends starting research with the subject's obituary in their local paper. How do you start? What comes next? Discuss your process.

"I also read obituaries. But I've had the good fortune to write about someone who is still alive; Astrid Lindgren. In that case, I read everything that anyone else had written by her, reread all her children's books and actually wrote a draft of my biography before I made a trip to Sweden to meet and interview her. By writing my book, I knew where there were holes in the text and information that I still needed. Astrid Lindgren gave me permission to write her story. I would never write about a living person without their permission. The Jewish Publication Society asked me to write a book about Izrak Perlman, but he refused to give permission and so although there is much material available about him, I turned down the contract."

Johanna Hurwitz

"I usually start in the children's section of my local library. I want a 'quick' read to get an overview. And I want to get excited about my person. Reading an obituary is the last thing I would do! Then I do Internet research...a fairly new approach for me. I find it very exciting to navigate through the maze of potentially helpful sites. I usually discover sites...books...and people and places, such as museums or national monuments connected to my subject. I start contacting these sites and these people. I write friends who might lead me to new sources. And I go back to the library and check out all the adult books I've learned about on the Internet...and more. One thing leads to another.

"At some point, if I can't find the books through the library or borrow them from friends, I consider buying them through a rare books dealer. The problem is that I love books and my house is overflowing with them. My 'newest' bookcase is under my bed—out of necessity!

"Travel is an important part of my research. I have a strong need to 'walk in the shoes' of the famous person I'm learning about. My books have taken me to many new and wonderful places such as New York/Hudson River Valley and the Catskill Mountains, for John Burroughs; Pennsylvania and the coast of Maine, for Rachel Carson; Wisconsin and various wilderness spots like Yosemite National Park in California for John Muir; and many Little House sites, such as Missouri, Wisconsin, and Minnesota for Laura Ingalls Wilder.

"I'd love to write about Jane Goodall, but only if I could go to Africa. And so far, no publisher has offered to buy me that plane ticket!

"I couldn't have written about Marion Russell in *Along the Santa Fe Trail* without seeing the wagon wheel ruts along the trail at Fort Leavenworth where she started, or Fort Union where she lived as a bride. The same goes for John Muir. It would be crazy to write about him without seeing Yosemite, where he spent so much time. Besides, doing research in the Yosemite National Park Library, located in the awesome Yosemite Valley, hardly qualifies as work!

"After doing the early research and travel, I get down to the challenging part—getting organized."

Ginger Wadsworth

"I start reading about my people at the Library of Congress—it's my favorite place and my good luck charm. I need to read a lot from many different sources about my subject before I feel comfortable beginning to write."

Beverly Gherman

"To write a book requires market research. I investigate publishers to see who published books like the one I want to write. I target them, and send in multiple submissions. My cover letter emphasizes that I will have an index, as list of sources, maps, chronology, and related information like a bibliography of the author's books. After the contract is signed, I read books about the subject and check those books' bibliographies. Next, I compile a list of sources and a list of where the subject has lived or visited. Then I write to these places—libraries, museums, historical societies, tourist bureaus, and newspapers. Often I've written to more than 100 places for each subject."

Angelica Carpenter

"The research process starts in all sorts of ways, but reading the obituary for Wilma Rudolph was the direct inspiration for *Wilma Unlimited*. With the six 'Lives of' books, the artist Kathryn Hewitt and I work out the selection process with much research, outside consultation, debate, and even argument! We have to like the people—either them as human beings, or their work—because we'll be spending so much time with them. We want the people to be, in some way, accessible to young readers. I prefer dead people: I like to write about the structure of their whole lives. (And also, they can't sue for talking about things like underwear!) Finally, we try for a balanced list—crossing countries, eras, boundaries, etc."

Kathleen Krull

How do you choose a beginning and find the order in your book?

"So far, all my biographies have been written in chronological order. However, I usually open each book with a vignette to introduce young readers to that person. For instance, in *Laura Ingalls Wilder, Storyteller of the Prairie*, the book opens with Laura as an adult, reflecting on her childhood days as a pioneer. She decides to write her memoirs for her daughter, Rose, having no intention or clue that her words would evolve in the classic 'Little House' series."

Ginger Wadsworth

"Chronological order isn't interesting, but you don't want to get too far away from it, because a different order would be confusing for children. With a biography, I try to organize life events so it reads like good fiction. Authors must relate their subjects to the time period in a way that children can understand. To tackle the history of an era, I look first for general, reputable overviews. Time-Life books are especially helpful."

Angelica Carpenter

In biographies written for young adults, how do you handle "touchy" subjects—like the person's sexuality, when that shapes the person to a great extent?

"In biographies for older readers, I never ignore 'touchy' subjects. For instance, I wrote that John Burroughs fathered a child with a housemaid who worked in his home. He later adopted the boy, Julian, and he and his wife raised him. It only takes up a small part of my book, and rightfully so. The most important issue is about his nature essays and the impact they had on readers in America. That is what I focused on.

"Over the years, I have been asked about Julia Morgan's sexuality, about why she never married. I don't talk about it in my book. I did not discover anything about her sexuality during my research, and I don't know why she didn't marry. All I can do is speculate, but not in my book. I do know that she was 100 percent committed to her career. And at the same time (1904-1957) when she was an architect, she was one of a handful of women in a male-oriented field. The female architects who did marry often gave up their careers to raise families. In my opinion, Julia Morgan had to choose between marriage and architecture...and it had nothing to do with her sexuality."

Ginger Wadsworth

"O'Keeffe lived with the photographer Alfred Stieglitz for six years before they married. A friend of mine said if I wrote about it, my book wouldn't sell in some states. She was teasing but in earlier years, it was more difficult to say indelicate things. I think today's kids are more used to unconventional relationships. I also think they need to know about the many aspects of people—being a great artist, doesn't mean that the person will also be kind or giving. I want to show the total person."

Beverly Gherman

"Lewis Carroll is controversial as he, like other Victorian photographers, sometimes took nude studies of little girls. Little girls were regarded as asexual and symbols of innocence.

"I am writing about this subject in a matter-of-fact way. For my Robert Louis Stevenson book, the editor would not include a picture from Samoa, probably taken by RLS, of a family maid, sitting topless in front of the fireplace, with Stevenson's wife, Fanny, who was wearing a muu-muu. The editor said that no librarian or teacher in America would buy the book if it contained such a picture.

"Today, though, I think we're to the 'warts and all' stage of biographies for children. So we don't cover up subjects' flaws as much as we used to."

Angelica Carpenter

What are some specific difficulties in writing biographies?

"There are lots of difficulties in writing biographies. Sometimes, the subject didn't do anything famous for most of his/her life. Laura Ingalls Wilder didn't start to write her famous '*Little House*' books until she was sixty-two. I had to write about her entire life, but emphasize her early years, then leap to her last years.

"There is usually a fee for permission to quote from that famous person. And photographs have a price tag. One of my jobs is to get a general idea of the cost early on in the project. If it is going to be too costly for quotes and/or photographs, a publisher might say no.

"In the case of *Julia Morgan, Architect of Dreams*, only twelve photographs of her exist. The publisher relied on other photographs of her blueprints and her buildings. Just like us, publishing houses have budgets, too, and must decide on how many and which photographs they can afford to include in the book.

"I love reading murder mysteries...unraveling clues. Writing a biography has some of the same feeling, believe it or not. I try to be a 'detective' and find out everything I can about that person –both good and bad– and put it all into a book. When *John Muir, Wilderness Protector* came out, it got a review that made my day. The reviewer said it 'read like a novel,' that it was a page-turner. My objective is having my readers wanting to turn each page to find out what happens next."

Ginger Wadsworth

"I had to ask Georgia O'Keeffe's permission to use her quotes and photographs. She refused both. So I took out the quotes, paraphrased and purchased new pictures. That was my first book and I was devastated, but it taught me a lot about the process of writing and rewriting biography.

"In an interview, Justice Sandra Day O'Connor told me she used to get 'terrified' whenever she tried something new. Later she wanted to change it to read that she was a little bit afraid, but I told her that I thought children could identify with her intense feelings. She allowed me to leave her words as she had spoken them. I felt I had discovered something new that others hadn't written about her and that has become my goal with all my books.

"People tell me that I should stick to writing about people who are long dead. Then I won't have to worry about dealing with these kinds of things."

Beverly Gherman

"The issue of possessiveness comes up in many literary clubs and museums. In one club, an officer refused my request for help because he was already helping a different author to write a book on the same subject. Most club members are kind and generous. This person did not represent the club's true policy, but for a time, I thought he did."

Angelica Carpenter

"The one difficulty I've experienced repeatedly is finding information about the subject's childhood. Kids, and adults too, I think, love to learn what famous people were like as children, when they were still powerless and little. But if the information isn't there, it's not there.

"Sometimes I'll speculate. For example, in one article I described a park with a set of stairs on a path, and imagined that my subject must have loved going up and down the stairs. I knew the stairs were there from newspaper articles. I knew my subject lived and went to school nearby. So I put the known facts together with a 'must have,' without saying it was true. It is possible to learn about the era and the environment and put that together with sparse facts about your subject, as long as you're careful not to present as fact anything you don't know to be true."

Ann Manheimer

To make the story as real as possible, some biographers advocate inventing dialogue. What is your opinion of this technique? If you are in favor of it, how do you choose to use it and when not to use it? Does real dialogue cost money?

"I don't invent dialogue and put it in a biography. In my opinion, created dialogue belongs in another format—historical fiction, history mysteries, a story about a famous person, creative nonfiction, etc. It's unfair to young readers to have them believe that the dialogue is true.

"For instance, I'm still mad that a reviewer claimed that I had created dialogue in *Julia Morgan Architect of Dreams*. I did extensive research, using oral histories at the University of California at Berkeley's Bancroft Library, and can document each quote.

"And yes, real dialogue costs money. I had to pay the University of California because of my direct quotes from the oral histories relating to Julia Morgan. The Muir-Hanna Trust charged me fifty dollars for every 300 words that John Muir spoke. And today, more and more libraries and museums, or even trusts, are well-aware of the importance of charging these use fees. The fees help pay the library staff, make it possible to maintain the other archival materials."

Ginger Wadsworth

"When I started writing in the eighties, you couldn't invent dialogue as had been so common with earlier biographies. I do like using quotes to bring my subject to life, but I have to know that they are accurate and are available in at least two different places. Whenever I quote or use ideas from others, I give attribution in my notes."

Beverly Gherman

"The rules say you can't. But Diane Stanley can. One librarian calls her books 'storiographies.' Jean Fritz also invents dialogue. I don't do it. But the rules allow you to quote any written source, even though that may have been made up.

"For instance, Frances Hodgson Burnett invented a lot of dialogue in her autobiography. We quoted that a lot. Sometimes I get around this rule by asking rhetorical questions. Lewis Carroll wanted to become a priest but worried about his speech impediment, which made it hard for him to read aloud or preach a sermon. How could he be a minister? While he's wrestling whether or not he'd make a good priest, I used questions like: How could he read the Bible aloud or preach sermons with his speech impediment? How could he become a priest when he loved to go to the theater?

"In my books, I use as many quotations as possible, arranged to resemble dialogue. Research shows that children choose books with a lot of quotation marks, expecting dialogue."

Angelica Carpenter

How can you put everything vital in a biography without overwhelming the reader?

"My goal is writing short. I look for the essence of my subject. Kids don't need to know every date or detail. But I want them to get the sense of the person. With Norman Rockwell, I was sure his son would tell me that he and his brothers resented his father's working night and day and not having time to play ball with him. Yet when I talked to him, he said that wasn't the case at all. They often modeled for him and they felt he was always there for them in his studio. So we mustn't assume anything."
Beverly Gherman

"You can't! It would be totally boring. That's the power of being a biographer...of deciding what stays and what goes."
Ginger Wadsworth

"You have to be selective about what you want to cover. I have sticky notes by my computer with nine or ten categories I want to include. If something is really interesting or funny, but does not fit the categories, it has to go."
Angelica Carpenter

How do you advise writers to "pare down" the material?

"Look at your future audience. Juvenile biographies can be for first graders on up through high school. Consider the age of your readers. What have they learned in school so far? For example, if you're writing about Abraham Lincoln, have the students studied the Civil War? How much do they really know about the issue of slavery?

"You might want to focus on just one event or a part of their life. For instance, I have studied Eleanor Roosevelt. Her childhood was tragic. She lost both her parents and was raised by her grandmother. Eleanor was plain and shy. Eventually, she overcame her difficult childhood to become one of America's most admired women. So, I would emphasize her childhood."
Ginger Wadsworth

"Some subjects have been written about extensively. I haven't selected anyone like that, but if I should, I would try to find the best adult biographies written and would still go to primary sources for my material."
Beverly Gherman

"I play detective, by which I mean I am a heavy user of the library. I read mostly secondary sources and scour them for juicy details that make information come alive. I'm taking the fruits of other people's labors, the most scholarly biographies I can find, and looking for the 'good parts.'

"When researching Beethoven, for example, one day I read that his favorite meal was macaroni and cheese. This homely tidbit gave me my focus: concrete details that kids ages eight to twelve could relate to, anecdotes that would humanize these iconic figures, what you would have noticed about these eccentrics if you'd been their neighbor. What did they wear? What did they do in the middle of the night? How weird was their family life? What did they crave? What about girlfriends and boyfriends? And what about their hair? If there is a magic key to what I do, it's this: After I soak up all the information, I don't use it all."

Kathleen Krull

Do you have any tips for writing the biography?

"I was very closed-mouthed when I began writing. I was afraid to tell anyone who I was writing about. Once I felt more confident, it became a tremendous asset to talk and let serendipity lead me along. Justice O'Connor told me about growing up in Arizona and what it was like to be isolated on a ranch there. Once she was ready to go to school, she went to live with her grandmother in Texas. I actually found friends [of hers] from El Paso when I told one person who had grown up there."

Beverly Gherman

"Get a travel guide to places where your subject lived or traveled. Find pictures of the place so it gives you the feel of the land. My mother, who was my coauthor, made us put the five senses into every chapter."

Angelica Carpenter

How do you organize your research?

"I buy boxes from office supply stores and a huge supply of manilla envelopes. While working on a biography, I use these boxes as file cabinets. These 'file cabinets' sit on the floor next to my computer. And I have to be *very* organized. Files might include: magazine articles, photo information, quotes, lists of books, a timeline, a file for each chapter, correspondence, interviews, Internet material, etc. I also keep a shelf or two for just that project. I keep all my books, including library books, in that area."

Ginger Wadsworth

"I like long lives! In order to handle eighty or ninety years, I always do a timeline and break the years into decades."

Beverly Gherman

"As I take notes, I make sure that each entry includes a source, indicated by an abbreviation. I keep track of the abbreviations in the long version of my bibliography, entering each source in the bibliography as I finish taking notes on it. I also note where I got the material and the call number, if any, in case I need to find it again. *You must document every word of your text.*"
Angelica Carpenter

"I have no organization whatsoever. I have a file though. I think the trouble with researching is you tend to go on and on. When I'm ready to write, I'll research until I feel I have a grasp of it. With *SOS Titanic*, I went to Ireland because that's where it was built. I went to the Ulster Folk Museum where they have all the Titanic memorabilia. They had a huge diorama of a sinking Titanic there. It was a tremendous help. They gave me pamphlets and I bought nonfiction books about it. I use everything I can. You have to research for a contemporary book too, but it's usually not so difficult."
Eve Bunting

What happens if you get sources that disagree with each other?

"Sources often disagree and it's difficult to know which is accurate. The rule is you must have at least two sources for every fact you use. Sometimes you have to admit that there are questions: it could have happened this way or that way. There is no certainty."
Beverly Gherman

"It happens all the time! Dates are the biggest problem. I am continually checking and rechecking my sources. If I can't find the answer, I usually have to make a judgement call, often based on the caliber of the source. I also use a lot of qualifying words, like 'sometimes,' 'often,' 'probably,' etc.

"I often ask an expert to read a draft of my text. Sara Boutelle, a professor of architectural history, read my book on Julia Morgan. Shirley Sargent, an expert of Yosemite and John Muir, read my book on John Muir. John Burrough's then ninety-two-year-old granddaughter, Elizabeth Kelley, read every word of each draft on my manuscript about him. If there were mistakes, believe me, she let me know. Nearly blind, she studied each sentence with a magnifying glass and wrote her answers in shaky penmanship, but with details about why I was incorrect. I always acknowledge the experts in my books."
Ginger Wadsworth

Since writing a biographer is like being a detective. What are some 'sleuthing techniques' that you can share?

"Although I never discuss a novel in progress, I've discovered that it pays to tell everyone I know when I am working on a biography. In this way I've made some good links to people who knew my subject. When I was writing about Anne Frank, a neighbor who was a German refugee in Amsterdam before World War II, told me that his mother played cards with Anne's mother once a week. 'What language did the women speak when they were playing?' I asked him. When he told me 'German,' which is what I suspected, I knew that I could surmise that when Anne's father wrote her a birthday poem, he would write it in his native language. Someone else hearing that I was writing about Leonard Bernstein told me he had dated Lenny's sister. In this way, I've been able to pick up useful anecdotes."

Johanna Hurwitz

"For interviews, come prepared, but plan to be flexible. For example, an eighth grader who wants to be a writer, recently interviewed me in my home. He came prepared with questions and a tape recorder. I showed him my office, my books, and then we sat down in my living room for the actual interview. Although he asked a few questions from his list, he felt 'brave enough' to be creative. He noted that I own lots of paintings related to nature and wondered why. He also wondered why I am 'Ginger' when I'm listed as 'Virginia' in the telephone book. A good interviewer has a script, but doesn't necessarily stick to it.

"When I visited Laura Ingalls Wilder's home in Mansfield, Missouri as part of my research, I took three docent-led tours through the house. The first time, I listened to the docent. The second and third times, I looked at everything beyond the roped off areas. Outside, I wrote notes about the color of Laura's dishes, the style of furniture, the art on the walls, the titles in the bookcase, etc. I always look for those kinds of details."

Ginger Wadsworth

"I try to make fresh, contemporary choices from my research—little ironies, the opinions of the neighbors, amusing juxtapositions, details like hair and underwear. I take advantage of present-day openness to mention odd habits, sexual orientation, addictions, gossip and rumors, strengths and weaknesses and other behavior perhaps 'unmentionable' in the past. The text must get to the point quickly, so all the 'boring parts' must go."

Kathleen Krull

Choose one of the books you've written. Whom did you interview for the book? How were they helpful? What kind of information did they provide?

"Most of my biography subjects have been dead for quite awhile and there weren't friends and/or relatives to interview. However, for *Rachel Carson, Voice of the Earth*, I flew east to meet Rachel's best friend, Shirley Briggs. I had sent her a list of questions prior to my arrival. And I had been warned that Miss Briggs was very protective of her friend. I met her in Bethesda, Maryland. Miss Briggs had my questions on her desk. I sat down.

"She immediately pounded both fists on her desk, shaking everything, including my nerves. 'You do not know anything about Rachel Carson,' she shouted.

"I was shaking inside! Somehow, I calmly said, 'But of course, you are right. And that is why I have come three thousand miles to meet you and learn details about Rachel Carson.'

Over the next three hours, we talked. Miss Briggs worked her way through my questions. With each answer, she told a story, then another story, and over the course of the interview, I learned about Rachel Carson as a person."

Ginger Wadsworth

On Poems and Poetry

Brevity
"I know what I like. Brevity is wonderful. More images of characters. My poems are completely character driven. I write poetry in the style of vignettes."
Angela Johnson

Word Picture
"A good poem is one that transports me to another place, one that makes a picture in my mind. It makes me feel I am there, in the moment the poem captures. If the poem is about a party, I will get hungry. If the poem is about a dog, I will see her in my mind."
Janet Wong

Relationship
"A good poem creates a relationship—a connection between the poet and the reader that falls into some intangible and indefinable place outside of 'words'— maybe that's why the form has been around for so long...it's something we can't really explain."
Susan Hart Lindquist

Unexpected Angle
"A good poem says something new, fresh, surprising. Even when its subject has been written about many times (how many new subjects are there?) poetry invites you to consider it from a new perspective. A poet is a little like a photographer who shoots a subject from an unexpected angle.

"Poetry is also a gift to the ear; it's something to listen to. There's pleasure in the pure sounds of the words, in the way they fit together and interact—like the notes in a musical chord."
Alice Schertle

Rhythm

"What makes a good poem? When I sigh, or shake my head at the beauty of language or the amazing clarity of metaphor. When the words either break my heart, or bring a smile to my face. A good poem makes me feel like I've been there, or have felt the same way as the poet did. It makes me look at something in a way I've never looked at it before. It surprises me. Additionally, a good poem should have good rhythm. Good music, when it's read silently or aloud. It should feel good in your mouth; good to your ear. Rhyme can be a compelling element of poetry, but words should never be forced for the purpose of rhyme."

Rebecca Kai Dotlich

Made the List . . .

"I've published some of my poetry on my web site. One day I got an email that said, 'I have a web site that lists the worst poems on the web, and you're on it!'"

Bruce Balan

Images

"Forty years ago, when my son was ten, he was diagnosed with a chronic disease. I often worried myself sick about the possible prognosis. I decided I couldn't stand all those negative thoughts and had to figure out a way to drive them from my mind. I was determined to keep my brain busy concentrating on something else. I would write a book in verse—a sixty-four-pager, the popular length in those days. I actually woke with the image of the title in my mind.

"The mental calisthenics of creating was demanding and began the pattern of my poetry-writing process. It is a matter of juggling rhythm, rhyme, sense (or non-sense), and plot or concept. Each word selected has to make the best possible contribution to the unity of all these factors. In several of my books, the elements of math and science are also included. Numbers are one of the most difficult concepts to bring off successfully in poetry. Those words are completely inconsistent in number and accent of syllables and are very limited in rhyme possibilities. They often have to be worked in, in other parts of the lines instead of at the end—a tricky business!

"Writing poetry is truly a selecting, assessing and manipulation process using the best possible words—and a limited number of them. My favorite tools for choosing the right ones are my *Synonym Finder* by Rodale, which is much better than a thesaurus, and a rhyming dictionary. In my opinion, rhymes should repeat the same sound exactly and never be forced with not-quite-right choices. Nothing destroys the credibility of a poet more than improper rhythm or rhyming. My advice to aspiring writers is to read lots of poetry and practice, practice, practice!"

Joy N. Hulme

Snippets

"The process of writing a poem starts when I get a snippet of an idea, usually by observing children in action at my local elementary school or in the neighborhood. I've found that an idea that might be considered "slim" for a picture book is often wonderful for a poem. These ideas go in a folder and are pulled out at poetry-writing time. Before writing a poem, I usually know the twist at the end, or an unexpected element within it. Then I hear a rhythm in my head that fits the words I want to start with. The revisions go on and on. Part of my process is reading the poem to a good friend of mine who is a professor of poetry and understands my style and philosophy."

Betsy Franco

Know Thyself

"Pay attention –sometimes to big ideas and sometimes to tiny details, but always to yourself and how you feel about them."

Susan Hart Lindquist

Brainstorm

"I find a topic. I think that some of the best topics are the most innocuous and obvious, but overlooked. For instance, I've written poems about grumpy teachers, or icky babies, simply because these are obvious topics. A writer should not overlook the obvious.

"I brainstorm every possible word, phrase, rhyme, idea, possibility that could possibly go with the poem. Then I start trying to coalesce these fragments into any sort of coherent form. I particularly look for great rhymes and rhythms, phrases with lots of velcro. I write, I unwrite, I write, I cross out, I write, I throw away and start over, and eventually, painfully, I begin to put together a poem. If it isn't painful, like a long distance runner, I'm not trying my hardest, not doing my best. Eventually, after countless rewrites, it becomes a finished product. Never is it truly finished, but finally I reach a point where literally I have no more mental or emotional ability to take it any further."

David Greenberg

How?

"I try to select just the right words and images when I'm writing a poem. I write for myself and the reader. I'd like to think that someone reading my poems will feel like they know me through my poetry, or know themselves better.

"But what comes first? It might be something I remember, or something I see. A bit of an overheard conversation. Just one word in a song I'm listening to. A poem can be sparked by watching a waterfall, holding an autumn leaf, or remembering my grandfather's attic. I grab pencil and paper—I love notebooks—or I go right to the computer.

"I begin to write words on the page, playing around with groups of words and how they sound together. I try to compare one thing to another. *What does it remind me of?* Even as a child, I did this. The poet in me appears at many different times, in different ways. Sometimes it hides, and I don't like that!

"If it rhymes naturally, great. If I can make it sound as if it rhymes naturally, great. But if it doesn't want to rhyme, it doesn't. I actually prefer to write in rhyme because I have a form, a structure. But if it doesn't want to rhyme, it doesn't. But I also enjoy writing and reading free verse poetry.

"I also go to the thesaurus frequently. It's like a treasure hunt of words. Magical and many words. If you were sewing and you had a basketful of buttons in every shape and color, you'd keep trying different buttons in different places. *Which button fits best? Which seems spectacular?* I pull words out and put words in."

Rebecca Kai Dotlich

How can you encourage the poet within yourself?

"Partly it's a matter of breaking down that resistance to poetry that a lot of people feel, the idea that it's somehow distant and formidable—untouchable. I think a lot of beginning poets feel they have to find a 'poetic' subject to write about, something ennobling or profound. A better idea is to look around and recognize everything, even the most mundane and familiar things as possible subjects for poems.

"Read poems. Read old poems, new ones, funny and serious poems, hard poems and easy ones. Read the same ones over and over again. Read them out loud. And allow yourself to dislike some poems. Not every poem will speak to everyone."

Alice Schertle

"Write from your own life; use specific memories to create a poem. Write from the moment; small moments. Offer the reader details. If you peel an apple, think of it as the start of a poem. What does the skin feel like? How does your hand shape itself around the knife? What does the peel look like? What can you compare it to as it winds itself around and off of the fruit? A merry-go-round of scarlet skin? What does the apple look like now that it didn't look like before? Smooth, bald, white creamy, naked, ghostly, etc."

Rebecca Kai Dotlich

"A funny thing happens as we get older; we grow satisfied with the language of old images. Listen to a child explain the moon, or a skinned knee, or how it feels to be lonely."

Susan Hart Lindquist

Poetry with
Lee Bennett Hopkins

Lee Bennett Hopkins has created many books for children and adults. His autobiography, *Been to Yesterdays*, received the Christopher Medal and a Gold Kite Honor Award. He founded the Lee Bennett Hopkins Poetry Award, which is presented annually. His Lee Bennett Hopkins Reading Association Promising Poet Award is an international honor given every three years. His other titles include *Spectacular Science: A Book of Poems* and *My America: A Poetry Atlas of the United States*.

You are passionate about poetry. What fuels your passion?

"Poetry is a literary form we must include in our writing and in our studies. It's a heritage from the time of Mother Goose rhymes to contemporary poets. A great deal more can be said in a few lines, in a few words sometimes, than in an entire novel.

"There's more happening than ever before, in poetry. More children's poets have emerged in the '90's than in any other decade."

What makes a good poem?

"Something that blows your head off! When you read a poem and it knocks you out, and you say, 'That's it!' In doing anthologies, people ask what criteria I use. I tell them it's the 'ooh factor.' When I go, "ooh," then it's a good poem!"

Can you share your process on how you compile your anthologies?

"Most books I do are based on books I wish I had when I was teaching. I start with a theme. Then I search through original books of poetry. Everything from A to Z—Adolf to Zolotow! When I've exhausted that, I look through anthologies. I also have a group of people around the country, whom I fondly call my 'take-out poets.' Jane Yolen, X.J. Kennedy, Karla Kuskin, and others. I tell them a theme I'm working on, and often they write original poetry for me, so readers will see new work. I think that's important. Not that I don't like the old, Edward Lear, Robert Louis Stevenson. But I want to give a fresh approach to my books, so that readers have something new to look forward to."

Some poets say good poetry must be written out of angst. What are your feelings regarding that statement?

"It depends on the poem. There are poems for happy times, and sad times, and for the reflective and the whimsy. Poetry is a genre as wide as prose."

How do you write a poem?

"I start out with an idea and then I jot down a lot of words and phrases that may not make a any sense whatsoever. It could be a long, long page of isolated words, phrases, and thoughts. I let it sit for awhile, and then sometimes a word or phrase will jump out. Sometimes that is the basis for the poem. Some poems come full-blown; others take months, and some don't come at all!"

What's the best advice you've heard regarding writing poetry? The worst?

"The best advice is to read poetry. Read a great deal of it. I think that way, a writer will find his or her own voice by reading as much as possible. The worst advice, is the old adage of one has to write a poem that no one knows what it means. So the professor can dissect it and analyze it!"

Rhyme

Don't Force It

"I spend a lot of time searching for that perfect word. I print out my manuscript when I have a rough draft and I carry it with me everywhere I go. I always have my rhyming dictionary with me as well. When I first wake up in the morning, I grab my manuscript and pencil and I go over the verses. I use a thesaurus a lot too, so I can find the word to help characterization, time period, and flavor. If I can't find the right word, then I work for a set of rhyming words that fit the story idea that I want to tell and try building a verse around those rhyming words.

"Sometimes my stories have to change. I won't write forced rhyme—words put in there just to rhyme. If the word doesn't fit the story, it gets eliminated. That's one of the reasons it can take me so long to write a book."

Verla Kay

What Do You Want to Say?

"As I research, I make outlines and outlines of my outlines. I'm given the number of pages that will be in the book and I have to decide what information will go on which page. When I have decided what I want to say on each page, I then put it in rhyme. Sometimes that's easy to do and sometimes it takes forever. The more information I have, the easier it is."

Ruth Heller

Clap to the Beat

"Read lots of rhymes! Read Jack Prelutsky. *Alice in Wonderland*. *Jabberwocky*. *The Walrus and the Carpenter*. Robert Louis Stevenson's poems. If you find something you like, use your hands to clap it out. When you really get going, jump up and down to the rhythm! Write a couplet. They are easy to try."

Sarah Wilson

Perfect Fit

"Often I select the rhyming words first, then fit the verses to them. Sometimes running a rhyme through the alphabet, such as dine, fine, line, mine, nine, pine, vine, wine, will turn up unexpected word combinations, and ideas for another verse or another book! Read good rhyme by other authors, to see how they play with words. The best rhyme also has rhythm."

Deborah Lee Rose

Jingle All the Way

"Rhyme does not come naturally to me. Very often, unfortunately, the first lines come to me in rhyme. I try to forget them! I try NOT to write it in rhyme. But once it gets in your mind that way, it's hard to change it. When I start a book in rhyme, I live with this jingle in my head constantly. It drives me crazy! It is not effortless for me.

"When I wrote *Flower Garden*, my husband and I were in the market buying plants. We had all these plants in the shopping cart and I said, 'Garden in the shopping cart, doesn't it look great.' And he said, 'Oh, Eve, you're starting it again. You're rhyming a picture book.' I said, 'No, no no!' At the check-out stand, I said, 'Garden on the check-out stand, I can hardly wait!'

"I tried to put it into prose, but it wasn't right. Sometimes you get caught in a trap with a rhyming book. But children really like them."

Eve Bunting

Get the Beat?

"It is hard to teach rhyme. You have to hear it, listen to the natural beat of language, the way syllables are stressed, the way words that don't look anything alike can rhyme. You have to be able to read back your rhyme in a natural voice. If you've got the beat right, it won't sound forced. You can't invert your sentences just to make the rhyme work. A fluffy bear, he wanted to be. That sentence would naturally be 'He wanted to be a young, fluffy bear.' Changing it around to make a rhyme never gets past an editor.

"Also, a surprising rhyme is always better than a common one. The more syllables in the rhyming word, the better. Anyone can rhyme bear with chair. I would rather rhyme teddy bear with underwear. I often rhyme the last one or two syllables only, especially when rhyming in Spanish. If you can't hear the difference between a good rhyme and a bad one, you probably won't be able to write in rhyme. Read it out loud, over and over, until it sounds absolutely perfect. Have others read it to you, as well."

Susan Middleton Elya

Happenstance

"Writers hoping to write rhymes for children need to immerse themselves in Mother Goose and Dr. Seuss. And they should remember that the best rhymes are those where the flow of the words sounds natural, and, oh, by the way, they just happen to rhyme. Too many writers try to twist the phrasing and contort the sentence structure to force the rhyming words to somehow fit at the end of the line. It sounds unnatural. I agree with those poets who believe that poetry is an oral literary form and should flow like real speech."

Tedd Arnold

Rhyming Dictionary

"I believe that 'rhyme' is simply a style, a voice, a method of writing. Whether you're writing in rhyme or in prose, you still need to have a good story to tell. If you have the story, the words will come. Sometimes they come in prose or free verse, but other times they come in rhyme.

"To rhyme, all you need is a good rhyming dictionary. Then you need to choose the most interesting, most surprising word rather than an obvious, predictable one. The hard part about writing good rhyme is to make the lines scan smoothly, so that when they're read aloud, the story sings and doesn't bump along. Play around with the meter until you come up with one that works for the tone of your story."

Marisa Montes

Strike the Right Note

"One of my favorite activities is writing songs. It makes me reach for words and expressions. I also write down lines from songs because those lines have found a rhythm in our language.

"Even though some of my rhyming books start with a set of words I love, I almost always have to back up and ask myself what the story is. Sometimes I don't have one because I was so sure the rhyme would warrant a book.

"Read other books that rhyme and if they make you cringe or you're bored after awhile, you've learned what you *don't* want to do. Some of the best rhyming books I've read are by David Milgrim because, although they are for young people, their message is for everyone. And you're not even aware of the rhyme until you're part way through the book.

"Rhymes need to be active, even in a quiet book. They need to move forward. Use a word menu, a rhyming dictionary and a synonym finder. I like to write song parodies, and found it easy to write *Hark! The Aardvark Angels Sing* in text, and easy to write it in song, but the challenge was to write it so that it could be read as easily as it was sung. It took hard work to hit both slots with the same words.

"Look at a long list of words in the rhyming dictionary. *Can a story could be written from them?* Example: A Little Novella about Cinderella. She had two ugly stepsisters Stella and Della, and very mean stepmother, Queen Isabella."

Teri Sloat

Read the Masters

"I think writers should be careful with rhyme—it's so easy to force it. The best way to understand rhyme is to read a master like Jack Prelutsky or to read a current anthology of poetry for young children."

Betsy Franco

Say it with Music

"Rhyme is like music. It has to lilt along. If you don't have the musical sense when you're reading rhyme, it won't be good. I look at rhyming like a ballad. I like words to read like a lyric, like a song. In order to get that, you have to listen to a lot of music and read a lot of rhyme. Feel the words. Feel the story. Become the story."

Margaret O'Hair

Goofy Word Doodles

"I wish I could say I had a process or an acceptable technique, but the truth is, a lot of my rhyme comes from being bored. I have a non-writing day job that requires me to sit in on a lot of meetings where I don't actively participate. Since I can't draw or doodle worth a darn, I end up playing with words. And when I play with words, I end up playing with rhyme. Perhaps there is a certain freedom in thinking that it is just a bunch of word doodles so there is no real pressure.

"You have to be completely free to be goofy when you want to work with rhyme. Again, like most things, to *write* in rhyme, you have to *read* in rhyme. One thing you can do is take a nursery rhyme or song that you are familiar with and rewrite it with your own words. The familiar pattern will help you with the initial rhyme."

Susan Taylor Brown

Play Word Games

"The best calisthenics for rhymsters are anagrams, palindromes, spoonerisms and puns. Simply messing with language at its elemental level, particularly at the level of sound, fosters an ear for rhyme."

David Greenberg

Music to the Ear

"Read good poetry out loud. Dissect good rhymes. Spend time with a good kindergarten teacher! Listen. I love to try to rhyme weird, multisylabic words—so much of it is just a matter of taking a risk. The bad thing that happens when you start doing this, is the tendency to want to make *everything* rhyme. It's so pleasing to the human ear—good rhyme is playful, it goes inside, and begins to work with body rhythms—naturally, like blood pumping through your heart."

Susan Hart Lindquist

Surprise!

"Try to use unexpected rhyme. Something that you haven't seen a hundred times before. This isn't easy. Cat and mat are expected. As is ham and jam. Look at the possibility of using the two or three syllable word instead. Use a rhyming dictionary for help. Then it is all trial and error. See if it fits. Begin with what you want to say and THEN find a rhyme that sings it.

"For the most part, let making sense lead you into the rhyme. Unless, of course, it's a nonsense poem, but even then there needs to be good reasons for the chosen words and rhymes."

Rebecca Kai Dotlich

Kid-like

"Be short and simple. In my book, *What does the Rabbit Say?*, a sentence can be two words. 'Ducks quack, cows moo, chickens cluck, doves coo.' Use words with kid appeal. Like lollipop and words that have k's in them."

Jacque Hall

Tools of the Trade

'The best advice is to make sure your rhyme sounds natural and not forced. Two of the things I keep with me are a thesaurus and a rhyming dictionary. Let's say you want to rhyme the word 'sleep' but you can't do it. Think of synonyms.

"I collect musical recordings. Today the great master is Stephen Sondheim. I love Cole Porter, Johnny Mercer, Lorenz Hart. I also have books of lyrics by these folks. The rhyme structure is incredible. There's a book on Cole Porter where they show his hand written notes—crossed out words that didn't work. Read good lyrics and poems, and when you're working on your own material, jot down potential rhymes.

"Have a good ear for music. I'm not a musician, but I've sung and listened to a lot of music. One of the mistakes people make is putting too many beats or emphasizing the wrong syllable in their stanzas. Read your work aloud. Does it sound natural? Don't force the meter!"

Marilyn Singer

Lights, Camera, Action!

"When I first started writing, a screenwriting teacher told me that if I wanted to be a screenwriter, I should be willing to devote ten solid years of my life to writing scripts, before I ever expect to earn a living doing it. It's a difficult profession, where decisions are rarely made by creative people, you get very little respect as a writer, and everyone and their dentist thinks they can do a better job than you. If you're writing scripts for fun, or just for the experience, that's fine, but if you're expecting to earn a living at it, then be prepared for lots of hard-knock schooling.

"That said, I still write scripts every chance I get. Some have been made, some have been bought but not made, and some have never sold. I would tell the beginning screenwriters to expect lots of disappointment, punctuated by moments of sheer elation, and the occasional big deal. It's worth it, if you can handle all the disappointment in between."

Neal Shusterman

Lin Oliver has been Senior Vice President of Television and Home Video at MCA/Universal, and currently runs her own production company. She has written, developed and produced feature films, television movies and series television, including *The Trumpet of the Swan, Finding Buck McHenry, A Christmas for Fort Zack,* and *Aliens Ate My Homework,* based on Bruce Coville's best-selling book. Her projects have included interactive laserdiscs that garnered Grammy nominations for Best Children's Video. She has been Executive Producer of *Harry and the Hendersons,* which 72 episodes aired weekly on Fox Television. She's also written books for children, and if this isn't enough, she is co-founder and Executive Director of SCBWI.

What prompted you to go into the film industry?

"In college I majored in English literature with the intent of being a writer. I won a television comedy writing contest at UCLA. That automatically moved me into writing for television."

How did you and Steve Mooser happen to start the Society of Children's Book Writers?

"I spent two years writing for television, but it felt vapid and pointless. So I auditioned for a writing job, and Steve and I were hired. In the '70's there was federal money to develop a kindergarten through sixth grade reading program. Each of us wrote seven or eight novels and 100 short stories with controlled vocabulary. We had on-the-job training to learn how to write clearly, develop a story line. It was very fortunate for us. I'm sure there were only two jobs in the world writing for children, and Steve and I had them both!

"He was a journalist and I was a television writer. We tried to learn more about writing for children, so that's when we formed the Society of Children's Book Writers, SCBW. [The I for Illustrators was added later.] We did it for ourselves. We just called great authors, like Sid Fleischman. He came! It was my first exposure to authors. I learned that people who work in children's literature are kind and strive for excellence."

How did you get back into film?

"After the government job, I was hired as an executive at Universal Studios, developing interactive video discs. They wanted someone to write pilot programs that were interactive to use in schools. They had the right idea. Kids want to interact. The field of interactivity took off, so they offered me an executive position. I had just sold my first trade children's book. So I had a conflict, but I thought I'd never get this opportunity again. I stayed there for eleven years. I really learned about film and television. I was eventually Executive Vice President of MCA-TV. (Music Corporation of America—the parent company of Universal Studios.) As time passed, I found myself drawn to family programming. Most of my efforts to developing this field, including working with Stephen Spielberg's Amblin Entertainment.

"After eleven years I left the executive ranks to become an independent producer. I've specialized in writing and producing movies and television for children and their families."

Have you written original stories for film, or do you write adaptations?

"Both. I love to adapt scripts from good books. I did a television series based on Don Freeman's *Corduroy*, and a feature film based on E.B. White's *The Trumpet of the Swans*. *Finding Buck McHenry*, a film I produced for Showtime, was from the book by Al Sloat. And I'm beginning to adapt Louis Sachar's *The Wayside School* stories for a television series."

What advice do you have for children's writers who want "break in" to Hollywood?

"Most people want the easy way. There isn't any. The most common error that people make, is that people have *an idea* for a film or television series. Maybe they've written a couple of pages or a treatment. Almost always that doesn't work. If you're new at something you have to prove yourself. Everyone has good ideas. There's no shortage of good ideas! It's all in the execution. I'm sure editors find the same thing. Show me! For someone who is starting, they have to work really hard to produce the script. If you want to be a writer, you have to write!"

How can writers turn their novels into screenplays?

"Study the craft like you do writing a novel. Read Syd Field's *The Art of Dramatic Writing*. Or use the other route. Submit it as a book to a producer. People submit to me all the time. The book gets optioned and then there are the decisions on who should write the screenplay.

"Most typically, the author is *not* the one who does the screenplay. It's a very different medium. Many novelists can't write screenplays. Screenplays are scenes—dialogue and action. Often, young adult authors write internal coming of age stories. They write psychology, not action. Movies are called moving pictures for a reason! Surprisingly, I've found that picture book writers make better screenwriters. They are trained to tell a story without words, using images."

How do producers find projects if authors don't submit them?

"People in Hollywood read *Kirkus* and *Publishers Weekly*—they scout books."

Do you have an amusing anecdote about your work in this industry?

"One of the things that happens when you produce or write for children, you come against people who don't know the field of children's literature. So you pitch wonderful, famous books that buyers don't necessarily know about or appreciate.

"When I first pitched *The Trumpet of the Swan*, I thought, how hard will this be to sell? Everyone will clamor for it! Well, most of the people I talked to didn't know about E.B. White. I went in and told the story. I said, 'A trumpeter swan is born without a voice.' The studio executive said, 'We just did a movie about a goose, which had disappointing box office. I can't buy *The Trumpet of the Swan* because poultry just doesn't sell.' He was dead serious! I thought, 'You can't have this book even if you *want* it. You don't deserve this!'"

Can you comment about censorship in the film industry?

"There is a lot of censorship in film and television for children.

"They censor peculiar things. When I started writing animation, you couldn't have belly buttons on television. Now there is great sensitivity to stories that are construed as using witchcraft. There is a lot of talk about morality, then a gratuitous 'moral' tacked on the end of a show; but the shows present a great deal of titillation. Kids are given a very mixed message. We know this will entertain you, but we'll tell you what we think you should be thinking or feeling after you've been entertained!

"Then there are people who have notions on what children can or can't handle. When I talked about writing a movie about twelve-year-old boys, I was asked, 'Do you feel qualified to write kid-speak?' I believe there is an emotional truth that cuts through any of the jargon. It's a very subtle prejudice about kids—not giving them enough credit. If you pander to kids, the kids will reject it. I think it's the same with books, too. The trick of relating to children is to really be inside the way kids feel. That's what Judy Blume is so good at. Her characters express what the kids are feeling."

Photography

What are some tips can you give to authors who aren't professional photographers?

"I took courses from National Geographic and these are their tips.

"Never put your subject in the middle. This really improves your photographs immensely.

"Put your photo a little off center. It makes it different from others.

"For every horizontal photograph you take, stand the camera upright and take a vertical of the same subject.

"Never take just one picture of any subject. You can wrap the words around the photo in different ways.

"Then there's the rule of three. If you have your choice of photographing a number of subjects, there's something visually interesting and symmetrical about the number three. So three people, three flowers, three trees. It adds balance. In my book, *Among the Orangutans*, I took a picture of one orangutan and three trees in the background.

"You can have people move around. Stand this way, come up front. Direct people."
Evelyn Gallardo

"My husband, Ed [Radlauer], was self taught. He never snapped a picture he couldn't sell. I took a photo class from John Sexton who had been a student of Ansel Adams. I also learned a lot from the art director with whom I worked as an editor.

"We never could have photographed with an automatic camera. Ed never could have taken a drag racing picture with one because it won't let you take the picture until you're in focus. For a motor sport, you snap the picture real fast. Then if you have time, you do it again and look at all the edges of the frame. You might not realize that some branch is sticking into the picture or someone is violating park regulations. Ask yourself, 'how would it look to a kid?'"

Ruth Radlauer

"Invest in a camera that is much smarter than you are! Before going to Costa Rica, I bought a Canon Elan system with three lenses and a strobe for about $2,000. That investment has paid for itself MANY times over. Also, burn film like it's paper. Shoot from every single angle. Try different exposures (bracketing). Go out and shoot in different lighting. For my book, *Monteverde Science and Scientists in a Costa Rican Cloud Forest*, I shot at least fifty rolls of film and came out with seventy-five to a hundred really good pictures. Most of what you shoot will be crap, but if you get one or two good shots per roll, you're doing well."

Sneed B. Collard III

How to Write a Series

These days, many series have been written by one author who then assigns later editions to ghostwriters, such as *Goosebumps,* and *The Babysitter's Club*. Sometimes series books are all written by the same, original author as with *The Borrowers* and *Anne of Green Gables*.

Stephen Mooser, Linda Joy Singleton, Johanna Hurwitz and Kathleen Duey comment on their own writing-for-series experiences. Following their comments, you'll find an interview with a master of suspenseful series, R.L. Stine.

Tell us about your experiences with writing a series.

"For the *Treasure Hound* books I proposed the whole series. I had a couple of chapters of the first book written, and a true treasure at the end the kids could look for. It was a package thing. After I had done a couple of novels for Dell, they asked me to do a sports series. I ended up writing baseball stories that involved monsters. They asked for a monster series next, so I wrote the *Creepy Creature* Series. Next, they just wanted sports, so I wrote *The All Star Meatballs*.

"The series I most enjoyed was the *Creepy Creature*. One of the things I like about series, is that with each book, you get to know the character better. You can create any situation and the character will write the story for you. Like with (the television show) *Seinfeld*. The success of the series is that someone developed four really interesting characters. Then almost anyone can come up with the situation. What's really hard for a series is creating the characters."

Stephen Mooser

"My first series, *My Sister the Ghost*, was sold as one book. Then it turned into a three book sale and at the end, I had four books in the series. Then my editor at Avon asked me to write a cheerleading series. I never would have done it if she hadn't asked. That four book series turned into a six book series. I knew nothing about cheerleading, so I went to a cheerleading camp, read books about cheerleading, read a cheerleading magazine and I even took a ballet class, since I thought there were a lot of dance movement in cheers.

"My cloning series was different. I came up with the cloning idea because I thought it sounded marketable and it appealed to me because the topic of twins and doubles has always appealed to me. The idea took ten months to sell. At first they asked for three books, then later it became five."

Linda Joy Singleton

"I never planned any of my series. *Busybody Nora, Much Ado About Aldo, Class Clown, The Adventures of Ali Baba Bernstein* and *The Hot* and *Cold Summer* were each written without the intention of writing anything else about the same characters. But in each case I discovered by the end of the book that I knew much more that I wanted to share with my readers. Most recently I've written about the friendship between a guinea pig and a squirrel. That was *Peewee's Tale*. Almost at once, I found myself writing a sequel, *Lexi's Tale*, and already ideas are jumping about my head about a third book. It seems another series in the making!"

Johanna Hurwitz

"I knew that I didn't want a day job. Multi-title sales seemed like the closest thing to job security one could manage in children's writing. I have learned a great deal from writing my series books and am proud of them all. With one six-title exception, my series writing has been from my own concepts—not multi-author, in-house or packaged. I keep creative control and am sole author. Except that the *Survival* series is written with dear friend and collaborator Karen A. Bale."

Kathleen Duey

What does it take to make a successful series pitch?

"Connections, luck, and really knowing the market. Have strong writing skills. Most series are offered to established authors. Editors are hesitant to do a series with an author that doesn't have a track record. But on the other hand, I know of instances if someone writes one book that is strong and compelling, it can go on to sequels and a series."

Linda Joy Singleton

"Series pitches need to be sharp, focused, and reflect a grasp of market. Publishers seem to commit to two to four books at a time, so it is wise to design your plots with story arcs that can be completed in two to four book spans. If sales of the first few warrant more, a second contract will be signed. I have sold nineteen *American Diaries* in twos, threes and fours, amending the original contract each time. If you want to sell a series, hone the original concept until it seems markedly different than what else is being sold. Come up with something new and interesting, with enormous child-appeal. Write a blazing pitch/synopsis/concept page, then synopses of the first four to six titles. Include sample pages, or, if you are new, a finished first book."

Kathleen Duey

What can an author do to make her series successful?

"Run naked down Broadway! It helps to be a celebrity to begin with.

"Seriously, though, it is best if the publisher can put a lot of promotion behind your series to make it successful. It's very difficult, otherwise, for an author to find an audience. I've tried everything. I've done bookmarks, I speak at conferences, booksignings, I have a web site. While all of this helps, the numbers need to be so huge that it is an uphill climb."

Linda Joy Singleton

"Series success is no different than general success as an author. The first concern is the quality of your work—if the books don't appeal to readers, no amount of promotion will help. After producing wonderful books, the task is to make your work known. To begin promoting your work, contact local bookstores to plan events to showcase the books. Learn to speak well. Visit schools. Put your own money behind your career if you can. If you are lucky, your publisher will help you promote. If you are like the vast majority of us, you will be virtually on your own. Promotion is the second half of your career. Resign yourself to learning about it and spending a significant portion of your time at it."

Kathleen Duey

What is it like to ghost write for a popular series?

"Ghosting (for the *Sweet Valley Twin Series*) is the hardest writing I have ever done in my life. It's very much like trying to imitate someone's voice—speak another language. And you have a group of editors with their opinions of what the language should sound like. They're all jumping in with their suggestions to rewrite what you've done. Three editors worked on one book! They ask you to overwrite because they expect to cut a good part of it. And they change a lot. It was a good discipline and a learning experience. I was proud I had this little bit of history with this series."

Linda Joy Singleton

"I have never done real ghost writing. I did write under a pseudonym once, completing six titles for Avon's *Spinetinglers* series. There were five or six of us, all writing under the name 'M.T. Coffin.' M. T. as opposed to 'full.' Nudge, nudge. Get it? It was fun. We had advance and royalty agreements held our own copyrights and signed standard publishing contracts—just no byline on the cover. I have rarely written anything work-for-hire."
Kathleen Duey

Should an aspiring writer become a series writer?

"Series writing can be a good place to break into the business. And it is educational. You will learn deadline-discipline, plotting, character development, and much else that any fiction writer needs to become good at. You will learn to be prolific. But if your grand dream is winning the Newbery, rave reviews and literary acknowledgment—and if you have the luxury of *not* making a living at this—I don't recommend series writing for long. Some people get stuck; they lose their drive for excellence in the deadline dash. If you do write for in-house series, *always* deliver a good book, one you would be happy to see your own name on.

"If you sell your own series, make sure that your contracts don't stipulate the publisher being able to hire other authors if it takes off. Quality control, quality control quality control! Protect your name and reputation; keep your work standards high even if the books are pure entertainment. And if you feel yourself getting sloppy, get out."
Kathleen Duey

What can an aspiring writer do to become a series author?

"Write one strong book or write for an established series to build a reputation with editors."
Linda Joy Singleton

Featuring R. L. Stine

R.L. Stine is one of the best-selling authors of all time, with his *Goosebumps*, *Fear Street* and *The Nightmare Room* series. His first book, *How to be Funny*, was inspired by *Mad Magazine*. He graduated from Ohio State University and was an editor of *Bananas Magazine* before he began writing books full-time. In his free time you'll find him in his New York City apartment playing pinball.

Your first book for children was How to Be Funny. *What advice do you have for writers who would like to* write *funny?*

"Keep away from my book. No one liked it. I wrote joke books for twenty years. *101 Monster Jokes. 101 Cafeteria Jokes.* In bookstores, there are categories for every type of children's books—sports books, young adult fiction. But not humor. You can't sell them in bookstores. Most of mine were sold from school book clubs and book fairs. When *How to Be Funny Came* out, I'd go into a bookstore and ask where it was. They'd say, 'Oh, I think that's in performing arts.'

"I had my first book signing for *How to be Funny* in a Doubleday Bookstore. I wore a suit and bunny ears. There were stacks and stacks of *How to Be Funny*. No one came over! I sold zero books. I don't think kids would come to a man wearing bunny ears.

"My wife and I used to write lots of funny books together."

How was collaborating?

"A nightmare! Jane is still my editor. How would *you* like to be married to your editor? Plots are the only things we fight about. We work totally differently. She starts writing in the middle, then the end, then the beginning. I have to write from the very first word and do everything in order. She locked me in a closet once! That was our last collaboration together as writers. She left me in the closet!

"We work well together now. We've done over two hundred books together. I have many editors in addition to Jane."

You outline your plot before you begin to write. Can you talk us through your plotting process?

"It's just me sitting with a pad and pen. It's kind of mysterious. I have general ideas and I think of the ending very early on. I know a basic premise and then the ending. Then I know how I'll go back and fool the readers. I know how to get the kids from figuring out how the book is going to end. I make a list of characters and a cheat sheet where I describe them all. Then I start the book. I outline the action in each chapter. I have to revise the outline maybe once or twice. Then, when I've done all of the hard work, it makes it easier to write quickly. I enjoy the writing part.

"I used to hate outlines. I'd fight it. Now I can't work without them. Kids tell me they start a story and then they don't know where to go and where to end. I say that's why you need an outline. They think it's like cheating to know the story in advance."

With regard to craft, how can writers create exciting action/adventure scenes? How can writers build suspense?

"I think if you're doing a thriller, chances are the plot is going to be pretty absurd. My plots are ludicrous. In order for the reader to believe the story, you've got to give them something very real to accept what is going on. I work hard to make sure the kids in my books are very real kids. They can't sound like some old guy trying to write kids.

"The secret with my books, is the close, personal point of view. Generally I write in first person, told through one person's eyes so the reader comes to identify with the character. When the character is scared, the reader is scared."

What are the most important elements in a horror story? Are there different standards for various-aged readers?

"My standards are there have to be surprises. The reader has to be shocked. The story can't be linear. The reader must say, 'Oh my God, I never thought *that* would happen!' There have to be a lot of twists and surprises. Every chapter ending is a twist. It ends on some cliffhanger. The challenge is coming up with new surprises."

What can an aspiring writer do to become a series author? What makes a winning series proposal?

"I think you have to really know the reading audiences. You have to know a middle grade from a young adult. You have to know the younger reader books. You have to be really familiar with the market. Study the bookstores and the series that are out there. Which ones aim at girls and boys? Then it's a matter of a good idea that can sustain itself over a large number of books."

Can you talk about your experiences with bringing your stories to television?

"I've had mostly good experiences. I'm proud of the *Goosebumps* series. It was on TV for four years and had five or six prime time shows. It was the top rated kid show for three years. They did a wonderful job. I didn't do any of the scripts, but it was fun for me to see what other people would do with my stories. It was very exciting!

"Another television series is based on my *Nightmare Room* series. This is the first live-action show the KidsWB has ever done. There are some from the original books and some new stories just for TV My wife and I read every script and make comments and changes. It's fun. It's an interesting process that's very different from writing a book. It's so collaborative, with many people involved."

Collaborating

Patricia McKissack and her husband, Fredrick McKissack, have co-written over fifty award-winning books, including *Sojourner Truth: Ain't I a Woman?*, *Jesse Jackson: A Biography*, and *Christmas in the Big House, Christmas in the Quarters*. Married for nearly thirty years, they live in Missouri.

How do you and Fred begin a project?

"My husband does most of the research in our partnership, but we work closely together. We usually like to read an adult book to get an overview of the subject. An autobiography, diary or journal is one of the best sources for finding biographical information. If there are family members still alive, we try to make contact. We try to travel to the person's hometown or other significant places in his/her life. It is always interesting to walk in the footsteps of the person you're going to write about. Museums, libraries and historical societies are helpful places to visit by e-mail or in person. We are always on the look-out for related books on the subject, records and documents, letters and journals. They help us reconstruct a life.

"Here is an example of how the above description works. While researching the playwright, Lorraine Hansberry, the author of *A Raisin in the Sun*, we contacted her sister. She provided us with the Hansberry family history and personal stories about the family. Lorraine Hansberry died at age thirty-five, but she kept a journal and it was later published, entitled *Young, Gifted and Black*. We read that. Her former husband was listed as her literary administrator, but he was dead. Ironically, Hansberry's literary estate is now being managed by her ex-husband's second wife! It was through this contact that we were able to get pictures and permission to use quotes from Hansberry's work. Interesting process.

"Each story presents its own set of challenges. When we researched black whalemen for our book, *Black Hands; White Sails*, we visited Whaling Museums at Nantucket, New Bedford, Providence, Mystic Seaport, Boston, Plymouth, and Bath, Maine. We traveled to San Francisco, Seattle, and also Barbados looking for information. For two summers we visited Martha's Vineyard's Whaling Museum and the Whaling Museum at Sharon, Massachusetts, gathering information from primary sources and interviewing people who were authorities in the field.

"We use the Internet to research, too, but it isn't as trustworthy as print resources. Whatever we find on the web, we check and double check. We are very concerned with accuracy.

"Fred does the most of the research described above. Of course, when we travel I always go along. Then, I use the facts that we've gathered to develop a story. Two heads are better than one! We see things differently, but it's a good thing. Seeing our work from different points of view helps strengthen the project.

"Fred's a detail man. Fred likes to find the shoe size of people; their favorite color, grades in school, etc. Those are often his interview questions. Success is really in the details.

"We have accumulated a tremendous reference library. We also have a computerized calendar program, so we can find the month and day of every A.D. year. Our good reviews often mention the interesting details that Fred's able to find. For example, I will write: 'It was March of 1863.' But he will check the weather reports from that time period so that I can improve the sentence: 'It was a cloudy and windy Tuesday in March of 1863...'

"Adult books can be very boring for a young reader, because their interests are different. We try very hard to bring the subject alive for the reader by making the action immediate and the story real."

How do you know what to include?

"Our editor is always very helpful in tightening our manuscript. After working on a piece for months, we are too close to it. But our editor is seeing it with a fresh eye and helps us work out the kinks. We also measure the interest level of the information. Is this something a sixth grader would enjoy knowing? If not, we usually don't include it. Then, sometimes we do."

What do you do with the material you cut?

"I recycle all research three or four times. We spend too much money and time to get one book out of three years of research. So I usually get a biography, historical fiction piece, and sometimes a picture book for one research."

ON WINNING THE NEWBERY

"My sister said the best thing. When she found out *Hope was Here* won the honor book, she remembered in fifth grade, when a school librarian told her just to look for the gold and silver stickers. Now I have one of those! When the stickers came, I thought of putting one on each cheek to make a fashion statement! When the phone call came, they called at 8:00 in the morning. I thought it was a telemarketer. I was in my pajamas. I didn't get out of my office until 4:00 P.M.; the phone just didn't stop ringing."

Joan Bauer

Do you have any advice for authors who would like to collaborate?

"I wouldn't advise it! Seriously though, it must be a natural fit. It's as important as choosing a husband or wife. If writing is your career, I wouldn't trust just anybody to help me with it. With Fred and me, it is a perfect match. He has a very inquisitive mind. He loves planning and organizing. I love the drama of story—developing character, setting, action and idea. I use a broad brush stroke with lots of pain. Fred uses a small brush with contrasting colors that highlight. That's the best way I know how to describe what we do and how."

Judith Ross Enderle and Stephanie Jacob Gordon met in a UCLA writing class. After writing for *Highlights for Children* magazine, they've written many books for young people from picture books to young adult novels. They've coauthored books such as *What's the Matter Kelly Beans?*, *Six Sleepy Sheep*, *Two Badd Babies* and *Six Snowy Sheep*. They've coedited the Fox magazine, *Totally Fox Kids* and served as story editors for Fox's *Rimba's Island*. They've also written scripts for Lin Oliver Productions and Viacom.

How did you get the idea to collaborate?

"We were taking a writing class in genre fiction and decided that it would be fun to try a story together. We had such a good time that we decided to write all our stories together."

Discuss the process of collaboration on a picture book. Is it different from the way to collaborate on a young adult novel? How?

"All of our collaborations start with brainstorming—deciding on characters, plot, setting, etc. With a picture book, one of us will write the first draft and give it to the other person to rewrite. This process continues back and forth, reading the text aloud after each revision, until we are satisfied with the story and the way it sounds. With a young adult or middle grade novel, we create a chapter-by-chapter outline and divide up the chapters. Each of us works on our chosen chapters then we put them together and read aloud to make corrections and changes. One of us will then put in the revisions on the computer and we read aloud again and again until we are satisfied with the flow of the novel."

How do you handle the business side of writing? Do you both have the same agent?

"We do our bookkeeping on the computer, using Microsoft Money for Personal and Business Accounting. In a separate Word file, we track our speaking engagements and editorial work and when we bill and when we are paid so we know if something is past due. We have the same agent, who negotiates our book contracts and handles subrights. Having an agent gives us more writing time."

What is the best aspect of collaborating?

"The best aspect is the excitement of brainstorming and having someone else to share the writing experience."

The most difficult?

"The most difficult is working out the differences in how we each see a story direction so that we are both happy with the outcome. We always say that whoever types last gets the final word!"

Finish this sentence. You should collaborate with another writer . . .

"When you can put the resulting work above all else."

You should not collaborate if...

"You have to be in control of every word."

Has the collaboration changed your friendship in any way?

"Our friendship has become stronger. We've been collaborating for over twenty years. We are like sisters."

What's your best advice for authors who would like to collaborate?

"Have the same goals, agree on the same set of writing rules, keep in mind that you want the best book possible and respect each other's abilities."

With regard to your writing styles and processes, how are the two of you alike?

"We are both goal oriented and give 200 percent when we say we will do something. We are perfectionists when it comes to our manuscripts, though not necessarily that way in day-to-day life. We both love to play with words and to write books that make young readers laugh."

How are you different?

"One of us is a better speller and good at descriptive details; the other is a stronger plotter."

Why did you decide to write with a pseudonym? I notice you use both of your names on the books you write now. This must have been a conscious change. Can you comment on this?

"Jeffie Ross Gordon came about when we wrote a book for the Scholastic *Sunfire Series* of historical romances. There was no room on the cover for two names. The editor asked if we wanted to leave one name off, but we said absolutely not. Instead we created Jeffie by combining Judy and Stephie for Jeffie; Ross is Judy's maiden name; Gordon is Stephanie's last name. We used this name until we started writing picture books. When we went out to publicize *Six Sleepy Sheep* and *Two Badd Babies*, a bookstore owner called our publisher and said they were expecting a guy named Jeffie, then two ladies showed up. Our publisher suggested we go back to using our separate names, so we did...the end!"

Writing for Children's Magazines

Kelly Milner Halls is a full-time freelance writer. Her work has appeared in *Booklist, Child Digest, Fox Kids, Guidepost for Kids, Highlights for Children, Teen PEOPLE, US Kids, Kid City* and dozens of other publications.

How did you come to write for children's magazines?

"I studied journalism in college, and I thought I'd write for adults. Then I realized I didn't want to look for the 'dirt' on people! The first article I wrote was on dinosaurs, because my children liked dinosaurs. It took me two and a half years to sell it. *Children's Digest* bought it, exactly as it was written. I hadn't been reading the markets right."

How should you read the market?

"Read the magazine you're writing for. Can you garner passion for that particular editorial voice? Can you write in their style? If you can't, move on. Does the magazine use 'kid speak?' Slang? *Chicago Tribune* likes to sound fresh. 'Bling bling' is slang for diamond, so the *Trib* might want you to use it in your lead; back it up in the article later—be sure the kids know what it really means. Fox Kids is the same. They say, 'If Bart Simpson would love it, so would we!'"

As a different market example, what does Highlights Magazine *want?*
"They like an 'editorial moral residual'—a beautiful, almost unspoken tone that makes kids be better people."

How many children's magazines are published today?

"There are 125 listed in the *2001 Children's Writer's & Illustrator's Market*. But I think there are probably more than that, not to mention websites."

Of those 125, which are the best magazines for new writers to break into?

"Any children's magazine with 'briefs' or specialized sections are easier for new writers to crack, because they have such a steady need for topical material. If you're willing to start small, you've got a shot."

Which writing for children online markets can you recommend?

"I do a workshop on writing for online sites. It's tough to know who will pay and who won't. There isn't a lot of black ink on Internet ledgers yet. But if there is an editorial staff listed on the website, they will often consider freelance submissions. Look for the editorial staff and ask—shoot them an e-mail."

Kids, Teachers and Authors Say and
Do the Darn'dest Things...

Many authors present assemblies and writing workshops to children in schools.

Glad You Asked

"At one school I said, 'You can ask me anything.' So one boy asked, 'What did women do about menstruation in the Middle Ages?' The teacher said, 'Bill! Sit down!' It was a good question. Kids ask questions about what is really on their minds if they are encouraged. And I think it's a good thing."

Karen Cushman

Another Good Question

"I asked a kindergarten class if anyone had read a book Shirley Climo had written and I had illustrated called *The Korean Cinderella* and a little voice said, 'North or South?'"

Ruth Heller

OOPS!

"Giving gold panning demonstrations makes school visits fun and interesting. I'm still blushing at one demonstration I gave, though. I had just finished my demonstration at a newly built elementary school and when I dumped the five gallons of gold panning water down the drain, neither the teacher nor I knew the sink's hole wasn't connected to any pipes yet! Water started flooding the classroom and there was a lot of laughter as I scurried around stopping it. Thank heavens it was just clear water!"

Verla Kay

Big Fan

"I was signing books while at a school, and there was a boy who had missed my presentation, for he was in a different grade. He came up to me and said, 'I love your book! It's the best book I've read in my entire life!' I felt pretty good. This was great. My ego was totally puffed! Then he asked, 'When are you going to write the next *Harry Potter*?'"

Katie Davis

Doodling Around

"One hot afternoon, several years ago, I went to a school in Northern California. I usually draw for kids, so I stood up in front of this huge group of kids and I started drawing. Right in the front row, a kindergartner yelled out, 'Does this guy know what he's doing?' It was very quiet. I went on. Two minutes later, he says really loudly, 'Is he *sure* he knows what he's doing?'"

Thacher Hurd

Roll Out the Carpet

"When my first book was published in 1986, I visited a Long Beach low-income school. I was told the kids were practically gang members, and could not afford to buy my books. When I arrived, I found a red carpet—literally—lining the sidewalk. There was a representative from every single class. Each student gave me something...pictures they drew, letters, flowers. They all shook my hand and treated me like royalty. They said, 'We never liked to read until we read your books!' These kids *knew* reading was important. They came with pennies and nickels and quarters in baggies to buy books. Those hand-warmed pennies meant a lot to me."

Lee Wardlaw

Tenderhearted Everywhere

"Years ago, I was invited to speak at a Catholic school. I must have shown them a riddle book, for a boy asked me 'What's black, has a million legs, and red beady eyes?' I said, 'I don't know.' He said, 'I don't know either but it's creeping up your leg!' The nun apologized and made the boy write me a letter of apology. But it was a good riddle and I've used it since then—but not at Catholic schools!

"*A Pocketful of Seeds* was loosely based on my friend Fanny Krieger's story. Her family all died at Auschwitz. When that book came out in 1973, people didn't know much about the Holocaust. Fanny and I spoke to a sixth grade class. We told them the police arrested people because of how they looked. They kept asking, But what did you do wrong? It was very hard for them to understand that innocent children were being sought and murdered.

"Then we visited a tough middle school. We were a little nervous about our reception. After our talk was over, children started asking careful questions. A young man asked 'How do you know your sister isn't still alive? Have you looked for her?' It was very touching to see these tough kids bringing so much tenderness and sympathy to her."

Marilyn Sachs

Cheap Money

"I tried to dissuade children from going into children's book writing because there isn't much money involved. So I'd tell them I'd work months and months and I'd only get an advance of three thousand dollars. Well, I thought that would be discouraging to them. But it wasn't! They thought, Wow, three thousand dollars is a lot!"

Stephen Mooser

Kiss and Tell

"As I talked to a large assembly, two teachers in the back were making out! I said, 'Would the adults in the back please stop talking.' Later the man apologized to me and said he was going to make amends to me in front of his class. I thanked him and said, 'I'm sorry, but I just couldn't concentrate.'"

Ruth Radlauer

Undercover Narc?

"A visit day could run from the superb, to what the hell are you doing here? At one school, a secretary asked me, 'Are you a narc?'

"The children I write for are quite literal. While speaking at an Oklahoma prison for juveniles, a fight broke out among a group of boys in the back of the room. It was over what brand of motorcycle was in the picture!

"One school had converted their entire front lobby into a shark's mouth. In the cafeteria there was a live horse! Parents had kids select a picture from one of our books and the kids drew the picture with textile paint on cloth. We have that fifteen- by fifteen-foot quilt hanging in our house.

"In North Carolina, a school I visited was by a river. When I got there, the teachers and kids were fishing! I joined in. For lunch, we ate the fish."

Ed Radlauer

Hand in Hand

"At one school, in between assemblies I chatted with a third grade girl. A fire drill went off and she took my hand to lead me to her class outside. She said to me, 'I'm never going to wash my hand again!'"

Suzanne Williams

Affair to Remember?

"At one library visit, one kid asked me if my husband cheated on me, would I get mad and would I put it in a book?"

Marilyn Singer

Marine Wait

"It was the worst week of my life in Texas. That very first day, there I am looking stiff in my brand new boots, when I started telling a story to the little kids. One kindergartner was so over excited, she threw up on my boots. As they were dragging her out of there, she screams, "But I want to see the famous *otter*!"

Jane Yolen

Curtain Call

"I went to a third grade classroom and a boy met me outside of class. He handed me a rope. I went into the classroom and I discovered I was to be Muriel from my book, *World Famous Muriel*. The class had pictures of banana peels pasted on the floor and, on the chalk board behind a screen, they had drawn an elephant in a zoo enclosure, a monkey in a cage and a flamingo in a pond. They handed me a hat and there was someone who was the queen and spoke her dialogue. I had to remember the dialogue for Muriel!

Sue Alexander

Moo to You

"At my first school visit, everyone was dressed in cow paraphernalia as a tribute to my book, *Moonstruck: The True Story of the Cow Who Jumped Over the Moon*. The principal had on cow pants, the PTA ladies had on cow earrings. There was a cow centerpiece on the table, cow cupcakes to eat, cow mobiles hanging from the ceiling, cow murals on the walls and cow dioramas on the table. This was not California anymore. This was cow land."

Gennifer Choldenko

Sad Realities

At another school, I talked to a second grade in the library and I asked if anyone had any questions. Some of the kids were sharing. A little boy wildly waved his hand at me and he said, 'My daddy beat me this morning.' I said, 'I'm so sorry, honey.' After the class left, I told the librarian I didn't know what to say. She said [the boy's] social worker took the boy away five times and five times they returned him [to his family]. That incident has stayed with me for years."

Sue Alexander

Book Helps

"I've had a number of incidents where someone will wait until everyone else is gone. They may walk up and burst into tears. After *Chinese Handcuffs* came out, (it's about a young girl who was molested by her biological father and by her stepdad.) A girl came up to me after everyone else had gone and said, 'I didn't have this experience, but I read this book and I thought you knew me. It's the first time I had an idea that anyone else knows about [this abuse].' I said, 'You know a lot more people than you think know it. *They* are the reason I write it.' Later, she wrote to me and said she got into therapy. At which point, as far as I'm concerned, bring on the critics!"

Chris Crutcher

Who Are You?

"The best was in Taft, California, where I was treated like a family member and loved every minute. The strangest [school visit] was contracted and pre-paid by a local school librarian who was out of town when I arrived. The date on her confirmation letter was right, but no one in her school knew who I was or why I was there. A puzzled principal finally opened a small, closet-like room and made the announcement that classes could be brought there to 'hear about books.' I never saw a single teacher, as they'd been given a free period, or anyone else. It was like the Twilight Zone! Only a grounds-worker said goodbye when I was finished and finally able to leave!"

Sarah Wilson

Autograph Please?

"I love it when they ask, 'Are you famous?' I respond, 'No, are you?'"

Eve Aldridge

Sharing Time

"A kindergartner raised his hand and asked me how my manuscripts get to the publisher. I told him that I mail and sometimes fax them. He asked, 'What's a fax?' So, I described it. Then a little girl raised her hand and said, 'I have a fax machine.' I broke down laughing as eighty hands went up and a roomful of children started shouting, 'I have a fax machine too!'"

Bruce Balan

Calling All Janitors

"At one school, I was talking to a library full of first-graders. One little tyke sitting on the floor in the front row, kept tugging at my trousers. I assumed he was intrigued with the dimes in my penny loafers. Just the week before, an older youngster had asked about them and I'd explained how I taught school in an unsafe area. The dimes were in case I ever got mugged. My theory was that they would go unnoticed by a mugger and since phone calls were only a dime then, I'd have money to make a call.

"Fully anticipating a question about the coins in my shoes, I looked down and asked the first-grader, 'What would you like to know?' He looked up, smiled and said, 'I think I'm gonna be sick.' And in a blink, he vomited all over my shoes.

"The moral of the story, expect the unexpected when visiting schools, or move to the other side of the room when someone tugs on your trousers."

Larry Dane Brimner

Got Voice?

"I had been doing a long stint of school visits, so I lost my voice. But this was the last school to do. All the teachers wanted to talk to me, so I wrote down that I had to save my voice. The teachers were very alarmed. After all the kids packed into the assembly hall, I croaked out my presentation. I sounded horrible! The kids giggled; the adults were horrified. They [the adults] stayed that way, but the kids adapted. It pinpointed the difference between grownups and kids!"

Elaine Marie Alphin

Pantomime Perhaps?

"When I tell students how to interview if they are going to write biographies, I emphasize that they should prepare everything ahead of time: be sure their equipment is working, that they have fresh batteries, etc. Yet I recently spoke at a school where they have a wonderful new multipurpose room, but the acoustics were so bad, the students couldn't hear me! So it's true, always come prepared for anything!"

Beverly Gherman

Let's Pretend

"I talk about how, when I became an adolescent, I felt embarrassed that I wanted to play with my fantasy world. I didn't know it then, but I was getting ready to be an artist. I tell kids, if you feel embarrassed, don't be. It just means you have an active imagination. If I weren't making a living at this, three hundred years ago they would have put me in a loony bin for drawing flying grandmothers! It's okay, because books are respected; but it's really just pretending. Imagination is good! Value it. Love it."

Elisa Kleven

Make Me a Star

"We were signing copies of an early picture book, *Six Sleepy Sheep*, when a man rushed up to the front of the line. He put two wrapped packages down along with a large manila envelope. He told us, 'My daughter just loves your book.' Then he left. His daughter wasn't with him and he didn't buy a book or even have one autographed. The packages contained celery soup (which was mentioned in the book). The manila envelope...you guessed it...contained his picture book manuscript."

Stephanie Jacob Gordon

Real or Fake?

"When we were speaking at a school, one of the children raised her hand to ask a question. When called upon, she asked, 'Do you know the real Judy—Judy Blume?'"

Judy Ross Enderle

Magic Touch

"Once, a girl who had just received my autograph on a slip of paper, came back around behind me and rubbed the paper across my shoulder, so she could tell her friends she touched someone famous!"

Deborah Lee Rose

Get in Line

"There's a wonderful page in Helen Lester's *Author: A True Story*, that I have framed in my office. She is pictured sitting next to 'a very famous author' at a book signing. 'Her line had no end. Mine had no beginning.' Well, that was me at my first book signing, for my picture book, *When Molly Was in the Hospital*. My table was right next to Janell Cannon's at the California Reading Association Convention, the year Janell won the California Young Reader Medal for *Stellaluna*. There were more than a hundred people in her line, but I sold only three books that hour! Fortunately, I was able to laugh about it even then."

Debbie Duncan

Birds and the Bees and...Snakes?

"I was at a school when a second-grader raised her hand and asked, 'How do snakes make babies?' I looked at the teachers for guidance and they were busy trying to disappear into cracks in the wall, so I decided to just plunge ahead, using words such as 'penis,' 'vagina,' etc. I heard a few giggles, but the kids handled it no problem. That made me realize that it's the *adults* who have most of the problems with controversial subjects. Kids are just fine with it. This experience also inspired my follow up to *Animal Dads*, the book *Making Animal Babies*, which, by the way, many children's librarians are informally banning from their libraries because it contains the words 'sexual reproduction.'"

Sneed B. Collard III

Word for Word

"I remember one visit very vividly, because I learned a lesson from it. I was writing a series of dinosaur books at the time. One little guy helped me out with the questions. He knew more than I did! I said, 'I think I better take you home with me.' At the end of my talk, the little boy stood with his jacket on, waiting for me to take him home! Children can be quite literal!"

Eve Bunting

Philosophy Lesson

"My book, *Made in China*, is about Chinese inventions. It is written for upper elementary and middle school students. However, I often give presentations to entire elementary schools. I had told a kindergarten class the story of a great flood that covered China. Afterwards, I encouraged the students to ask questions. There were none. I pressed on, knowing young children can be shy. 'I am an author. I write books. Maybe there is something you would like to know?' A little girl jumped up, excited. I waited for her question, glad she had broken the silence. 'There is one thing I want to know,' she said. 'Who made God?'"

Suzanne Morgan Williams

Seeing is Believing

"I put on my long dress and sunbonnet and visit classrooms as Abraham Lincoln's stepmother, Sarah. I tell stories about my life and about Abraham's growing years. After one performance, a first grader came up to me and said quite seriously, "Tell Abraham hello for me."

Tekla White

Anticipation

"As my own children grew up, I tended to evolve with them and their changing concerns of high school, college, girlfriends, cars and so on. But by visiting elementary schools and classrooms, I have been able to stay in touch with my picture book readers. I visit schools a lot and have had many adventures—as any teacher knows what can happen on any given day. But one fond recollection is about an event that *didn't* happen.

"When I speak with older grades, I talk about the publishing process. I try to make it visual by having kids volunteer to come up front and represent various people in the process—the author, the editor, the publisher, the printer and so on. By the time I'm finished, I have a row of eight or nine kids up front holding various props and wearing little signs naming whom they represent.

"Once I had a group of about 150 third graders all seated on the floor in front of me. When it came time to pick each volunteer, I was met with a sea of frantically waving hands, as is always the case with third graders. I had already picked children to portray the author, the agent and the editor. The fourth person in my demonstration is the publisher and I happened to pick the waving hand of a pale-looking little girl. I noticed a quiet grumble ripple through the audience when she stood up.

"When the girl came forward and took her position in line as publisher, the children seated on the floor in front of her squirmed and tried to scoot backwards, like she had cooties or something. It occurred to me that maybe I had chosen a very unpopular child. It happens sometimes that I inadvertently pick someone that is, perhaps, the victim of teasing or something. I always feel bad when it happens. And I never cease to wonder how these kids let themselves get swept up in the excitement of the moment and raise their hands on the chance that they will be picked to come up front only to find themselves on public display before their tormentors.

"But the show must go on! And my presentation continued to its conclusion without event. Afterward, a teacher hurried up to me. 'Oh, I'm so relieved!' she said.

"'What?' I asked.

"'I was worried,' she said, 'when you picked Sarah as your publisher.'

"'Why?' I responded. 'She did fine.'

"'Yes, that's why I'm so relieved. You see, all year long, so far, whenever she's been called up to the front of the class—well, it's been so stressful for her—she's suffered projectile vomiting!'

"That explained my nervous audience scooting backwards! They probably weren't able to focus on a single word I had said once Sarah got up front. I expressed to the teacher that I shared her relief, both for the audience and for the child, that she made it successfully through it all –and that maybe some kind of healing had taken place! But in the back of my mind, there was a disappointed ten-year-old thinking, 'Whoa! Dude! That would have been really cool!'"

Tedd Arnold

Mushy Talk Leads to...

"One time, while speaking at a school in Colorado after lunch, I showed my slides and talked about the book, *Feathertop*. It's a Nathaniel Hawthorne tale that has romance in it. Everything was really quiet, and then I said, 'She took one look at Feathertop and fell in love with him!' Just as I said that, a kid throws up when he hears the word *love*. Everybody laughed and ran away from the kid who got sick. Some of the kids thought the word *made* him get sick! Kids *do* react funny when they hear that word."

Daniel San Souci

Chauffeur

"One class decided I was rich and famous because I had a driver picking me up. My husband!"

Teri Sloat

Contagious?

"The 'Catching Cough' happened at one school. Soon after my presentation to a huge audience began, one child in the back of the room hacked a legitimate cough.

Before the germs even had time to fly across the room, it was echoed by another. One by one, other fake coughs joined the chorus until there was no way I could continue to be heard, even with a microphone. It took the intervention of the principal to restore order."

Joy N. Hulme

Older but Wiser

"One girl came up to me, grabbed my hand and said, 'Mrs. Bauer! I always thought you'd be younger.'

"I'm impressed with the quality of questions kids ask me. I was in a school in California, and a seventh grader stood up and asked, 'If you were going to describe yourself in one word, what would it be?' I said, 'Overcomer.'

"I've been doing a lot of traveling, and I really feel good about what I'm seeing in schools. Kids are understanding stories. They have important insights and they care about the world and big ideas. I have a great deal of respect for adolescents. I think sometimes the media paints them as not having the depth that they have."

Joan Bauer

You Name It

"One day in upstate New York, someone asked me where I got the name 'Cricket' for the character in *Teacher's Pet*. I explained that I borrowed the first name of a teacher who I once worked with at a school in New York City many years ago. That very same afternoon, in another school about twenty miles away, a woman came up to me after my talk and introduced herself. 'You don't know me,' she said, 'But you used to work with my sister-in-law. Do you remember Cricket . . .?'

"Another experience, also pertaining to the use of names was when I revisited a school in Pennsylvania. Sitting with the teacher at lunch time, I was told that ten years earlier I had remarked that I would someday borrow the last name of one of the teachers: Boomsma. 'Are you still planning to use it?' I was asked. I told them that in the meantime, my son had gotten married and that my daughter-in-law had a very good friend with that same last name. 'I don't want to embarrass her,' I said. 'What is the name of your daughter-in-law's friend?' I was asked. 'Victoria Boomsma.' Suddenly a dozen voices shouted out in unison. 'Vicky? Your daughter-in-law knows Vicky?' Imagine—Victoria's mother was the woman I had met. And the name 'Boomsma' will be showing up in *Lexi's tale*."

Johanna Hurwitz

Ageless

"I'm often asked, 'Do you know Laura Ingalls Wilder?' Or 'Are *you* Laura Ingalls Wilder?' Now, I know I'm not twenty-five, but am I as old-fashioned-looking as the pictures of Laura Ingalls Wilder or that old-looking?

"At one school in Sacramento, California, I was totally honored. Each grade did a program related to one of my books. They sang songs, and dressed in appropriate outfits."

Ginger Wadsworth

Secret Love

"I love it when I am at a school and a very bold child comes up and whispers, 'I used to hate poetry, you know; but now I like it!'"

Janet Wong

Cool Compliment

"I was talking to some children and I was telling them how I get ideas for books. I said I used my own childhood memories. Since I'm an older man, I said, 'Would you believe I was once a child?' One first grader said, 'You *are* a child!'"

Bernard Waber

Zip It?

"There was a time when there was construction going on outside while I was trying to give a presentation in a basement library, and dirt kept being pushed into the window. There was a time I was speaking in an open classroom environment, and the first graders on the other side of the partition were singing "Kumbaya." Then there was the time I realized five minutes into my presentation that my fly was wide open, and I wasn't about to zip up while sitting on a stage in front of 200 middle schoolers, knowing that even if I was discreet, the Lavolier mike would broadcast it throughout the school. Thus, the rest of the presentation was an exercise in trying to keep my tie strategically positioned!"

Neal Shusterman

Kid Power

"When I appear at schools I talk about what kids the audience's age were doing a hundred years ago, two hundred years ago, etc. I focus on their importance, their power, and the human legacy of courage. In a middle school last year, a boy stayed after the session to hug me, wordlessly, then turned and ran out of the auditorium. I asked a teacher about him and found out he had tried to commit suicide a week or so before. You never know how you will touch children's lives. There is a huge responsibility in writing for children—and enormous joy, of course."

Kathleen Duey

Anatomy 101

"I've been asked questions on how to draw things. In one school, we had a big discussion on how you can draw a nose. How do you draw a nose? Do all noses

have hair, or just the teacher's? Do you really need to draw nose holes? If it is a part of the story that something comes out of a nose, then you need to draw the holes! That's when I love saying goodbye and leaving the teacher with the kids!"
R.W. Alley

Giddy with Fame
"At one school, a cluster of kids in the Story Readers Club chatted with me as I was signing books after school in the library. Suddenly I heard a soft, 'Thunk,' but thought it was a book falling off the shelf. A few moments later, a tallish African American third grade boy staggered to his feet and said, 'Did you see that? Did you see me faint just then?' He leaned over to his little sister who was beside me. 'Didn't I just faint?' he said to her and she nodded. 'Wow,' he continued. 'I've never seen a famous person this close before, since the time Stevie Wonder came to our school.'"
Alexis O'Neill

Always One Skeptic
"I was talking to older kids and they were filing out of the room. A few kids were around the desk where my books were displayed. One little second-grader came in, and marched down to the desk. He poked an older boy who had heard my talk.
"'Who's she?' he asked.
"The older boy replied, 'She wrote this book.'
"His eyes narrowed as he picked up my book.
"'So you wrote this book?' he said to me.
"'Yes,' I replied.
"He turned, holding the book so I couldn't see it.
"'So what's your name?' he asked."
Zilpha Keatley Snyder

Above Ground
"One day I was walking across an elementary school playground, dodging soccer balls and watching the kids, when a little boy came racing up to me all disheveled, panting, red-faced. He came screeching to a halt in front of me and said, 'Are you a living author?'"
Alice Schertle

Unspeakables
"I love the questions kids ask. Two stand-outs are: 'Do you ever get death threats? And 'What kind of underwear do *you* wear?' Sometimes kids will ask truly meaningful, perceptive questions about writing or methods—beyond 'where do you get your ideas.' This is always thrilling."
Kathleen Krull

Actions Speak Louder

"My favorite school visit situation was touching rather than amusing and it happened on the Monday after a school visit instead of during the visit. As part of my school presentation, I show the kids how to make 'things' out of bread dough clay, based on a 'thing' that my main character makes for his mother in my book, coauthored with my husband Kevin, called *The Birthday King*.

"I gave my presentation on Friday, bringing a large container of examples of 'things' Kevin and I made at home. The following Monday I received an excited call from a second-grade teacher. She told me that she had a problem student who, in the past, had refused to share anything with the other students. But he had worked all weekend and taken the theme of our book—cooperation—to heart. On Monday morning, he showed up with a large container just like mine. It was filled with several 'things' he had made by himself, and he proceeded to give one to each of his classmates. It was nice to know that when we go home after our school visit, we leave something of ourselves behind in the hearts of the children."

SuAnn Kiser

Mystery Meal

"I will always remember the school that arranged for the visiting authors to eat lunch with a small group of children that had distinguished themselves in some way. I thought this was a great idea, until I found that the planner had taken it one step further and was also serving the authors the same cafeteria meal as the children. The mashed potatoes had the consistency of sand soup, and the desiccated mystery meat sandwiches on stale over-processed white bread was a chef's nightmare! Needless to say, I readily shared my meal with my voracious table-mates, and was never happier to go hungry."

Kevin Kiser

Picture This

"School visits create so many memories for me. There was a girl in a New York school who touched my life in a way I can't describe. I have her picture right here by me when I write. She makes me smile. Then there was a boy in fifth grade once who came up to me quietly and whispered that he had something to give me. He offered me his school picture, with his name and age on the back. He asked if I would keep it...always. I still have his picture.

"Poets help to spread the word, the joy of poetry in schools. We need to talk to our children more about poetry; give them poetry every day. Parents are tired at night, and prefer to read simple, short picture books to children at bedtime. Why not give them a poem? Or even read the same poem each and every night for a week, adding one new one besides? The child will know that poem by heart, and so will the parent. What a gift!"

Rebecca Kai Dotlich

Pajama Party

"During one kindergarten classroom visit, I came dressed as Flossie from *Flossie and the Fox*. I told the story. When I got to the part where the Fox asks Flossie, 'Of course, I'm a fox, and a little girl like you should be terrified of me. Whatever do they teach children in schools these days?' Before I could give Flossie's answer, a little girl answered, 'Not very much.' I lost it for the first time as a storyteller! I had to stop and chuckle. She wasn't being a smart aleck. She was being honest. That was one of the most memorable visits for me.

"I usually don't stay with strangers while working, because you never know what to expect. In one case, we stayed with a teacher. Her home was lovely and there were private guest quarters. After working a long day, I was exhausted an had one thought in mind—get to bed. Without warning, there was a knock at the door. My hostess informed me that she had invited a group of neighborhood children over to hear a bedtime story from me. She had even prepared cocoa and cookies. Of course, she had never mentioned any of this to me. *What to do?*

"One look at the children and I couldn't say no. There they were on the living room floor with freshly pressed p.j.'s—some brand new with the folds still in them. They had their various bunnies, blankets, and bears who had come along with them to hear a story told by a real author. How could I say no? I didn't. I sat with them and read *Messy Bessey* and giggled and drank cocoa. It was a delightful fifteen or twenty minutes that could have been so much better had my hostess warned me ahead of time. Oh well, perhaps she thought it was better to ask for forgiveness than permission."

Patricia McKissack

Selling Your Books to Publishers

Are there secrets to getting your book published?

Wave of the Future?
"Try writing e-books. You don't get paid—you get a cut. This market will get popular when kids discover they can have books on something that's like a Game Boy. Maybe it will make books cool to read."
Linda Joy Singleton

Buyers Wanted
"Commercially, I always had the market in mind. Because I found out in a very early stage at my career, at no time, at any editorial conference, did the publisher ask what is *in* the book. The only question ever asked was who is going to buy it? One publisher even prided himself by saying, 'I've never read a book I've published. The editor has done that.'"
Ed Radlauer

Follow the Leader
"Follow your editors around. If they move to another house, that might be a good lead."
Cynthia Chin-Lee

A Networking We Go
"Information about trends is on the web now. Read the *Publishers Weekly* 'Children's' issues. Network. Go to conferences."
Ellen Jackson

Don't Skimp

"I use really quality paper clips and nice quality recycled paper for my cover letter so it looks great."

Bruce Balan

Be a Pro

"Read. Make it easy for the editor to say yes by presenting your work and yourself in a professional way."

Elaine Marie Alphin

One Way

"Get an agent. She stuck with me for six years until the book sold. She believes in my writing."

Kathryn Reiss

Double Duty

"Use your research to write more than one project. The research you do on a book can lead to a lively article for a magazine. If you are any kind of photographer, submit photos with your article. Being paid for artwork as well as writing can double your income."

Connie Goldsmith

In the Right Place

"Keep your manuscripts circulating. Subscribe to newsletters and e-mail lists. Go to conferences. You never know when you will be in the right place at the right time."

Tricia Gardella

Blinkin' Fish

"Changing genres has sometimes helped me sell a book; for example, I originally used the idea that fish don't blink in a concept book manuscript. I ultimately sold *Why the Frog Has Big Eyes*, a Pourquoi tale in which the climax of the story depends on this scientific fact."

Betsy Franco

Poetry Apostle

"Don't rush to write themed collections of poetry. Write poems that matter to you. My first collection, *Good Luck Gold*, was completely unthemed, and it is my favorite of my collections. It's not the most cohesive collection—I would say that *Behind the Wheel: Poems about Driving* is the best, in those terms—but it's the collection where I took the greatest risks, in terms of the breadth of subject matter. Write ten times more poems than you need. Soon enough, you will find that certain themes appear in your writing, and you can then assemble themed collections, which seem to have a better chance of finding an audience. And when your first collection is published, perform those poems everywhere you can: schools, libraries, community centers, museums. Become a poetry evangelist!"

Janet Wong

Don't be afraid to ask

"Ask editors, 'What do you need?' And if you get an answer, listen!"

Kathleen Duey

Marketing and Publicity Tips

Your work on the book doesn't stop once you've sold it to a publishing house. Then you have to get people to *buy* it. Read what these authors have to say about the marketing world of children's books.

Target Practice

"One of the best ways children's authors can promote their books is to attend conventions for professionals in their target markets—educators, librarians, and children's booksellers. Another is to make sure the online booksellers are posting full and accurate information on your books. This is even more important than having your own web page, because people who find your books on Amazon are most likely wanting to buy books, while your home page visitors are most likely looking for freebies!

"But the best way of all to promote your books is to keep new ones coming out. That's vital for keeping your name in front of the children's book community."

Aaron Shepard

Interact with Kids

"Because nonfiction is used in schools and libraries, those are good places to promote it. Some authors prefer to speak on the conference circuit where they have direct contact with teachers and librarians. I prefer to go to schools where I can also interact with children."

Caroline Arnold

Write!

"Each book you publish helps sell your other titles, so keep writing and submitting."

Deborah Lee Rose

Just Say Write

"Marketing is of no interest to me. I write books to please myself and hope other people will like them well enough to buy them—or check them out of the library."

Mary Downing Hahn

Word of Mouth

"This is a very frustrating issue for me. If you're not already famous, publishers won't put much marketing money behind you, so it's all up to the new writer. If you're rich, you can hire a good publicist and concentrate on writing. If you're not rich, but you have lots of energy, you can do lots and lots of school visits and require that the students have purchased and read your books before you go to the school to speak.

"But then, when do you have time to write and submit your manuscripts? So my tips is to spend your time writing and write the best, most unusual book you can, and word of mouth will make your book a best seller."

Marisa Montes

Evelyn Gallardo is the author of *How to Promote Your Children's Book* as well as books for children: *Among the Orangutans, Endangered Wildlife,* and *Jane Goodall's Animal World –Gorillas.* She's also a professional photographer, whose photos have appeared in *The Dark Romance of Dian Fossey,* and periodicals such as *Ranger Rick, ZooLife,* and *Animal Magazine.*

When should an author start promoting a book?

"A year before the book is published. Prepare promotional materials and compile a press kit."

What should be in a press kit?

"It should include a brochure, a biography page, letterhead and business card, a press release, (you can ask your publisher's marketing department for one) and a content sheet. The content sheet should be a one page description of a presentation you can do at a school. Another thing that looks nice is a head shot which makes the media much more likely to run a story if they have a picture to go with it. Something that makes a nice representation is the catalog ad. If it's a half page, cut it out and paste it on a separate sheet.

"When you go to an interview, be sure and bring your press kit. Have them in your car no matter where you go. If someone from the media shows up, you can give it to them. When a reporter reads it, they should be able to do a story about you without even meeting or talking to you."

What is the most effective way to help my publisher sell my books?

"School visits. Authors may sell thirty to three hundred books at one school in one day. The average is seventy-five books. Booksellers love to have book sales like that. That builds your audience when you go to schools. The children are eagerly awaiting your next book and you've become *their* author. They feel they have a personal relationship with you. Plus they want to read your book because they met you!

"Another way is to get a web site. You really have to have one. I get a lot of school visits from my web site. If you're terrified of public speaking, you don't have to do it. Get yourself a web site and put your energies in promoting your site."

My web site doesn't get me many school visits. What should I do?

"Get your web site listed on author directories such as WritersNet (www.writer.net) and AuthorsDen (www.AuthorsDen.com).

"Contact organizations that place performers in schools through printed catalogs. Performers must apply and audition for each chapter before being added to its roster. Check out their web sites for more details. One good example is the roster of Young Audiences (www.youngaudiences.com) There are thirty-three chapters across the United States. Traditionally they have placed musicians and artists. Over the last few years they've been including authors. You audition for them for free. When you are hired through them, you get paid your fee. They add a percentage (which can vary in different chapters) on top of this.

"Doing school visits ten years ago was almost unheard of. Now more school districts have become aware that authors are available. Maybe in ten years everyone will do it! I did an informal survey. I asked 2,000 adults if any of them ever had an author visit their school. Only two said yes. And both of them said it was a very profound and memorable experience."

How can I make the most of a radio or television interview?

"Watch interview programs. My best advice would be to put three main points you want to make on an index card. No matter what, during the interview, mention those three points. Politicians are good at this. They rarely answer the questions they have been asked.

"There are bridging techniques. If you don't know the answer to a question you could say, I don't know about that, but what I do know is this. People will really benefit by looking at my web site. My book *How to Promote Your Children's Book* gives you good bridging techniques.

"Prepare ahead of your interview. Don't keep mentioning the title of your book over and over again. Don't be stingy and say you'll have to read about it in my book. Be generous in what you say and people will be more likely to read your book. Lean forward in your chair toward the interviewer so you look interested. Bring several copies of your book so they can stack them up and take pictures of them. And if you want school visits or gigs speaking at conferences, be sure to mention it. Let people know you are available. An example would be, 'I do lots of school visits. At one school, one student said....'"

What's your best advice about school visits?

"Make everyone's job as easy as you possibly can. Two months before the visit, send a master book order form. It's an order form with copies for both the school and the student. This way there can be pre sold books before you ever arrive.

"Kids are so media inundated. Everything is fast paced. So you can't expect to stand up there and be a talking head. Make your presentation highly visible. Make it interactive so they can share a bit of the spotlight. Call them up to the stage. Say their name into the microphone. If you're having fun, the kids will too."

Author/Editor Relationship

Familiar Pick-up

"It was the big evening—my first meeting with an editor. I arrived at the busy San Francisco restaurant and sat down to wait. The editor was ten minutes late. Or was he? Maybe he was already here. I didn't know what he looked like, so how could I tell? All I knew was the slow Midwestern voice I'd heard on the telephone. A glance at the bar revealed several men sitting alone. Could one of them be my editor? Along with the clink of glasses and the murmur of low voices, I heard a distinctive Midwestern drawl. I scanned the bar, freezing when I discovered the source.

"There, with a leggy blonde on each side of him, sat a middle-aged Lothario clad in skin-tight jeans, his shirt unbuttoned to the waist. A cigarette hanging from one hand, he clutched a beer in the other, winking and nudging his companions as he talked.

"I gasped. Mother was right. Going to the big city all alone to meet a man was *not* a good idea. I longed to run out the door, but I did have a book contract and I'd be darned if I'd let my distaste for him ruin my big chance. I stood up and held my head high. As I strode across the room, I noticed I had an audience: the other single men at the bar.

"'Excuse me,' I said with as much dignity as I could muster.

"He stopped mid-boast to assess me. 'Well, hello there, sweetheart.' Gold chains hung down his hairy chest.

"I shuddered, but maintained my composure. 'Are you Jerry? From Illinois?'

"'Pull up a stool,' he gestured with his beer.

"Oh no. My worst nightmare had come true. My stomach churned as I used the stool to balance. I turned to sit, when he added, 'I'm not Jerry. But join me for a drink. The name's Steve. From Iowa.'

"'You're not Jerry?' I said louder than I intended. My hand flew to my heart. 'Oh thank God!' As I hurried back to my seat, I looked up to see my audience having a grand time, laughing and elbowing each other. One man laughed so hard he cried. When the real Jerry came into the restaurant (looking like an editor, if you know what I mean), I was so relieved, I hugged him.

"'People here in California sure are friendly,' he said.

"'Not as friendly as people from Iowa,' I assured him."

Elizabeth Koehler-Pentacoff

Thank an Editor Every Day

"For the most part, 99 percent of editors are underappreciated. Just like authors, they have learned how to critically look at stories and improve them. All my books are better because of editors. I may discuss things, but generally I respect editors and follow their suggestions."

Stephen Mooser

Knees Knock, Nails Chewed . . .

"In the beginning I was scared of editors. First time I'd meet them I'd be tongue-tied. Now I realize they're really kind people and they have my manuscript's best interest at heart. You need to listen to what they're saying. But sometimes you have to stand up for your work, if you have a logical reason for keeping a scene a certain way."

Lee Wardlaw

Whatever Works

"If two people agree something isn't working, then you have to look at it and change it in your own way. Try to be appreciative."

Marilyn Sachs

Guidance with Your Book

"Finding my editor was a great piece of luck. She's about my age, and an English major like me. We think a lot alike. I trust her judgement. Like me, she wants my books to be as good as they can be. She always says to me, 'This is my opinion, but it's your book' which makes me willing to work with it. We work very well together."

Karen Cushman

Opportunity to Learn

"If you are a good student, you'll learn a lot. You have to absorb the lessons. If the lesson is that your character is cutesy or too talky or you don't sound natural, then you have to purge that from yourself. I totally thank Liz Gordon for teaching me that. Other editors taught me other things."

Marilyn Singer

Line by Line

"For me, one of the most valuable experiences has been sitting down with my editor, Robert Warren, at Harper. We sit for two or three hours going over each line of a book. He's a terrific editor and he doesn't say it's good when it isn't. Every author needs someone to look at their book objectively and yet be a supportive co-creator. It's hard to have someone else read your book and tell you what it *really* needs. Every book needs something, and every artist has a person they go to for their honest thoughts."

Thacher Hurd

Love, Love, Love

"I love my editors!"

Eve Bunting

Famous Editor Wowed!

"Charlotte Zolotow was one of my editors. She was incredible! I remember, we had lunch one day, I had finished a novel with her and I said, 'You know, 'I Can Read' books have been around since the '50's. How come no one has done an 'I Can Read' poetry book?' She literally dropped her fork on the floor and said, 'What an idea! Go for it!' And now I'm working on my seventh—a book about pets. I started that poetry series."

Lee Bennett Hopkins

Dig Deeper

"Nancy Paulsen is fabulous! She doesn't rewrite for me. She offers. She knows what I can do. She gives me an extraordinary amount of freedom. In *Rules of the Road*, there was a discussion among some of the editors at Penguin Putnam that Harry Bender's death might be too severe. We worked that through and it made the story stronger. I've never been in an editorial situation when it hasn't made the work stronger—I've either learned how to make the story better or learned how to defend my work.

"Also, my first editor, Mary Cash, was just wonderful in how she helped me learn to dig deeper with my humor and not just be content with one-liners. She challenged me again and again to burrow deep. A fine editor is one of God's greatest gifts to writers. I truly enjoy the editing process."

Joan Bauer

Book Signings

When Loretta Ichord (*Hasty Pudding, Johnny Cakes* and *Other Good Stuff*) agreed to appear at a bookstore in Berkeley, she thought she'd be talking to children, parents, and teachers. Imagine her surprise when hungry homeless men filled the empty chairs. Since her performance centered around making colonial johnny cakes for the audience, the men stood in line for the free food! They reappeared several times, depositing extra johnny cakes in their well-worn pockets. One never knows what one might encounter at a book signing.

Complimentary Fan

"At one bookstore, a child in line for my autograph announced that he was a kindergartner. He pointed to one of my books on the table and said, 'I like the pictures.'

"'So do I,' I said. 'But I didn't draw them. An illustrator did.'

"He seemed puzzled. 'If you didn't draw the pictures, what *did* you do?' he asked.

"'I wrote the story,' I explained.

"As I signed the inscription in his book, I noticed him studying the first page intently. He was too young to read. What was he thinking?

"He looked up at me in awe.

"'Wow,' he said. 'You sure are a good typer.'"
Elizabeth Koehler-Pentacoff

Favorite Author

"At one bookstore, a woman my age raved about me being her favorite author when she was a child. Since we were probably children at the same time, I just smiled and thanked her."
David Lubar

Independence

"Try to do independent bookstore signings, because they're the ones who will hand sell your book."

Lee Wardlaw

Sorry, Melville

"One boy came over and put *Moby Dick* in front of me. I said, 'But honey, I didn't write that book. He said, 'It doesn't matter. I just need your signature.' So I signed it *I wish I had written this book*. And I signed my name."

Marilyn Sachs

Through a Reader's Eyes

"At a bookstore there was a family with three little girls. They loved *The Midwife's Apprentice*. The youngest child, a five-year-old, listened to the story every night with her big sisters. She said what she liked best was that the whole story was about a cat. For her, that was what this book was about! A book is collaborative process between the author and the reader."

Karen Cushman

Have You Been Cloned?

"With an unusual YA series, *Regeneration*, about clones, you never know what to expect from readers. At one bookstore, I was getting ready to leave when one man walked around and around. He stared at my book and said to me, 'You know, people already *have* been cloned.' Then he walked off before I could ask him if he knew this was a personal experience!"

Linda Joy Singleton

Bat Attack

"Booksignings are sometimes quite an adventure. I've even had critters attack me! I did one book signing at a country fair in Washington when we had a massive thunder, lightening and hail storm. We were in a huge metal building and a bat got rattled out because of the noisy hail. As he flew down around us, I waved my sweater like a matador cape, trying to shoo him outside. Another time, in a park in Sacramento, a squirrel bombed acorns on me."

Verla Kay

"I reach parents to come to my book signings because of my book, *Thank you Mr. Falker*. A lot of children struggle with disabilities. Parents will say how much their child has benefitted to know that I struggled through it."

Patricia Polacco

Lost Chance

"The experience I've had at a book signing was that I was waiting for J.K. Rowling to sign my copy of her book. The person guarding Miss Rowling recognized my name inside my book. She proceeded to tell me how much she loves my book, *Say Hola to Spanish*. She talked just long enough to keep me from being able to speak to J.K Rowling! By the time I turned to her, she had finished signing and had moved on to the person behind me. It was ironic and frustrating to be recognized at an inopportune time. Then I realized that truly famous people must feel that way all the time."

Susan Middleton Elya

Lost Art

"I ran into my old high school boyfriend who brought his three kids. I did a signing in my hometown, where a girl I babysat for brought her daughter and brought some drawings I had done for her years ago. She had put them into an album."

Ashley Wolff

Beep Beep!

"One time I was placed really badly in a store—at the end of the checkout line, so that nobody saw me until they were already done shopping. The manager, trying to be helpful, but not interested in moving me, told me about the last signing he'd done, which, apparently, had sparse sales. The author was probably in the same place I was! The clerk said it had been a book about cats, and so the author began trying to attract business by meowing loudly. Since I was promoting *The Beetle and Me* at the time, I considered honking or beeping, but couldn't quite get started!"

Karen Romano Young

Let Me Entertain You

"My most pathetic signing was at a bookstore in a mall, scheduled at the same time as a performance of male dancers. People literally ran past the bookstore to check out the provocative music!"

Dian Curtis Regan

The Price of One's Worth

"My favorite odd incident occurred in a small mall in Vermont. The turnout had been slow and the store's owner asked me to sign several stacks of paperbacks in case someone wanted one later. While I was signing, I noticed several teenagers watching me. One strolled over and asked why I was writing in the books. I told her I'd written them and was autographing copies for the store. Mildly impressed, she lingered a while. Finally she asked, 'Will these books be more valuable after

TOO NICE

"Everyone is too nice! It's hard to take. I get kind of emotional. There are hundreds of people standing in line. Parents are so grateful. They say, 'Thank you. My son never read a book in his life until he read yours.'"

R. L. Stine

you die?' I told her probably not. Obviously disappointed, she and her friends sauntered away."

Mary Downing Hahn

Stand By Your Mom

"When I was signing my first book, Zilpha Snyder was next to me. She had a long line of people waiting for her to autograph her books. My six-year-old daughter stood in front of my table and told me *I* needed a line!"

Teri Sloat

Matchmaker

"At a public library, a boy came in and said to me, 'I'd like to introduce you to someone. This is my uncle. He's single and you're single, and you need to marry him. Then my mom would get off his back because he's single and I'd get free signed books.'

"The uncle was tricked into coming! The kid was so great; he was completely and totally not bothered by the fact we were so embarrassed. I said to him, 'I'll give you a signed book, but you can't keep finding women for your uncle!'"

Angela Johnson

Fan Mail Is Nearly Reward Enough.

Some Letters Put You in Your Place

"In one letter I received, the child wrote: 'I love your book about drag racing. But I've got to go now and read another book. Remember, you're not the *only* author.'"

Ed Radlauer

"Not long ago I had a letter from a boy who greeted me this way: 'Dear Mr. Big Shot Writer.'"

Sid Fleischman

"Dear Mr. Greenberg,

"My teacher told me to write you a letter. My favorite poet is Shel Sylverstein. Not you.

"Love, Amy"

David Greenberg

Others Make You Smile

"Are you a *living* author?"

Alice Schertle

"One child wrote, 'I'm 11 years old. How tall are you? Do you like younger men?'"

Deborah Norse Lattimore

"Sometimes kids ask, 'How many books do you write in a day?'"

Ruth Radlauer

"I created a quiz on my web site. It is called, 'Have you been cloned?' The questions are exaggerated. Basically, if you get most of them right, it says there's a possibility you've been cloned. It's just fun. One fan e-mailed me and said she got all ten right! That's not possible! I told her it made me laugh."
Linda Joy Singleton

"A youngster explained he was writing because it was an assignment to write to a living author. He chose me and further explained he would get extra credit if I wrote back to him. His letter continued with all the usual questions about ideas and writer's block, then he signed his name. In a postscript he added, 'If you're dead, just ignore this.'"
Larry Dane Brimner

"Recently, I got a letter from a child whose school I'd visited. It read:
"'Dear Mr. Collard,
"Tank (sic) you for coming to our school. You didn't have to.'"
Sneed B. Collard III

"'Dear David,
I would like to know how old Abe Lincoln was when he died? How old was his wife when she died? How old were his children when they died?'
"Whoever wrote me that letter, was clearly obsessed with death. Perhaps a loved one had just died or was very ill. The writer would have been better served if he had spoken to a therapist, not me!"
David Adler

Stars in Their Eyes
"One girl asked that when I made the movie of my novel *Time Windows*, would I call her so she could play the lead part of Miranda!"
Kathryn Reiss

"I've received fan letters from girls who want to play Sammy in the movie!"
Wendelin Van Draanen

Dear Mrs. Edison...
"I got a letter addressed to Mrs. Thomas Edison, but sent to me because I wrote a biography on Edison. The writer wanted to know about how my husband invented the lightbulb!"
David Adler

A Few Truthful Letters

"Dear Mrs. Reiss,
"You are not my favorite author. But you are my second favorite author."
Kathryn Reiss

"I got a letter from a child who said, 'My teacher is making me write to you.' It made me laugh."
Joan Holub

"I received an email from a girl who said she and her best friend were going to college. She said *Cherry Migration* was their favorite book when they were growing up. That made me feel old!"
Bruce Balan

Readers Can Identify with Book Characters

"In the Amy and Laura books, Amy always knocks over her milk. A child wrote to me, 'I'm a lot like Amy. Do the mops in Amy's house smell sour?' She really felt like she was talking about a living child."
Marilyn Sachs

Familiarity

"The best letter from a young reader says, 'Do you live around here?' I don't, of course, but I love it when the story seems that real to them, and about them."
Richard Peck

Friends?

"Dear Mr. San Souci,
"Do you like Shaquille O'Neal?"
Daniel San Souci

Some Letters Can Be Rewarding

"The best letter I've received so far was from a blind fourth grader. She couldn't see my presentation. I do a lot of drawing. But she wrote, on her Braille typewriter, that she loved to hear my stories. I figure that if my love of reading and for books can make a blind girl like my work, which is very visual, I must be doing my job."
Doug Cushman

"After I got done with one talk, a little girl said, 'Can I shake your hand?' I said, 'Of course.' After we shook, she turned around, held her hand up in the air with her other hand on her arm, saying, 'She touched me!' I got tears in my eyes and I thought, no honey, *you* touched *me*."
Verla Kay

"I got a letter last year from a woman who red my books as a child and now she's introducing them to her children. That went right to my heart. And I get letters from ministers and rabbis who have used *Nadia the Willful* in funerals for children."

Sue Alexander

Honesty the Best Policy?

"A second-grader wrote how much he enjoyed my books, and then he wrote, 'Good luck in the past.' A fifth grader from Florida wrote that she had two favorite authors—me and Judy Blume. She wrote me however, because she didn't have Judy Blume's address!"

Lee Bennett Hopkins

"'Dear R.L.Stine, You probably don't remember me. But just before you spoke at our school, I stepped on your foot.'

"I *did* remember him!"

R.L. Stine

Not Every Writer Is a Fan

"I love the ones that begin with, 'My teacher is making us all write to an author. I wanted R.L. Stine, but he was already taken, so I picked you.'"

"Or 'I've never read any of your books but some kids say they're pretty good, so maybe I will someday.'"

Mary Downing Hahn

"This one is my favorite:
'Dear R.L. Stine,
I've read forty of your books. I think they're really boring!'"

R.L. Stine

"Dear Mr. Hurd,
I don't like your story, *Mama Don't Allow*. Opossums can't speak English or play a sax. Crocodiles don't wear suits and stand on their two hind legs. I think you should make more improvements.
Kathryn"

Thacher Hurd

"One of the first letters I ever got was from a boy in Kansas. I was so excited to have a fan writing me! I opened it and it said,

"'Dear Mr. San Souci,

"'Our class project is to write to our favorite illustrator. I wrote to my favorite illustrator, but he's dead, so I thought I'd write to you instead.'"

Daniel San Souci

Fun Fantasy

"Dear Katie Davis,

"I like to laugh and I like when you made me laugh. I had fun and I like to be funny. You are a really good illustrator and author. Were (sic) do you live? It would be cool if you were a super hero. We could call you Super Katie!

"Your pal,

"Ryan, First Grade"

Katie Davis

Nonfiction Idea...

"One little boy wanted to know if I ever wrote biographies of seven-year-olds!"

Sue Alexander

Love is Blind

"I get a lot of fan mail for pop musician Aaron Carter. Teen and preteen girls do online searches on his name and click on the links to my site that comes up. Then they email me saying how cute I am, and how they'd like to be my girlfriend, and such. I have to write tactful replies about not being Aaron Carter. The problem is, sometimes I'm not sure who they mean to write to!"

Aaron Shepard

Aspiring Book Publishers

"I get a lot of fan mail. It's a constant worry because they pile up. I read them all. Sometimes I feel guilty because I haven't answered them for awhile. If the letters stop coming, then I'll have something to complain about! I'm thankful for them. I have one letter from two little boys who are writing a book. They wrote and asked, could I send them a cover for their book and tell them how to put print on the page? Could I help them in any way? They could pay me because they have money!"

Eve Bunting

To Lee Wardlaw:

"Dear Lee,

"I loved your book *Corey's Fire*. Is Corey a real person? Could we have lunch? I would like to go to lunch with you because the cafeteria food stinks. If you take me out to lunch, take me to Sizzler.

Your friend,

Charlie"

"Dear Lee,

I have a very important question to ask you. When you're writing your book, doesn't your hand hurt from writing so much?

Love,

Jennifer"

"Dear Lee,

I like your books *Me + Math = Headache* and *The Eye and I.* I have written 32 books in four years. How many have *you* written?

Sincerely,

Tony"

"Dear Lee,

I have a personal question. Does your husband ever get jealous of your wonderful talents, and does he get mad when you have sold a book and get about $5,000,000 for it?

Yours truly,

Benita"

"Dear Lee,

I'm glad you came to visit our class because it was better than doing work all period. Thank you, thank you for coming!

Your fan,

Jason"

"Dear Lee,

I really liked your book *Seventh-Grade Wierdo.* It was so good I couldn't put it down. I even read it on the toilet!

Your friend,

Angie"

"Dear Lee,

How are you? I'm fine, thanks. I think you're the best author that I've read so far. But, I have a long life ahead of me.

Your friend,

Christopher"

To Dian Curtis Regan:

"In closing, it is most imperative to my sense of well-being that you continue writing monster books at a furious rate."

"I'm not even halfway through your book and I love it! I have read 52 books since August and yours is the best—so far. And I'm not just saying that to make you feel better."

"Hey! Try turning your books into movies!"

To Teri Sloat:
"I was so glad you came to our school. I thought all the good authors were dead."

"Would you bring a picnic lunch to our pumpkin patch next year? I'm allergic to peanut butter."

"I really like your colors that you use, but I could show you how to draw a dog better."

To Joan Bauer:
"Dear Mrs. Bauer,
My teacher said we have to write to a living author and I'm hoping you'll qualify."

"I want to congratulate you on becoming a successful authoress. This means that you've now become homework."

"I got this one from a 15-year old girl who didn't like to read:
'Dear Mrs. Bauer,
You should feel good about what you do, because it isn't every day that Holly Goldman picks up a book.'"

Emotional Connections/A Big Fan
"I received a very moving letter from a childhood friend of Anne Frank who had survived the Holocaust. I actually wrote about his woman in my biography and so it was quite amazing to have her write to me. She now lives in Israel and wrote saying that she felt I had done an excellent job in portraying her friend. That meant more to me than any book review I've ever received.

"When I wrote *The Rabbi's Girls*, I used the actual names of two young teen-agers who were killed in a tornado in 1924. A ten-year-old girl in California read my book and wrote to me. I saw from her last name, even before I completed reading the letter, that she would have been the great niece of that tornado victim.

"Most of my mail, however, is in a lighter vein. Children share events in their lives, tell me their favorite foods, and what they liked about my books. I frequently tell children that when I was growing up in the Bronx, in New York, I felt my life was very boring. I wished I lived somewhere exciting like Minnesota or Nebraska. Not too long ago, I got a letter from a fourth grader in Omaha who said he'd heard that I wished I lived somewhere exciting like Nebraska. 'Well, I live in Nebraska,' he wrote. 'And it's not that exciting!'

"Recently I got a letter from an eleven-year-old boy who told me he had a size 14 shoe and that he weighed 175 pounds. I dropped a note to my editor and told her that we could no longer assume that I was only writing books for small children."

Johanna Hurwitz

To Zilpha Keatley Snyder:
"One little boy wrote:
'I think I'm getting ready to write a book. If I do, can I use parts of yours?'"

"The only time I wrote to an author, they wrote back and said he'd been dead for three years. I hope you haven't."

"Why did you write this book? Is something funny going on in your house?"

From Role Models to Dog Kibble
"I get letters from deaf kids who read my Connor Westphal mysteries and they're very touching. They appreciate the deaf protagonist as a role model. Most of my mail is very positive. But every now and then I get a complaint that Connor doesn't ever seem to 'feed her dog.' I guess I need to include more dog food. . ."

Penny Warner

Glittery Effect
"Children are very creative in putting together fan mail packages. SuAnn and I have received letters that come out of the envelope trailing little bits of brightly colored glitter over clothes, desks, and carpets. Each sparkle is a little piece of joy and love for us—though we are eternally grateful for the power of our DustBuster! Perhaps the funniest thing about glitter-filled envelopes is that at least one aspiring author we know did the same thing with a submission to a publisher. I doubt that the editor who opened that envelope found the mess it made as charming as we did!"

Kevin Kiser

To Patricia McKissack:
"I get mail from many different places. I recently got a call from Madrid, Spain from a father who was delighted that he could give his son a book about Nzingha, an Angolan Queen. He was Angolan and his wife was Spanish. He was happy that his son now could read about a person who had been a leader in his culture. I also love the letters I get from students.

DIRECT EFFECT

"I was in Dallas one time, in the height of the *Goosebump* popularity. A teacher told me, 'Reading scores have skyrocketed in the last two years and we think it's because of your books.'"

R. L. Stine

"'Dear Ms. McKissack,

'I read *The Dark Thirty: Southern Tales of the Supernatural*. I thought it was going to be scary. It wasn't.

'Your friend, Jeffery'"

"'Dear Mr. and Mrs. McKissack,

"'I read your book because my teacher said I had to. But it was good, believe it or not!'"

Authors Were Once Children Too!

What did children's authors read when *they* were children?

A Peek into Another Reality . . .
"*Cotton in My Sack* and *Strawberry Girl* opened up a different world than where I was raised—in a Los Angeles suburb of no trees and lots of cement."
Karen Cushman

Riverboats and White Washed Fences
"Mark Twain was the great find of my childhood. As a Midwesterner, I needed to find an author from my part of the country—neither British nor New Englander. And I found a great one. I vanished into his *Life on the Mississippi,* and somehow never returned."
Richard Peck

Independence from adults . . .
"I read constantly. I loved *Heidi, Dr. Dolittle, Smokey the Cow Horse* by Will James, and *The Secret Garden.* I loved having a secret; a hidden place that no adult knows about."
Zilpha Keatley Snyder

Reading Was an Escape from Chores . . .
"As a child, I had the best intentions of cleaning my room. On a Saturday morning, I'd have a feather duster in hand, and head for my overcrowded bookcase. I have a vague recollection of feathers and dust fluttering in the air, so I probably attempted to dust my books. But before the dust could settle, I'd be stretched out on the floor, deep into an adventure. My favorite book has always been *Charlotte's Web.* But I also loved *The Borrowers, The All-of-a- Kind-Family* series, *The Little*

House books, *The Moffats*, *Pippi Longstocking*, *The Secret Garden*, and the Meg books by Elizabeth Ladd.

    Elizabeth Koehler-Pentacoff

A Medicine with a Spoonful of Sugar

"My mother was a librarian. Once I was at a conference where there was a panel of kids talking. One girl said her mother was a librarian. She said her mother was trying to force books down her eyes. My mom was like that! Although I resisted most of what she'd bring home, I did read two newspapers every day, loved *The Hardy Boys*, and my favorite book was—and still is—*Treasure Island*. I loved adventure stories that I ended up writing."

    Stephen Mooser

Not All Children's Authors Were Quiet Readers...

"I spent a lot of time in the school library, because I was such a disruptive kid in class. The teachers kept kicking me out. I was the class mouth. So in the library I read lots of science fiction, science, and nonfiction. My favorites were Asimov, Heinlein and the *Freddy the Pig* series."

    David Lubar

The Land of Make Believe

"I grew up in a small town in Ireland, called Maghera. My favorite books were the *Anne of Green Gable* books. I used to pretend I was Anne. But in my Belfast boarding school, I didn't do that much pretending. It wasn't conducive. I went to boarding school from ages seven until seventeen, which was traditional in Ireland. When I came home, though, I changed from being myself into becoming Anne."

    Eve Bunting

Reality Check

"I started writing when I was seven. I loved Eleanor Estes and Beverly Cleary. I wasn't into animal stories; I wasn't into anything that couldn't be real. I wanted to see myself in the stories.

I was raised in Los Angeles in the '50's and '60's. Los Angeles is a whole different country! I was in a situation that felt ideal: one third of my school was black, one third white, and one third Asian. I wasn't at the top of my consciousness. I wasn't reading stories about little black girls. When I wrote my first novel in the sixth grade, my character was black, but she had blond hair and blue eyes!

"People gasp when I tell them this, but as a child, if we were going to a really white section of the city, my mother would say, 'Act your age and not your color.' It didn't feel bad. It was just the way it was. That was my total awareness. I didn't know anything about civil rights."

    Karen English

The Best Christmas Present Ever

"My father and mother bought me all the Scribners classics. My brother, Bob [author Robert San Souci] and I lived out those books! Although we grew up in Berkeley, the trees around us seemed like the Eastern Woodlands. We became the characters in *Robin Hood, Treasure Island, Kidnapped*. We *were* the last of the Mohicans!

"Like most kids, we didn't have much money to buy people gifts. And we got tired of getting everybody little porcelain figurines from the thrift stores. My mother had a whole box of these well-intentioned but useless gifts. So we came up with the idea of making original books to give to parents and our relatives, one Christmas. Robert was into science fiction, so he wrote about Santa Claus with a broken down sleigh, and a flying saucer full of aliens helping to deliver gifts. He made ten blank books and handwrote that story in each one. I did the illustrations over and over, ten times! I think my mother still has one of the books, tucked away in the attic."

Daniel San Souci

Some Kids Were Already Writers . . .

"I was a Santa Barbara Beach Girl but I absolutely loved to read. I read to everybody—my mom, dad, brothers, my cat. I loved Dr. Seuss, *Go Dog Go*, and *The Grinch Who Stole Christmas*. Because I loved reading, I loved to write. I wrote my first book when I was seven. The protagonist was one-inch tall, modeled after Tinkerbell. I loved Peter Pan. I wanted to marry him!

Lee Wardlaw

Dream Fulfilled

"When I was a kid I wrote constantly. I wanted to have my own girl series like Judy Bolton. When I was thirteen, I started a pen pal relationship with the author of that series, Margaret Sutton. I wrote her a letter and she encouraged my writing. We met, for the first time, at my graduation party when I was seventeen. She was seventy."

Linda Joy Singleton

The Very Special Event

"As far back as I can remember, I've doodled and drawn and put small books together. My mother was an artist and a librarian, and very supportive and encouraging. My father let me use the family typewriter as soon as I'd learned the alphabet. This was a Very Special Event, which made writing simple stories a whole lot easier. I still type with the same three fingers I used when I was four and a half! I haven't been able to change the system.

"I loved *Alice in Wonderland* and John Tenniel's illustrations, Johnny Greulle's art and books, Laurent de Brunhoff's *Babar* and Garth Williams's art in E. B. White's *Stuart Little*."

Sarah Wilson

Secrets Turned to Ashes

"My dad helped me learn to read just before I started kindergarten and, once I started, I never stopped. In elementary school my favorite day of the week was "Library Day." I loved fairy tales, books by Jack London, C.S. Lewis, E.B. White, and *Nancy Drew* stories. I was motivated by *Harriet the Spy* to start keeping a journal. I now wish I had kept that journal—probably would be a hoot to read. But back at that time (fifth grade), I decided the contents were dangerous enough to warrant destruction in the family fireplace.

Nancy Barnet

SOS Atticus

"I loved to read and write. I kept a journal. When I was in junior high, I read *To Kill a Mockingbird*. I even remember where I was sitting when I read it! I was looking for healthy father figures, since my dad wasn't able to fill that role in my life. Atticus Finch was the guy! That book has affected the way I create character. I try to create characters that can be role models. I don't have Harper Lee's skill, but I do remember that we, as authors, can do something special for our readers through our characters."

Joan Bauer

Reading Was an Escape

"As a child, I had many favorite books. I did love one author in particular. Caroline Snedecker wrote about ancient Greece and Rome. My favorite was a book she wrote called *The Spartan*. It was about a boy considered a coward just as I was considered a coward. I read books about the ancient world because I didn't like the modern world I was living in."

Marilyn Sachs

The Library Was a Second Home

"As a child I loved adventure stories like *Treasure Island*. I also loved Daphne du Maurier's novels and short stories. I spent a lot of time at the library."

Loretta Ichord

"My mom often took me to libraries, and to this day I can remember the layout of my favorite library. I had been comfortable there. I still breathe a sigh of contentment when I walk inside a library."

Joan Holub

Of Ham and Eggs

"I read quite a bit when I was in elementary school. I was a Dr. Seuss fan, I loved *Green Eggs and Ham*, *Horton Hatches the Egg*. I read the *Chip Hilton* series

voraciously. It was like the *Hardy Boys*, but it was about sports. Then I read a series about famous people when they were kids. Daniel Boone, Kit Carson, Will Clark."
Chris Crutcher

Books Made School Bearable

"I was miserable in school as a child, partly because I was, and still am, a very slow reader. Basically, I went voluntarily for only one reason, to find out what happened next in the stories my teachers read aloud in class. I loved being read to— the rhythm of language, the magic of words and how they made stories unfold in my head. I think I can safely say that I never would have become a writer if my parents and teachers had not read aloud to me.

"As a small child I loved Thurber's *Many Moons*, Grimm's fairy tales, Kipling's *Rikki Tikki Tavi*, and Maj Lindman's *Snipp, Snapp, and Snurr* books. My mother read the *Little House* books, *The Little Princess*, and *Stuart Little* aloud. My father read the *Hollow Tree Stories*, *Treasure Island*, and *Icebound Summer*. The first book I remember reading by myself was the *Little Lame Prince*."
Susan Hart Lindquist

It's All in the Family

"My mother read to me a lot. As a child I was hypnotized by the cadences and the rhythms of her voice. The sound of her reading has influenced my writing and I try to bring a sense of rhythm into my own writing. It was magical growing up in a household in which my mother, Edith Thacher Hurd, wrote children's books, and my father, Clement Hurd, illustrated them. At the same time, it was a normal average suburban childhood. I loved to go to my father's studio and watch him work, slowly making his way through each picture in a book. In their quiet way, I think they taught me much about how a picture book works.

"My all time favorite book is *Sailor Dog*, by Margaret Wise Brown, illustrated by Garth Williams. I also loved *Ukelele*, a Golden Book, *The Little Fur Family* by Margaret Wise Brown, and *Ole* by the Daulaires.

"My father was low-key and a wonderful man. He enjoyed the success of *Good Night Moon*, but didn't make a big deal of it. He died in 1988 so he didn't see all of the phenomenon that the book has become. It's my part-time job now, managing how it is taken care of in the world. Sometimes it can be a burden to have your father have illustrated *Good Night Moon*! But it also gives me the chance to be involved in wonderful projects, such as the *Goodnight Moon* video that HBO did in 2000."
Thacher Hurd

Perfect Pioneer

"When I came home from school I listened very carefully. If I heard the sound of typing I had to be very quiet. My father was upstairs in his office and he was writing books. Because I had to be quiet as a child, it forced me to read, do my own writing, or be outside. I used to run away with my dog every afternoon and go exploring. I grew up in Southern California and a huge canyon wrapped around the side of my parent's home. I also went to the beach everyday. And it was only a couple of hours to get to the desert.

"I liked the Laura Ingalls Wilder stories, because I think I would have made a perfect pioneer. The way she wrote it sounded so glamorous in a covered wagon. It didn't sound hard at all! I read *Little Women* and the Margaurite Henry horse stories."

Ginger Wadsworth

Clattering Keys

"My earliest memories are not of Mom's cooking but of clattering of typewriter keys. My mother, Jean Shirley, wrote for children in children's magazine in the 1950's and children's biographies and nonfiction in the 1960's. We moved a lot, and wherever we went, she sought out writers' groups. I was always around writers. In each new town, our first outing was to the public library. We checked out as many books as were allowed to take. As a young person, I regarded librarians as obstacles—intimidating women with rules that made no sense to me. Children could check out just six books; children could not read the six books and bring them back for more on the same day; children could not check out books from the adult collection. My favorite books were the Oz books, *The Secret Garden*, Laura Ingalls Wilder's *Little House* series and Maud Hart Lovelace's *Betsy-Tacy* series."

Angelica Carpenter

Another World

"Early on I read many of the staples: *Curious George, Mike Mulligan's Steam Shovel, The Five Chinese Brothers* (before it became non-politically correct). I liked these for their entertainment value, and learned their lessons without knowing I was learning. At some point I discovered the Land of Oz, and spent a lot of time there. This was a wonderful, magical place where the unlikely was commonplace, and the impossible just took a little more magic. Later, I moved on to the world of Tom Swift (Jr.) And found it to be a wonderful, scientific place where the unlikely was commonplace and the impossible just took a little more science. I always try to write books that I would have liked to read as a child, and that I still like to read as an adult."

Kevin Kiser

Just Like the Kids in Line for the next Harry Potter...

"When I was little my parents read the Golden Books to me. I loved them! When I read on my own, I still loved fairy tales and poetry, Robert Louis Stevenson

and Emily Dickinson, the *All of A-Kind-Family* books, *Spider Web for Two* and *Nancy Drew*. I couldn't wait for the latest *Nancy Drew* books. I'd go down to the local candy store, where they sold some books. I'd race down to get the next one!"
Marilyn Singer

Illicit Reading
"I loved to read the things my mother hid in the closet! *Gone with the Wind*, *Tobacco Road*. Books she thought I shouldn't read. I was supposed to be content with *Little Women* and *The Secret Garden* and doing my homework. But since my parents both worked during the day, they couldn't control my reading."
Beverly Gherman

Undercover Readers
"I can remember hiding from my mother so she couldn't find me reading. I often hid a flashlight under the covers so I could read after lights out. We moved a lot, so I didn't have friends until I was in the sixth grade. Books were my friends. I was especially fond of the Oz books and anything with magic in it."
Verla Kay

"As a child, I read constantly, sometimes ten to twelve books a week. But a favorite one was P.L. Travers' *Mary Poppins*. I remember reading it snuggled under the covers with a flashlight. I loved the imaginative fantasy and adventure."
Joanna H. Kraus

Emotional Connections
"Books were always very important in our house. I can remember exactly where I was when I read *The Little Mermaid*. I was in bed and I remember the house I lived in. I couldn't have been more than six. It was the saddest thing that ever happened to me! I just sobbed and sobbed! It made a tremendous impact on me.

"Only a few years ago, I realized that my brother and I had never been read to. However, our parents were readers, we were surrounded by books, we were all library users and it never occurred to us not to read."
Ruth Heller

"My three favorite books from childhood are *Go Dog Go*, *The Lorax*, and *Charlotte's Web*. The reason for *Charlotte's Web* was because it was the first book I ever read on my own that made me cry."
Bruce Balan

Books were Salvation
"*Charlie and the Chocolate Factory* saved my life! I was badly teased in fourth

grade and my teacher would read this book every day. It was incredible. It allowed me to go into another world."

Katie Davis

Magic Carpet Ride

"As a child I was addicted to reading. I read *Little Women* and *Heidi* and *Anne of Green Gables* over and over. And I'd sit up in our apricot tree and read fairy tales and off I would go on a Magic Carpet to that wonderful land where every thing came out Right with Truth and Justice for *all*.

"Actually, I think my mother thought my reading was a problem. Once she told me, 'Real people *do* things. They don't just read about them!'

"Mama was raised by Finnish parents and the only reading looked on with favor was the Bible. My grandfather was a tailor and worked at home. My aunt said he would have her sit by him while he worked and read aloud from the Finnish Bible.

"'He couldn't have been paying very good attention,' she said. 'I skipped some and he didn't notice.'"

Laura Leonard

There Were Good Readers . . .

"I liked Kipling's *Just So Stories*, his *Jungle Books*, *The Burgess Book of Animals*, *The Burgess Book of Birds*. My parents gave me *Heidi* when I had my tonsils out at four years old. I liked *Arabian Nights* and of course *Anne of Green Gables*. Like many writers, I was a good reader at a young age. For my tenth birthday I was given a box of ten adult books that included *Gone with the Wind*, *Keys to the Kingdom*, *Giant*, and books by Pearl Buck. My parents never censored my reading, nor did they direct me toward children's books when I wanted to read adult ones."

Connie Goldsmith

And Non-readers . . .

"I was pretty much a non-reader as a kid. I was taught strictly phrenetically. Phonetically I became a reader when I was twenty-three. My husband, Ed, watched my eyes and said, 'You don't read right.' I remember reading the Greek and Roman Myths and Augusta Hewell Seaman mysteries."

Ruth Radlauer

"I came from a non-reading family, so I don't have memories about reading."

Gary Soto

Way of Life

"I didn't know anything about poetry as a child. I came from a very poor background. My father left when I was twelve, and Mother, a single parent, had to raise three of us. Survival was more important. We didn't read. I was a poor student. I hated school, partly because we moved around so much. Poverty was my way of life—not poetry!"

Lee Bennett Hopkins

"I didn't read much, for fun as a child. I played with friends, or worked at my mother's beauty shop, or watched TV. I usually read only if I had to, for book reports, and I forgot the books as quickly as a I read them. I certainly never read poetry in my own spare time; I hated it. Or I thought I did, though in all fairness to poetry, I really didn't know enough poetry to hate it. I think what I hated was having to analyze and memorize a poem—and then forget it, mouth open, in front of everyone."

Janet Wong

Some Read Adult Books...

"I loved *Understood Betsy*. But I didn't read children's books for very long. By the time I was eight I read mostly adult books."

Ellen Jackson

And Those Who Got in Trouble for Reading

"I had a very poor childhood but we had a copy of *Treasure Island* in the house. I read it until I practically memorized it. I learned to write by the frying pan method. My grandmother, who raised me, would whack me on the head with one. She'd say, 'Auntie isn't feeling well. Cheer her up and write her a funny letter.' Whack! My grandmother also thought reading novels caused a condition called 'softening of the brain.' So she ordered me to read only nonfiction. I had to sneak any fiction reading. My sister and I would read with a flashlight under the bed covers. One day my grandmother caught me reading a book of short stories by Mark Twain. She grabbed it and tore it in half. I never saw it again."

Ed Radlauer

The Movie or the Book?

"My favorites were and still are *Harriet the Spy*, *The Egypt Game*, the Oz books, *Charlie and the Chocolate Factory*, *The Little Princess* and *The Secret Garden*. When I was a kid, my father worked for Walt and Roy Disney. My dad told me to be on the lookout for books that would make good movies. I recommended Zilpha Keatley Snyder's *The Egypt Game*, and the story people at Disney fell in love with it. They approached her, but she turned them down. That taught me two big lessons. First, that I had good taste in books, and second, that the most important thing isn't a movie. It's the book."

Gennifer Choldenko

Strong Women Characters

"I liked *Anne of Green Gables, Little Women, Pippi Longstocking,* and *Nancy Drew.*"

Cynthia Chin-Lee

Storytelling Is Literature

"When I was young, I felt hopeless and dumb. I could draw very well, but I was dyslexic. Not only was reading difficult for me, but my handwriting would mistranslate. I couldn't do math.

"My people were storytellers. My dad's people were from Ireland, my mom's from Russia. They relied on spoken stories to validate themselves. Storytelling was what I was used to. I do remember sitting on my mother's lap, my ear near her breast, while she read. Her voice washed through me. I became part of the story.

"As a cute little girl, I could 'read' the room. Feel the tension or the joy. There lies the horror of artists—we are *too* aware. It's heightened awareness that can bring wonderful things and grief."

Patricia Polacco

Memories

"I remember learning how to read from that big red book of *Dick and Jane* fame. It really was big, at about two feet by two feet when opened up. I especially loved books by E. Nesbit and Madeline L'Engle, but read anything and everything including the cereal box. As an adult, I went to the library in search of my favorite book from childhood, not remembering the title or the author's name, only the great pictures. Of course, that book turned out to be none other than *Where the Wild Things Are* by Maurice Sendak."

Eve Aldridge

Turn Off the TV

"I was born into a military family that was accustomed to relocating often. This gave me a taste of the nomadic lifestyle. I spent the bulk of my first five years in Kodiak Island, Alaska. It was a grand time for me, largely because there wasn't any television. When I explain this to children today, I'm met with shivers and quivers and gasps. When I explain it to their parents, these reactions are even more pronounced! But not having television meant that as a family, we read books aloud in the evenings and frequently created our own stories.

"One of my fondest childhood memories, is of a younger version of myself atop my Dad's shoulders as he sits in his overstuffed chair, an open book in his lap. My brother is at his feet, while my mother occupies a corner of the sofa. The story begins and, after awhile, the book passes to my mother and then to my brother. My very favorite story was *The House That Jack Built*. I loved how each part was connected to the next, and how the whole thing grew and grew. Both of my parents deserve medals for the countless times they read that story to me. Today I look back on it and wonder if that's why I'm always building or remodeling houses."

Larry Dane Brimner

Army Brat

"I was born in San Juan, Puerto Rico, and at the age of four, began the traveling life of an 'army brat,' as my family moved to Missouri, then to France when I was seven, and finally to California when I was ten. My parents read to me when I was too young to read on my own, so I've loved books from an early age. But I really discovered books when we moved to France and our TV didn't work! I began checking out books at the school library during the year and at the Army base library during the summer.

"My favorite reading spot was the living room window of our small apartment, three stories up, leaning back in a chair with my feet propped on the radiator. I'd read for hours after school and during the summer, and when I looked up to daydream about the story, I had the most incredible view, directly in front of me: The Cathedral of Toul, where Joan of Arc (my beloved heroine) was tried for witchcraft. We lived a mere two blocks away. Even as a child, I was in awe every time I gazed out that window.

"My favorite books were *The Secret Garden*, *The Island of the Blue Dolphins*, *Follow my Leader*, *The Little Witch*, and a series of biographies about famous women like Annie Oakley, (who I wanted to be), Amelia Earhart, (who I also wanted to be), Betsy Ross (I passed on sewing the flag), Mary Maples Dodge, Dolly Madison, Pocahontas, Sacagawea, and others. I also loved mysteries, ghost stories, and anything to do with witches."

Marisa Montes

"I grew up near Maji, a remote village in the southwest corner of Ethiopia, and my mother home-schooled my sisters and me for the early grades. She's the one who taught me how to read. But even before I could read, my life was full of books and stories—my dad is a mesmerizing storyteller and also would read the Bible to us almost every evening, so the rhythms of rich language were seeping into my brain at an early age. My mother was the grammarian of the family and the person who loved fiction. We didn't have a lot of books in Maji, but the ones we had, we read over and over again: *Black Beauty*, *Winnie the Pooh*, *Caddie Woodlawn*, *The Water Babies*, *Little Women*, various collections of fairy tales, and others.

"When I went to boarding school in Addis Ababa in the fourth grade, I had a library to use for the first time. What a wonder! I remember reading all of the Louisa May Alcott books and—I think—every other book in the fiction section...at least once. Growing up without television, I was an avid and enthusiastic reader

who loved being pulled into the worlds created by the authors of the books I pored over, but I never met an author, nor did my teachers talk much about authors, so I never thought specifically about the creative decision-making and agonies behind the words and stories."
Jane Kurtz

Series Popularity
"I loved the *Curious George* books, the *Freddy the Pig* series, the Edgar Eager books, and *Nancy Drew*."
Ellen Leroe

For the First Time...
"When we lived in San Francisco, Dad and I went for walks on weekends. He would tell me stories, so then I'd think of stories to tell him. I loved reading *Sherlock Holmes* and the tales of King Arthur. I read them over and over again. I was in fifth grade when I read Mark Twain's *Connecticut Yankee in King Arthur's Court*, and I liked it so much I didn't want to get to the end. It's the first time I realized that, although I could read the book again, I'd never again have that same sense of discovery."
Elaine Marie Alphin

Ahh...The Library...
"I'd walk home from school with my nose in a book. I even read the backs of cereal boxes. And I reread everything. One highlight of the week was our trip to the library. It's *still* a highlight of my week. My favorite books as a child were the *Trixie Belden* Mystery Series."
Kathryn Reiss

Which Books Have You Read?
"Some of my childhood favorites were Dr. Seuss's early books, *Eloise*, *Pippi Longstocking*, and toward the end of elementary school, the works of Mark Twain. Other favorite authors, like Roald Dahl and Madeleine L'Engle, were a little after my time, so I had to wait a few decades to discover them. I also remember a *Golden Book of Myths and Legends*, with stories I used to retell to my sister on long trips in the car."
Aaron Shepard

Babar, Thomas, Tottie and Harriet
"I loved *Babar*, *The House of Dies Drear*, *The Doll's House*, and *Harriet the Spy*."
Debra Keller

Read 'Em All!

"The world of Pooh by A.A. Milne, *The Wonderful Flight to the Mushroom Planet* by Eleanor Cameron, *Rusty's Space Ship* by Evelyn Sibley Lampman, *The Golden Books Family Treasury of Poetry*, edited by Louis Untermeyer, *Nancy Drew* books, *To Kill a Mockingbird* by Harper Lee, and anything and everything in the library!"

Debbie Duncan

"My favorite books were *The Cat in the Hat Comes Back* and *A Fly Went By*. Later, it was *Stuart Little*, *The Boxcar Children*, and *Caddie Woodlawn*. I also loved all those biographies about Dolly Madison, Betsy Ross, etc."

Susan Middleton Elya

"*Little Bear*, the books about Edith the Lonely Doll and Mr. Bear, the *Betsy* books, starting with *B is for Betsy*, anything by Eleanor Estes, especially *Pinky Pye* and *The Witch Family*, Edgar Eager and Elizabeth Enright."

Karen Romano Young

"My favorite books as a child were the Andrew Lang fairy tale books, anything Arthurian, and all the dog and horse books I could find."

Jane Yolen

Remember the Read Alouds

"My favorite books as a child were the ones my mother read to me: *Mother Goose*, *A Child's Garden of Verse* by Robert Louis Stevenson, *When We Were Very Young*, *Now We are Six*,by A. A. Milne, nonviolent fairy tales and bedtime stories. As a youngster, I was too busy doing things (work and play) to have time to read about other kids doing them. As I grew older, I was a serious student but did not spend leisure time reading. Learning new things has always been a delight for me. I loved all of Louisa May Alcott's books."

Joy N. Hulme

Will the Real Nancy Drew Please Stand

"My favorites were *Little Toot*, *Alice in Wonderland* & *Alice Through the Looking Glass*, *Black Beauty*, *Call of the Wild*, *Nancy Drew*, (I WAS Nancy Drew), *Lorna Doone*, *The Prince and the Pauper*, *Little Lord Fautleroy*."

Tricia Gardella

Millions and Trillions and Billions . . .

"My childhood favorites were *The Poky Little Puppy* and *Millions of Cats*. I also spent hours studying the intricate illustrations in a fairy tale book I owned."

Betsy Franco

Old Reliables

"The best-known books that I remember loving were *The Secret Garden, The Phantom Tollbooth,* and anything by Mark Twain. Most of the individual titles I can remember are fairly obscure now—*The Red Feather* by Marjorie Fischer, *The Diamond in the Window* by Jane Langton, and *Journey to the Mushroom Planet* by Eleanor Cameron."

Ann Manheimer

How Many Favorites Do You Recognize?

"My favorite books were *And To Think That I Saw It On Mulberry Street, On Beyond Zebra, Charlotte's Web,* and *The Jungle Book.* I loved books about animals and books that rhymed."

Deborah Lee Rose

"I loved *Winnie the Pooh* by A. A. Milne, *Charlotte's Web* by E.B. White, *Put Me in the Zoo* by Robert Lopshire, anything by Dr. Seuss, *A Cricket in Times Square* (and its sequels) by George Selden."

Linda Kay Weber

"At first, I loved the series about the little twins who lived in foreign lands and did interesting things. Later on, I discovered *Little Women,* Clara Barton's biography, *Hans Brinker and The Silver Skates,* Dickens' *A Christmas Carol* and *Caddie Woodlawn.*"

Kathy Pelta

"The books that I remember loving as a child were the *Oz* books by Frank Baum, *The Rootabaga Stories* by Carl Sandburg, and *The Just So Stories* by Rudyard Kipling. I discovered poetry early because my dad read it to me. I loved it, but in no way did I exalt it, thinking that I wished to be a poet. In particular, I remember my dad read me *Archy and Mehitabel* by Don Marquis and Rudyard Kipling's *Poetry about War and Battle,* especially 'Gunga Din.' "

David Greenberg

"The Childcraft Library series, *Nancy Drew* books, *Treasure Island, Call it Courage, The Black Stallion, Island of the Blue Dolphins, The Secret Language* by Ursula Nordstrom, and *Tanglewood Tales* by Nathaniel Hawthorne."

Diane Matcheck

Funny You Should Mention . . .

"My favorite books as a child included the series books that were popular at the time. Especially the mysteries: *Hardy Boys, Nancy Drew, Mad Scientist Club,*

Encyclopedia Brown. But generally, I liked books that tempered a protagonist's struggle with humor. Humor can make all the difference between a book being poignant and a book being depressing. I also remember disliking books that had lengthy, flowery descriptions. Now I appreciate the prose, but as a child, I didn't have the patience."

Wendelin Van Draanen

Locked Out!

"I was a terrible student and all I did was read. When I was in the second grade, there was a wooden structure like a boat, on the school's playground. I read in there during recess. One day, I closed my book after everyone else had left the playground. The gates were locked and I had to scale the fence! I read *A Wrinkle in Time* a dozen times. I loved Zelpha Keatley Snyder's *Eyes on the Fishbowl*, and a book called *Black and Blue Magic.* When I was older, I loved big, juicy, romantic adventure books like *Jane Eyre, David Copperfield* and *The Scarlet Pimpernel.* I liked strong, narrative first person voices."

Franny Billingsley

On the Wild Side

"My summers were spent at a small camp in Northern Wisconsin. That's really where my love of nature and wildlife began. As a child, I had no intention of being a writer. It was the last thing on my mind! I majored in art in college, and later spent a number of years exhibiting, teaching, and basically being an artist."

Caroline Arnold

"Growing up, three of my four parents were biologists and they were always introducing me to the many wonderful creatures they came in contact with. My first love was snakes and I caught and kept many of them as a boy. I started reading Dr. Seuss books a lot and then the *Hardy Boys,* but there wasn't the wealth of middle grade and young adult books we have today. So by age nine and ten, I was pretty much reading adult novels. My first was *The Hobbit,* which is still one of my favorites."

Sneed B. Collard III

"I read almost all the available children's books in the library. My favorites were stories about animals including *Black Beauty* and *Beautiful Joe.* Studying the bird pictures in *Traveling With the Birds* by Rudyerd Boulton was a favorite pastime. I tried to match the pictures with the birds that perched on birdfeeders hanging outside a bedroom window. It was a difficult task since most of the birds in the book weren't native to Oregon where I lived."

Tekla White

Life Imitates Art

"I loved to make characters out of clay, paper, walnut shells. I built their environments, and I'd create a mural that would be their whole world. Over the years this type of imaginative activity got translated into making books. Now I'm still making characters, but instead of a dollhouse as a medium, I have a book.

"As a child, I loved *The Color Kittens*, Dr. Seuss with his weird architecture. I could get lost in those pictures! I loved *Eloise*, *Blueberries for Sal*. *One Morning in Maine*, for it's sweetness with a little sadness and loss. As an older child, I loved the Little House books. My very favorite book was and still is, *Charlotte's Web*. It has love, death, loss and rebirth."

Elisa Kleven

The Importance of Place

"Sometimes I think of the home I grew up in as a collection of my favorite places to read—on the front lawn, or on the living room rug with the sun coming through the plate glass window, on the screened-in porch when it was hot, or in the recliner next to the built-in bookshelves. A few favorites: *Little Women*, *Little Men*, and *Eight Cousins*, by Louisa May Alcott; the *Betsy-Tacy* books by Maud Hart Lovelace, and many historical novels. My all-time favorite is *The Witch of Blackbird Pond*, by Elizabeth George Speare, which I still reread every once in awhile because I love it so much. Of course, I also read series books like *Nancy Drew* and *Trixie Belden*."

Katherine Sturtevant

Reading Recipe

"I loved reading. It was my favorite thing to do on a rainy day. I used to fry Rice Krispies in butter and put salt on them. I'd lay on my bed and eat the Rice Krispies like popcorn and read a book. I've always associated laying on my bed with writing. That's how I write now."

Jacque Hall

Freedom to Read

"My mother read to me any time I wanted. I loved stories about Baba Yaga, Mary Poppins, and my favorite was *The Three Kittens*—they colored the town."

Teri Sloat

Like Father like Daughter

"I was one of those little four-year-olds who was drawing all the time. My dad was a watercolor painter. My family was artistic. My favorites in books were based on the pictures. Robert McClosky's *Blueberries for Sal* and *Make Way for Ducklings*, Garth Williams' *Charlotte's Web*. *The Tall Book of Make Believe*, which was a collection of poems and stories that Garth illustrated in color. The pictures tied it all together and made it into a whole experience.

"I also enjoyed my dad's books. They were in German, so I couldn't read them, but I *could* tell what was happening because of the pictures. I traced some of those drawings as a child."

Ashley Wolff

Exploring

"We had two sets of encyclopedias when I was a child; quite a luxury for my modest family, but my parents always made books a priority. One of the encyclopedia sets was meant for children and had all kinds of wonderful illustrations in them. I used to love to pull out a volume at random, open it, and find all sorts of new treasures and unknown worlds to explore. In terms of fiction, I loved all of my Little Golden Books. There is something wonderful about owning your own book and reading it over and over again, and at twenty-five cents, Golden Books were affordable to everyone. I still proudly display my original copy of *The Christmas Puppy* in my living room. When I got older I fell in love with *A Tree Grows in Brooklyn*, all the sagas of Pearl S. Buck, and of course, *The Outsiders*, which made me determined to be a writer."

Mary Pearson

Red Read

"*Anne of Green Gables* was a big favorite since I had long red hair, worn in braids, and people said I looked like Anne. I learned a lot about writing from those books. I vividly remember the love/hate relationship between Anne and Gilbert, and how it drew me in emotionally and made me keep reading.

"Other favorites: I loved ordering books from the Arrow Book Club. I could not sit still on those days when the big box from Scholastic arrived. It was never opened until the end of the day, which was excruciating! Favorites: The *Danny Dunn* books, *Miss Pickerel*, *Pippi Longstockings*, and joke books. And I love the fact that my own books have since been selections in the Arrow Book Club.

"I didn't discover my fantasy favorites until I was in my early twenties: the *Chronicles of Narnia*, the *Prydain Chronicles*, and *The Hobbit*. They were the books that influenced me the most as a writer, and are the reason I wrote *Princess Nevermore*."

Dian Curtis Regan

Reading Martyr

"My number one favorite book, which I remember reading over and over, was *A Little Princess* by Frances Hodgson Burnett. I used to sit under the plum tree in our back yard with a little piece of bread and pretend that I was Sara and starving, and all I had to eat in the world was this one little bun! My piece of bread! Even then I had quite an imagination.

"I also loved the *Oz* books by L. Frank Baum. I read all of them several times and wished there were more. For my birthday and Christmas each year, my godparents used to give me children's versions of the classics, so, thanks to them, I discovered Robert Louis Stevenson's *A Child's Garden of Verses* and *Treasure Island*, and Mark Twain's *The Adventures of Tom Sawyer*. Oh, how I wanted to have adventures, too! I loved books that transported me to a world different from my own."

Maureen Boyd Biro

Anywhere, any time . . .

"I read constantly, everything and everywhere: at school—when everyone else was doing math or geography, under the covers with a flashlight late at night, in a tree, on the couch, in the bathtub, walking home from the library, at other kids' houses, on the beach, on trains. But not in cars—to this day I feel queasy reading a map in a moving vehicle. Some of my favorites were the Pooh books by A.A. Milne, *Lassie Come Home* by Eric Knight, the *Sunnybank Farm* stories by Alfred Payson Terhune, *Tom Sawyer*, *Huck Finn*, *Anne of Green Gables*, *The Secret Garden*, *The Little Princess*, the *Moffat books* by Eleanor Estes, the *Melendy family* books by Elizabeth Enright, *Sherlock Holmes*, and yes of course—*Nancy Drew*, the *Hardy Boys*, and comic books (including Classic Comics)."

Mary Downing Hahn

Whatever You Do, Don't Read This!

"My favorite books were the *Nancy Drew* mysteries—all I could get my hands on. Perhaps I was so excited about them since they were hard to get in my town. The children's librarian allowed just a few on her shelves and told my mother that she did not consider them 'good literature for young people.' I borrowed from friends, received a few as birthday gifts and re-read all of them."

Caryn Yacowitz

Dick and Jane vs. Dr. Seuss

"I must have been an okay reader in school. I can remember in first grade when my teacher made me a word helper. Here's how it worked. The class would read silently from *Dick and Jane* books. If someone needed help with a word, they raised their hand. Back then, in 1954, students had their own small desks, arranged in tidy rows. When I saw hands up, I would scurry up and down the rows helping classmates to identify words. The words weren't much fun in those schoolbooks, but I felt pretty good about being a helper.

"Home is where I discovered real reading. I could read alone or Mom would read aloud. We couldn't afford to own many books, but I do remember having a couple of Dr. Seuss books or maybe I had brought them from the library. Great stuff! Not at all like *Dick and Jane*. Reading Dr. Seuss was amazing because his words were fun! But his books also helped me realize that reading isn't just about words. Reading is about imagination. The words are only a doorway. Reading is about getting inside the words and into magical, fantastical places. Reading is about meeting unusual characters and wild creatures that somehow live within the words. And that's fun!"

Tedd Arnold

Cover Girl

"I was fortunate to always be surrounded by books and parents who read. My father had owned a second hand bookstore before I was born. He sold the shop but kept most of the books and the walls of our apartment were lined with shelves. Both my parents and my grandmother, who lived with us, read to me and I vividly remember joining the public library that was just a short walk from our apartment.

"My favorite books were *The Betsy-Tacy* series by Maud Hart Lovelace. Imagine the thrill when a year ago a new edition of one of these titles, *Betsy and Tacy Go Downtown*, was published with an introduction that I wrote and my name on the cover of the book. That was something I could never have possibly imagined. Other favorites were *The Little House* books by Laura Ingalls Wilder and *Heidi* by Johanna Spyri."

Johanna Hurwitz

No Girly Girl

"I was a real tom boy as a kid. I grew up reading lots of science fiction, horror, and adventure stories, probably because that's what my dad and my friends, who were almost all boys, read. Also, that's what was most readily available in the town where I grew up in the 1950's. The public library was very limited, and there were no bookstores. Most of the books I read could be purchased at drugstores or variety stores. But I had—and still have—a genuine affection for the genres I mentioned above. I particularly adored the work of Ray Bradbury, Edgar Allen Poe, and Saki as well as Edgar Rice Burroughs. I also read pretty much the entire *Tom Corbett Space Cadet* series, and of course, *Tom Swift*. Also *Nancy Drew* and *The Bobbsey Twins*."

Nancy Etchemendy

Sweet Tooth

"When I was growing up, the things I read most were comic books. Archie Comics. They were wonderful. I got rotten teeth from eating candy bars and reading two or three comic books at a time!"

Angela Johnson

Siblings Led the Way

"I was the youngest of four children and I was much younger than my siblings. I tended to read what they were reading. I remember enjoying *Pinocchio* and *Heidi*."

Bernard Waber

Quirky Career Choice...

"As a child I loved to read all of the animal stories, like *Lassie Come Home*, *Where the Red Fern Grows*, and *My Friend Flicka*. When I was little I thought I'd think of names for paint colors or nail polishes when I grew up. I thought it would be a great job! Imagine! Getting paid for being creative. I thought nothing could be better."

Margaret O'Hair

Timeless Treasures

"I didn't grow up in a family of readers, so as a result, there weren't a lot of books in the house. I remember my grandparents reading the newspaper. I didn't own a lot of books of my own, but there was a used bookstore downtown and the owner didn't mind this kid coming in and reading his books without buying any. Of course there weren't any kids' books there, so I grew up on adult books. What I loved were the really old ones. The story didn't matter as much as the FEEL of the book. To see the copyright and know that it was over a hundred years old. I read a lot of poetry by people I can't remember. The one children's book I remember checking out from the library over and over again was *The Five Little Peppers and How They Grew*."

Susan Taylor Brown

Fortune Teller

"My favorite books as a child were *Charlie and the Chocolate Factory*, *The Lord of the Rings* trilogy, *Watership Down* and *Jonathan Livingston Seagull*. I knew from the time I was young that I would be involved in some creative field, either writing, music or art. Writing just emerged, over time, as the overriding passion."

Neal Shusterman

Gives you Goosebumps

"I read comic books and the entire shelf of fairy tales from my school library. I read the Norse legends, Greek myths and fantasy. When I was nine or ten I discovered science fiction. Ray Bradbury's stories changed my life. I met Ray Bradbury, and he said, 'All of my books have become children's books.' He was surprised. The scariest book I ever read was his *Something Wicked This Way Comes*. It's a terrifying book about two boys in the Midwest who sneak out of the house to go to a weird carnival."

R. L. Stine

Abracadabra

"I loved *all* books when I was little. Those little bug-marks were words? *Really*? And the words accumulated into stories? Pure magic."
Kathleen Duey

Read at your own risk...

"I cut my teeth, well, not literally, on the Lucy Crane and Marian Edwardes version of *Grimm's Fairy Tales*, illustrated by Fritz Kredel. Then I read every book that had a skull and crossbones sticker on the spine in the children's room of the Lucius Beebe Memorial Library in Wakefield, Massachusetts. Later, I wore the covers off the library copies of *The Secret Pencil* by Patricia Ward and *Wrinkle in Time* by Madeline L'Engle."
Alexis O'Neill

Picture Stories

"I was an only child, and I had to learn to amuse myself. From the first through the third grade, we lived near a sculpture garden. I became acquainted with the sculptress and she gave me books and encouragement.

"Looking back on it, these years were the ones I still look to when doing picture book work. What I noticed for the first time in a book, and really liked in *Sailor Dog*, by Margaret Wise Brown and illustrated by Garth Williams, was the way the words and pictures each told half the story. One didn't work without the other. As for *Wind in the Willows*, Shepherd's drawings in wonderful black and white really got to me, too. You didn't always need color."
R.W. Alley

Write from the Heart

"I loved so many books, the titles I think of at any given moment depend on the mood I'm in. The ones that come to mind today are the Mary Poppins books, *Little Women* (Laurie was my first crush), *The Wolves of Willoughby Chase* (which made my heart race)and *The Island of the Blue Dolphins*. (which made my heart ache.) *Tales of a Fourth Grade Nothing* never failed to make me smile."
Haemi Balgassi

Thirty-Two Nancy Drew

"*Mary Poppins*, *The Yearling*, *Nancy Drew* (I had thirty-two of those), *Little Women*. Also *Plastic* Man and *Little Lulu* comic books."
Alice Schertle

Calling all Genres!

"Around the house we had lots of Little Golden Books and inexpensive editions of classics. The first book I can remember reading is Robert Louis Stevenson's *A Child's Garden of Verses*, illustrated by Alice and Martin Provensen. Later favorites included historical fiction (Laura Ingalls Wilder; Elizabeth Speare's *Calico Captive* or *The Witch of Blackbird Pond*), biography (the Landmark Books series on people like Helen Keller, Elizabeth Blackwell, Susan B. Anthony; anything on queens), mysteries (the Famous Five series by Enid Blyton was thrilling), romance (Mary Stolz, Betty Cavanna), adventure (Scott O'Dell's *Island of the Blue Dolphins*), fun books like Louise Fitzhugh's *Harriet the Spy* and Astrid Lindgren's *Pippi Longstocking*. Above all, fantasy—especially Edward Eager's magical books and Carol Kendall's. I would have adored the Harry Potter books."

Kathleen Krull

Doodle All Day

"Books I liked: *Peter Pan*, *Davy Crockett*, *'Twas the Night Before Christmas*, *Mr. Fix-It*. Mostly I was a doodler—not a reader."

Paul Brewer

Love Affair to Scary Stuff

Freddy the Detective started my love of mysteries. I was eight or nine years old and fell in love with *Freddy the Pig*. From there I went straight to *Nancy Drew* and her clones. I wrote an interactive mystery for my neighborhood friends, but I guess I made the story *too* scary—they wouldn't come out and play after a while . . ."

Penny Warner

Undercover Picture Books

"As a child, my absolute favorite books were comic books and picture books of all kinds. From the very beginning, I was attracted to the marriage of text and illustrations. I taught myself to read and, according to my mom, when I finished reading my first picture book at the age of five, I closed it and calmly said, 'I'm going to write one of these someday.' My fascination with picture books continued into high school; where I would read novels in front of my friends, but sneak back to the grade school library during lunch hour to catch up on the latest picture books."

SuAnn Kiser

Skip to My Lou

"*The Gingerbread Man* and well-known fairy tales bring back some of the fondest memories of younger days. As I got a little older, some of my favorite books were *Heidi*, *Little Women*, *Treasure Island*, *Pippi Longstocking*, and the *Nancy Drew* Mystery series. I also loved *The Diary of Anne Frank*, and I had a fascination with nurses; read biographies of Clara Barton and Florence Nightingale more times than

I care to count. I don't remember reading poetry, but favorite nursery rhymes and jump rope chants were the poems I recited over and over again."

Rebecca Kai Dotlich

Lights! Camera! Action!

"I loved reading *and* movies as a child. I went to movies every Saturday and I was a big reader. As a small child, my favorite book was *The 500 Hats of Bartholomew Cubbins* by Dr. Seuss. I read all the classics, the series about *Nancy Drew*, the *Hardy Boys* and all of the *Oz* books. I loved *Anne of Green Gables* and *The Secret Garden*. The genre of young adult fiction was brand new when I was young, so I read adult books. I did read Beverly Cleary's *Fifteen* and it transformed my life! It was the first book I encountered about a teenager for teenagers.

"As far as movies, *The Blob* was the scariest! I remember that vividly. I also loved the Disney animated classics, like *Dumbo* and the sweeping epics, like *From Here to Eternity.*"

Lin Oliver

Storytelling Tradition

"When I was growing up, I never knew that my grandfather couldn't read. He was a functional illiterate who was much too proud to sign his name with an 'X.' He taught himself how to write his name and read road signs. And, he surrounded himself with books, magazines and newspapers. He loved holding the Bible and had memorized Scripture.

"My grandparents encouraged me to read. Daddy James (my grandfather) often had me read out loud to him. Imagine an adult willing to listen to a child stumble through *The Little Red Hen* and *Dick and Jane*! I was thrilled, because he was always attentive. I thought children read to adults in most families. I didn't know until later it was generally the other way around.

"Storytelling was part of my grandfather the way reading was part of me. I read him stories, and he told me stories. My grandmother told ghost stories and my grandfather told stories with my brother, sister and me as main characters."

Patricia McKissack

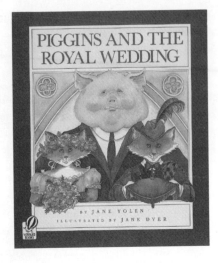

Featuring Jane Yolen

Jane Yolen has written every kind of children's book imaginable, and has won numerous awards. Her titles include *How Do Dinosaurs Say Goodnight?*, *Owl Moon*, *A Novel of Mary Queen of Scots*, *Encounter*, *Wizard's Hall* and *The Emperor and the Kite*. She has a B.A. from Smith College, an M.Ed. from the University of Massachusetts, and has completed her course work for a doctorate in children's literature at this university. She has been an editor of her own imprints and has taught children's literature and writing for children at colleges and writers' conferences.

Songwriter. Novelist. Poet. Teacher. Editor. Author of more than 200 books for children. Anyone who sees your accomplishments would be overwhelmed.

"This week I got four rejections from four literary magazines, one from *Scope*, a magazine for children, one from an editor turning down two picture books, and a possibility with a series I have, they may not take on the third book. It is important to know just because someone sounds overwhelmingly successful, it's still an everyday struggle."

How have you remained so versatile?

"I have a low threshold for boredom! The idea of writing the same thing—what Jo Rowling is doing—would drive me crazy. A big book on the same subject with basically the same plot. Locked into this. You might as well be working in a factory."

Let's talk about your book with Bruce Coville, **Armageddon Summer.** *How did that book come about?*

"It was my idea. I had an idea for a book about cults. Not a Jim Jones cult. I'm fascinated by well-meaning people in crazy cults. For some, the cult really *does* save them; for others it is absolutely the wrong place to be. I had the idea for a long time but I didn't know if I had the skills to do it. I kept putting it off. Then one day, I was in the shower, and I thought I'd ask Bruce. Of course he says I said, 'Bruce, I was in the shower and thinking of you.' But that's not true! That shows the differences between our senses of humor. Collaborating."

Would you discuss your experience with collaboration?

"There are many routes to collaboration. I've written short stories with one of my sons, a short story with my husband, stories with my daughter and many other projects. The questions that arise are all the same. The process and the way to solve them is different. One of the questions is always *who gets the last cut? Whose name goes first? How hard can I come down on my co-writer?* This is especially difficult if you are a mother of or married to your co-writer. In Bruce's case, we're best friends. But with Bruce, we are both on a similar path. We're both well-known writers. Those problems collaborating with him are different than when I collaborated with my daughter on her first books. One of the reasons is that *Armageddon Summer* is told in two voices. I think subconsciously, it was a way of getting rid of the problem of ego and final cut. We both had final cuts on our own pieces.

"My name went first, since the book was my idea. It might have been better to have his name first, since shelving, 'c' is better than 'y.' [Editor's Note: The Y books are often placed on the bottom shelves in bookstores and libraries.]

"Bruce loves to plot. I like to start off with a character and see where it will grow. He kept saying, 'We gotta plot.' Books that are adventure quest stories need to be tightly plotted. If you're writing a character novel, you don't need to sit down and plot.

"There was a period of five days when we'd done more than half the book, when he stayed in my house. We set up his computer downstairs and I worked in the attic. We ran chapters back and forth; we worked fourteen-hour days. It was intense! We stopped for food and to take walks. We didn't even make polite conversation. My husband was away. All Bruce and I talked about was this book. We felt like wet noodles at the end of five days. Although we didn't finish the whole book, we knew where it was going. It was exhausting and exhilarating! But if you have a bad heart, don't try this at home!"

The character Marina, in Armageddon Summer, *thinks a lot about her birthday, which has special meaning in this particular book. She sees the night as dark as chocolate cake with candles made of flickering stars. Do similes and metaphors come easily to you? How can authors learn to evoke poetic language in their novels?*

"I began as a poet. Even as a child, I wrote verse. In high school and college I thought of myself as a poet for the heart, and a journalist to make money. I've always thought in metaphor. Since the character of Marina was an Emily Dickinson nut, I was reading a lot of Emily to find the right poems and references. The more you read while you're writing, the more those metaphors rise up."

In Encounter, *you tell the story of Columbus through the eyes of a Taino boy. Did the point of view for this story come first?*

"Actually an editor called me up and said, 'In three years, the five hundredth anniversary of Columbus is coming up. I'm tired of Columbus sailed the ocean blue. Shouldn't we do a book in the Indian's point of view?' I said, 'Get someone from the Taino culture. But let me do some reading tonight and I'll call you tomorrow to point you in the right direction.'

"As I read, I discovered that fifty years after Columbus had landed, there were very few Taino people left. This population couldn't sustain itself. Some people in Puerto Rico have Taino blood, but to find a full-blooded Taino person was probably not possible. I knew that a Plains Indian or a Cherokee or any other Native American would probably not be able to tell the story with any more authority than I—if I did my research well enough. So I told the editor I'd do it, but we should get a native person, perhaps, to do the pictures. However, we never found the right one for the book. Then one day I was in an art gallery and saw David Shannon's work. He had a wonderful sense of place, which I felt we needed for this book."

In King Long Shanks, *your hilarious frog version of "The Emperor's New Clothes," did you think of the fairy tale and ask yourself, how can I make a twist on this?*

"I was talking to Vicki [Victoria Chess, the illustrator] on the phone. She said she always wanted to do a frog version of this story, because she could make him naked and no one would care! She asked me if I would write it and I said sure. Mainly, because we both wanted to see naked frogs!"

You also write rhyme—something that doesn't come easily for many people. What helpful suggestions can you make to other writers who would like to write rhyme?

"Read rhyme out loud. Better yet, get someone *else* to read it out loud. Read Mary Ann Doberman aloud. Don't try to be Dr. Seuss. Only Dr. Seuss can be Dr. Seuss. Read David McCord. Impeccable rhyme. If you read them out loud, you begin to understand the depth."

I love your Piggins mysteries. And advice for humor or mystery writers?

"Piggins was turned down by the first five publishers. Some said you can't do mysteries for that age child, or they didn't like Jane Dyers' pictures. That was her first trade book. We put it together, which is not the way one should do it! But sometimes you get a hold of an idea, even if people tell you *don't* do it, you won't know if you haven't tried! Don't stop things. It's just harder to find the right editor for something that is breaking the mold."

Many editors declare they are looking for a unique voice. How would you uncover the "story's voice" as you've described it?

"Listen. It's easy to impose your own voice on the story. Take time and get *in* there. Each story has its own color and sound. Find the right one. Sometimes you write the whole thing and you have to redo it. Sometimes you'll find something absolutely new.

"For years, I tried to write a little book called *Eeenie, Meinie, Mo.* First I wrote it in rhyme. One day I dropped the rhyme and found the metaphoric voice. When that happened it elevated the book and gave me the character of Eeenie in a way that I hadn't had a character before. But it took me ten years, from the time I started writing that dismal little rhyme, for the time I found the voice that let me see her.

"Take a story and put it in rhythmic lines. When I taught, I'd tell my picture book students to write their book as though it were a tone poem. Break it up into small breath spaces; write it down that way. You'll find all of the stuff you can throw out. You'll find moments of beauty you want to linger on. Other moments may be flat and dull. It's a trick that works! You don't have to leave it in the poetry form, you can turn it back to prose. The best writers of picture books are unconsciously writing the lyric line as if it were a poem. I remember Patty MacLachlan said she couldn't write poetry. But she *is* writing poetry. She just doesn't *call* it poetry. Fool the eye. Set it down as a poem. It makes you look at each small line, each individual breath space that's just taking up room."

Book Reviews

So There!
"Of my book, *Motorcycle Mania*, one reviewer said, 'This mindless book doesn't belong on a library's bookshelf.' It sold a quarter of a million copies."
Ed Radlauer

Light the Fire?
Apparently there is an association of vampire lit people. Someone found my book, *The Night of the Vampire Kitty*, and ordered it from Amazon. The review said, "This book ought to be burned, and so should the author!"
Stephen Mooser

Pay Back?
"For the most part, the journals that really love books have come out with good reviews. But one of my first reviews for *Hidden Talents* was so unbelievably meanspirited the only explanation I could come up with was that I had beaten up this person in high school and had forgotten about it. Or perhaps some critics just weren't sure how to respond to a book that devoted a whole chapter to setting up what I believe to be the largest lit fart in the annals of kids' books."
David Lubar

Sales Plummet?
"In the middle of an overall good review, a reviewer made a snide comment about one of my early books. I felt, there went a third of my book sales!"
Joan Holub

Disinfectant Please
"One interesting review I had was for a book called *Love and Kisses*. The text

is actually a round, with the message that love sent out always comes back; a girl kisses a cat, the cat kisses a cow and so on, until the cat comes back to kiss the girl. An English reviewer, hopefully tongue-in-cheek, referred to all this as 'very unsanitary practices' between animals and children!"

Sarah Wilson

READ THE GOOD STUFF

"A bad review is the another form of rejection. I don't read them and I don't believe them. However, I have no problem believing anything good said about me, my work, and my highly evolved sense of fashion."

Katie Davis

Mrs. to You

"My first, wonderful editor advised me never to respond to reviews. Then a review made her so angry that she wrote to the editor of the journal! The reviewer had criticized our book, *Frances Hodgson Burnett*, for calling the author by her first name. This practice was demeaning to women, they felt. Our editor responded with a heartfelt defense of our book (we called the author and her immediate family, men and women alike, all by first names) and of our publisher's non-sexist philosophy."

Angelica Carpenter

Squeaky Clean

"*The Beetle and Me* was included in a 'Squeaky Clean' list for young adults, which I find depressing. Not because I wanted it to be seen differently, but because someone perceived the need for such a list."

Karen Romano Young

Censorship

The Wizard of Oz, The American Heritage Dictionary The Diary of Anne Frank, along with books by Bruce Coville, Karen Cushman, Patricia Polacco, Zilpha Keatley Snyder, Gary Soto, and Jane Yolen, have all been declared unfit for school and library bookshelves by censors.

Jane Yolen's book about the Holocaust, *Briar Rose*, has been burned in Missouri by a pastor and his believers. Why did the censors object? Her book contains a gay character.

Bruce Coville's *Jeremy Thatcher, Dragon Hatcher* was taken off the shelves in Iowa for supposed satanic content. Why? The dragon ate chicken livers and Coville employed the colors red, black, silver and green.

All over the country, a wide-diversity of books is being challenged. Here are some anecdotes of how censorship has touched authors.

Disappearing Invitation

After a private school invited me to speak to their students, the principal had to call and *un*invite me. When I asked why they changed their minds, she explained that *Wish Magic*, the title of one of my books, was objectionable to them. Evidently the word 'magic' nixed my visit.

Elizabeth Koehler-Pentacoff

Dialect and the Supernatural

"*Mirandy and Brother Wind* and *Flossie and the Fox* have been censored for the use of dialect. *The Dark Thirty: Southern Tales of the Supernatural* has been banned because of supernatural elements in the stories. It is amusing to me that many of the people who criticize my use of African American dialect would think nothing of allowing children to read Burns, Riley, or Faulkner. All three authors used regional or ethnic dialects. My grandfather spoke in a rural Southern dialect that has its own rhythm and beauty. I see nothing wrong in it's use. I will continue to use 'his language' whenever it fits the story I'm writing.

"Besides, banned books are often the ones most read. Children, by nature, are rebellious. As soon as a book is banned that makes that book much more appealing to them and they become bound and determined to read it. I recommend that we teach children to make good choices and there wouldn't be a need to ban books. In our house, if a book contained information that was not in keeping with our values and beliefs, we shared that book with our children and we talked about it. As a parent who writes, it's been helpful to be a good listener as well as a writer."

Patricia McKissack

Monsters and Ghouls

"In Virginia, a principal told me not to bring my book, *Monster Mania*, which was about movie monsters. He said, 'The last author we had talked about ghosts. The school board refused to pay her and told her not to come back!'"

Ed Radlauer

"I wrote a series called the *Creepy Creature Club*. There was pressure put on libraries not to carry them and not to use them in the classroom. I spoke at one school in Mobile, Alabama. A couple of parents asked to excuse their kids. So they had to stand outside the room. It was unfair—the kids were singled out as being different.

Stephen Mooser

"A few years ago, I was invited to speak at schools and at a young authors' conference in a southern state. When I arrived, the coordinating librarian informed me that some of the teachers were boycotting the conference because they objected—not to any of my books—but to the *titles* because they contained the words 'ghost,' 'zombie,' 'monster,' and 'vampire.'"

Dian Curtis Regan

Pro Parent

"I had a nasty letter from a parent regarding *101 Ways to Bug Your Parents*. One father wrote and said,

"'How dare you encourage that behavior. I'm appalled my daughter was allowed to buy this book (through the Scholastic Books Fair). This book should be banned!'

"I wrote back and said, 'Sir, if you'd taken the time to read the book, you would have found the book is pro-parent and kids in the story learn bugging parents is not an appropriate way to deal with them. If you're having trouble with your daughter, here's what I recommend. Why don't the two of you read it every night for ten minutes before bed. Talk about the funny things and why certain things bother you. Communicate with each other!'

"He took my advice, and later wrote back apologizing, saying things were much better between the two of them, and that he actually found the book amusing. To his surprise, it also subtly taught valuable lessons. So I defused the situation. Parents need a sense of humor!

Lee Wardlaw

Pregnancy and Family Values

"A woman and her daughter picketed a school in Kansas, demanding *Dorrie's Book* be removed because they said the book showed bad family values. In that book, a family has triplets and I described the mother's pregnancy in detail. I thought it was a mild book. The principal and school board read the book and decided that the book was not offensive so they kept the book on the shelf."

Marilyn Sachs

Talking Animals and First Aid?

"In the South, *Charlotte's Web* has been censored. They say it's satanic to have animals talk. And Charlotte had children and she wasn't married. One librarian used white-out and bandaids to make diapers on the little boy in *In the Night Kitchen* by Maurice Sendak. She said, 'You just can't have children looking at this!' This same librarian used black felt-tip marker to black-out the breasts in Doris Gates' book on Greek goddesses."

Deborah Norse Lattimore

Take it as a Compliment!

"I wrote a book on evolution and received a letter complaining about it from someone in the Religious Right. Rather than being depressed about it, I was quite thrilled!"

Ellen Jackson

Celebrate Diversity

"We've got to teach children to respect each other. We need to show them *all* of the holidays. Celebrate lots of days! Otherwise children will pull into enemy camps, because they haven't been able to learn and experience each other. I worry that interest groups—one family—can walk into an elementary school and tell the principal they'll sue if a book isn't removed from the library shelves or if a holiday celebration at school conflicts with their beliefs. So the principal has to back down.

"My father was a born again Christian. It's not my belief system, but I respect it. My mother was Jewish. My own journey with God is my own.

"Down in the South, I was going to do a school visit and I had a death threat. A woman said if the children wished on my meteor, she would kill me! I refused to back down. When I have children wish on my meteor, the wishes are qualified. They can't ask for money. They can't change other people—but they can by the way they treat them! The children can't wish for possessions. In essence, the focus of the exercise is empowerment. Empowering them to believe the possibilities. We talk about hopes and dreams. One of them could be a doctor that discovers a cure for cancer, or the president of the United States.

"So we wished on the meteor. Every time the auditorium door opened, my heart stopped. We had guards. Eventually, I met with this woman. Because of my father, I knew what to say to her. They want to identify the demons that threaten their children, but they're identifying the wrong ones. Mankind with creativity is filled with light. Those who aren't, are quite dark. They want the darkness to stay away from their children. If the children can't identify the darkness, they won't know. The mother never even heard my presentation—she just heard via the grapevine. All the newspapers just said we wish on a meteor. She had a problem with the word *wishing*.

"Bob San Souci said some people wanted to ban Arthurian legends and Merlin in particular. He said to them, 'Can you show me the particular passage?' 'Well,' they said, 'We didn't read it. But sorcery is in the title.' They just *assumed* what the story was about. I'd have more respect for them if they read it.

"I talk about my dad—my old man. One woman said, "I love the book, but the title? You're calling your father an old man. Where I come from, the term is a derogatory term.' What I *meant* was an endearment. People will see a title and make assumptions that might not be accurate.

"I've done the wish segment in an Amish school. Not only the kids touched it and wished, so did the parents! And they gave me a wink! They knew exactly what it was about. Splinter groups gain power by scaring the hell out of the administration of schools. They have to give in or they wouldn't have the money to defend the case."

Patricia Polacco

Memorable Literature

"My book *Chato's Kitchen* made a banned list. They said it portrayed cats as gang members because they had bandannas on their heads. They put the book be-hind a cased shelf and kids couldn't have access to it unless they had a note from their parents. It was a lot of hoopla. But they finally reversed it. While many people defended me, I stayed clear of the ruckus. It was exciting that administrators, most of whom are non-readers, had a change of heart. They went back and read the book and learned it wasn't harmful.

"One of my essays was also part of a state test and a reactionary parent group said it was too violent. They searched the test. If the story had emotion, then it was bad for kids. Alice Walker's work and mine. They finally had to dump the test. Censorship limits students to a very narrow selection of work. Happy literature has no history. The most painful literature is the most memorable. I would be fearful of literature that whitewashed experiences."

Gary Soto

Disappearing Books

"Censorship comes in various forms. Most libraries have, or should have, in place a series of steps that parents and/or patrons can go through if they think a book unsuitable. Some people, however, streamline the process by stealing the ob-jectionable material right off library shelves. Sadly, some church pastors have even encouraged their followers to pursue this more streamlines approach.

"While I have never had a book officially challenged, one of my books, *A Mi-grant Family*, kept disappearing from the shelves at a public library. It turned out that a group took offense to what it deemed was my pro-migrant stance and rather than officially challenge the book, they simply removed it from the collection. Fortunately, the librarian was equally determined. Every time it disappeared, she reordered.

"In another case, I wrote three nonfiction books about a major taboo, homo-sexuality. I edited the first two, which were aimed at teens and were collections of writings by others about being gay or lesbian in America. Essentially, these books offered a beacon of light at the end of the tunnel. The third book was a history of the AIDS quilt, appropriate for children in middle school and above. Once again, these books were not challenged by any official process. Instead, I found myself the target of death threats and suddenly-cancelled speaking engagements. These speak-ing engagements were cancelled without so much as any investigation into the con-tent of my school and conference programs."

Larry Dane Brimner

Fear of the Occult

"*Time Windows* was banned in the San Diego Public Schools because of some fear that it was dabbling in the occult. My San Diego-based publisher called me, ashamed to tell me it was in their city. One small scene (from the book) was worrisome to a group of people. That scene had been *added* in revisions of the book."

Kathryn Reiss

Controversy

"I've never been censored, but some reviewers felt that *Smoky Night* wasn't suitable for children. They would call it The 'controversial *Smoky Night*.' Soon I thought that was the title of the book!"

Eve Bunting

Book Sales Affected

"The closest I came to being censored was in Kansas. A parent decided *Wait Till Helen Comes* advocated suicide. When the school board refused to ban the book, he appealed to television news programs and local papers. By the time I arrived in town for a week of school visits, I was famous. As a result, I sold a huge number of *Wait Till Helen Comes*. Fortunately, no one agreed with the man's interpretation of the novel."

Mary Downing Hahn

Civil Rights

"There have been organizations that thought my plays were too 'feminist' or 'civil rights' and chose not to produce them."

Joanna H. Kraus

Be True to You

"One school librarian decided she didn't want me to talk about *Squashed*. She said, 'It's a very nice book but I wouldn't want any of the overweight people to feel uncomfortable.' The whole point of the book is empowerment. But we never know where a story will concern a reader. The only thing we can do as writers is write the story and be who we are."

Joan Bauer

Out of Context

"My book, *The Rabbi's Girls* was temporarily banned by the Chicago Public Library because someone opened the book to a page in the middle and saw a derogatory statement about Jews. Eventually, someone else reading the entire book realized that I had not written an anti-Semitic book at all. In fact, quite the contrary.

"The National Christian Schools Association wrote to both me and my publisher to complain that the jacket on my book *Llama in the Library* made the subject look much younger than he is in the text. Since the fifth grade class studies about sex and an infant is born within the pages of my book, they didn't feel it as appropriate for second and third graders to pick up and read this book. As a result, they didn't include this title on their list of recommended reading for students although they liked the story and felt it was on target for fifth grade.

"I actually agree with them and it belatedly taught me something about the importance of a good jacket on a book. We try and teach children not to judge a book by its cover, but everyone knows that they do. Adults do too."

Johanna Hurwitz

Authenticity

"I had feedback that some people are concerned about the fact that I didn't censor my anthologies written my teenagers, while others are thrilled that I didn't. When I first started the books, one of the authors said he had read a lot about teenage boys, and he couldn't relate. On the same note, my oldest son said to make sure the books were compiled for teenagers, not adults. I decided that I was definitely shooting for authenticity above reader comfort, and that leaving out certain voices would defeat the purpose of the books."

Betsy Franco

To Quote or Not to Quote

"Although I haven't been censored in the traditional way, I was 'censored' by Susan Butcher, the dog musher, who did not give me permission to quote her when I was writing a sport biography about her. I believe she wanted to write her autobiography and other dog-related books, and felt that I would influence future sales if I quoted her. As a result, my book, *Susan Butcher, Sled Dog Racer*, contains no quotes. Children love reading about Ms. Butcher and anything related to animals, so I feel she did her young readers a disservice."

Ginger Wadsworth

Bottom Line

"I did have a school library refuse to offer copies of one of my books, though this was many years ago. This was my second novel, *Stranger from the Stars*, which is about a little girl in a small western town. She finds a stranded alien in the desert and helps his fellow aliens find and rescue him. In order to do this, the girl disobeys her parents. The PTA at this school felt that no book depicting a disobedient child should be offered in their library; it might set a bad example. It didn't matter to them that the heroine agonized over her decision, that she had excellent reasons for it, or that she saved someone's life by doing it.

"If that book were in print today, I'd expect it to be censored in many schools because the heroine, who spends a lot of time on her own in a desert frequented by cougars and wild dogs, carries a .22 rifle. I doubt it would matter that she follows every rule of gun safety and would never dream of pointing the rifle at a person, let alone shooting someone.

"I've had one letter from a parent who objected to *The Power of Un* because it depicts children going to a carnival by themselves at night without getting mugged or abducted. It didn't seem to matter to this parent that Un is not set in the inner city, or even in a suburb. It is set in the safety of a small town where everyone knows everyone else.

"People are very protective of children, and it's easy to understand the motivation. But I believe it's a terrible mistake to be so protective that we daren't allow children to think or act on their own. There is no more effective form of self-defense than resourcefulness and the ability to make good decisions. Those are learned skills that get better and better with practice. If we don't allow children to practice by thinking and acting as individuals in situations where mistakes are acceptable and relatively harmless, they can never be wholly functional."

Nancy Etchemendy

"Have I ever been censored? Gosh, I hope so! Once, a nun in Boston said that the language in my first novel was disturbing to her because she thought I wrote in vernacular. To her, white children would not understand that novel. She was telling me I only wrote for a certain population of people. Basically, she called me a racist. It's best to totally ignore those kind of things. You're putting voice to something that is so stupid. I wonder if she even read the book."

Angela Johnson

Limited Perspective

"On occasion, I've been told that parents have complained that I've used the 'H' word, and the 'D' word in my books. My response is that I take my responsibility as an author very seriously, and I only use those words when no other words will do. One notable incident came last year when a reading teacher friend asked me to speak at her school in New Jersey. Apparently the head of her school PTA went to the local Borders and dug up my novel *Thief of Souls*, which is not young adult. It isn't even in the young adult section of the bookstore. The parent made a big stink about me coming to the school because the book was not appropriate for sixth graders, so my visit was cancelled. That would be like judging Steven Spielberg's career by 'Poltergeist' and concluding he was a horror film maker.

"All censorship, I believe, is a manifestation of limited perspective, and people fighting to keep the perspective of their children limited. While I believe a parent has the right to say what their own child can and can't read, it is wrong to try to control what other children can read."

Neal Shusterman

Top Ten List

"I'm proud to say that *Goosebumps* made the top ten list of censored books of the decade! Most of these stories [of censorship] never got to me. They happened in small school libraries. I've been amazed there hasn't been more of a problem. Reading teachers and librarians have been so supportive of my books. They're thrilled kids are reading!"

R. L. Stine

Golly Gee Whiz!

"My books have been excluded a few places because of minor swearing by some characters; '*damnation!*' in one book, a single use of the expression was enough to get it ousted. One book was disallowed because of the use of the words 'hell' and 'demon;' a religious girl thinks—as she is watching people leap and panic in a fire— that this is what demons in hell must look like.

I was once refused a school visit because of using the word 'flophouse' for a cheap hotel. I always wonder if these people want me to have a hard-living stage coach driver scream '*fiddlesticks!*' as the team plunges over a cliff or to pretend like all the world is affluent and safe and that children were never exposed to anything less than wholesome. I have never written anything I thought worthy of censorship. Indeed, I do not believe in censorship outside the home. If you don't want your kids to read something, fine. Adults and other people's children are beyond your jurisdiction."

Kathleen Duey

Remember Mother Goose

"When my first book of poetry, *Slugs*, came out, it was banned in countless places. Apparently people thought it was too gross or violent. Of course, probably in most cases these people were going home and reading Mother Goose—one of the most violent, misogynistic books around—to their tender impressionable little ones."

David Greenberg

Style Choice

"I censor myself. I ask myself, *is this wholesome?* I know a lot of writing today is sophisticated for teenagers. I don't want to be that sophisticated."

Karen English

Author Attacked on Stage! Golly!

"My husband was on the Internet and he found a list of the fifty most censored books of the 1990's. I had two on that list: *The Headless Cupid* and *The Witches of Worm*.

"All of my Newbery Honor books have been attacked. Most of the attacks that I have been made aware of are on *The Egypt Game*. There are hearings with teachers and parents, but usually, the books are retained.

"My books aren't censored for violence or sex or inappropriate language. It's simply because they touch on the supernatural or are at least suspected of doing so. Actually, there is no hint of any supernatural event in *The Egypt Game*.

"A young teacher in Michigan used *The Egypt Game* for her class. She got midnight phone calls and people spread ridiculous rumors about my book. These people claimed that the name of the Egyptian God, Set, is really another name for the devil! And that the book encourages the worship of Egyptian gods. I think these people don't understand the meaning of the word *game*.

"Once, I was personally attacked on stage. A woman came up to me, grabbed me, and put a box of matches in my hand. She said this was a gift and that I was going to repent and burn all of my own books. That was a bit disconcerting.

"I think there is an organization that sends out names of books and authors to fundamentalist groups. Subsequently they tend to find supernatural tendencies in any book by that particular author. Even in realistic stories.

"I heard of one self-appointed censor who claimed that my book *Cat Running* was an attack on American parenthood, because the father, in the book, was domineering and the mother was weak and ineffective. One editor told me that when these attempts at censoring have occurred, all of my books in that particular area sell out immediately!"

Zilpha Keatley Snyder

Close to Home

"I've only been censored in a minor, though very personal, way. One of my sisters is very conservative, and she told me that she could not feel comfortable inviting her friends and neighbors to a book signing because *Jakarta Missing* has 'the occult' in it. I was completely surprised! To me, *Jakarta Missing* is a story of a girl asking the big questions of life, including the question, 'Do human beings really have any way of affecting what goes on in the universe?'

"Dakar throws herself into a magical kind of quest to test the limits of her control, but there's no indication that the magic actually works in any way. What she knows for sure, by the end, is that such things as kindness and loyalty and friendship do somehow send magic splinters out into the universe to multiply goodness. In my mind, *Jakarta Missing* is a highly moral book about people who care passionately about people all over the world and about finding answers to life's spiritual questions, so I was caught off guard by my sister's censorship.

"The other experience I had that helped me understand how censorship happens was a woman who wrote to me after a school visit expressing dismay that I had written *The Storyteller's Beads*, a book that in her opinion, glorified the idea of Israel as a haven for the dispossessed—an idea which has helped Israel justify its policies toward the Palestinian people."

Jane Kurtz

We Suggest Writers Read

What books should you read if you like to write? The following books and periodicals, have been recommended by the authors included in this book. Although not all the suggestions are specifically geared for writing for children, good writing is good writing, no matter who the audience will be.

"Favorite books that help me to write include Laurie Henry's *The Novelist's Notebook*, Dr. Eric Maisel's *Fearless Creating*, *The Persons, Places and Things Spelling Dictionary* by William C. Paxson, and *Legacy, A Step-By-Step Guide to Writing Personal History* by Linda Spence.
Elizabeth Koehler-Pentacoff

"The best reference for (writing) kids' books are other kids' books. And Strunk and White."
Thacher Hurd

"My favorite book is my thesaurus. I tend to get carried away. I'll read a different word, and soon it's an hour later and I'm still reading the thesaurus!"
Eve Bunting

"My favorite reference books are a series called *Writers Guide to...Everyday Life in the 1800's, Everyday Life from Prohibition to World War II, Everyday Life in the Civil War*, and so on. These books are a treasure of information about specific time periods, including the very details and facts a writer needs to bring the past to life."
Mary Downing Hahn

"My favorite reference books are the ones about slang, especially those that date the words. It helps me pick which ones to use to give the flavor of the times. I also like *Roget's Thesaurus*, so I can choose words that are a little off, a little different from the current word, to suggest a different place and time."
Karen Cushman

"Reference books for me are good books. My favorite book is *To Kill a Mockingbird*. I also love *The Color Purple* and *The Prince of Tides*. Another book, by John Irving, is *Trying to Save Piggy Snead*. And *The Things They Carry* by Tim O'Brien. It's a group of short stories that is a novel. It will knock you over! One of these stories is how to tell a true war story. It's instructional along with the story. You're right in the middle of the story and you're watching him make a decision and write it."
Chris Crutcher

"Read Strunk and White on a regular basis. Read it over and over again. Also read Robert McKee's *Story*."
Bruce Coville

"When I was growing up, one of the books a sculptress gave me was a simple book on cartooning. The cool thing is that it was the best reference book I ever got. It made you focus on how facial expressions and body movements can be constructed, without scaring you with anatomy details like nose holes!"
R. W. Alley

"When I'm writing about the past, as in my book *Fair Weather*, about the great Chicago World's Fair of 1893, my best reference work is the Montgomery Ward catalogue of that period. It will tell you more about how people lived than any history book. And what things cost."
Richard Peck

"There is no substitute for the publications put out by Society of Children's Book Writers and Illustrators."
Kathleen Krull

"For naming characters, my favorite reference book is *The Baby Name Personality Survey* by Bruce Lansky and Barry Sinrod, which provides the stereotypes and images that names convey. This is far more useful to me as an author than the usual derivation and literal meaning information given in most baby name books."
SuAnn Kiser

Recommended Books

Ackerman, Diane, *Natural History of the Senses*
Alphin, Elaine Marie, *Creating Characters Kids Will Love*
Asher, Sandy, *But That's Another Story*
Barzun, Jacques & Henry F. Graff, *The Modern Researcher*
Bauer, Marion Dane, *What's Your Story?*
Bayles, David & Ted Orland, *Art and Fear*
Bernays, Annee, *What If*
Boetig, Donna Elizabeth, *Feminine Wiles*
Bradbury, Ray, *Zen and the Art of Writing*
Brandt, Dorothy, *Becoming a Writer*
Browne, Renni & Dave King, *Self-Editing for Fiction Writers*
Cameron, Julia, *The Artist's Way*
The Chicago Manual of Style
Children's Writers and Illustrator's Market
Cleary, Beverly, *A Girl from Yamhill*
Corbeil, Jean-Claude, *Visual Dictionary*
Delton, Judy, *The 29 Most Common Writing Mistakes and How to Avoid Them*
Dils, Tracey, *You Can Write a Children's Book*
Disney Animation, *The Illusion of Life*
Elwood, Maren, *Characters Make Your Story*
Epstein, Connie, *The Art of Writing for Children*
Esbensen, Barbara Juster, *A Celebration of Bees*
Field, Syd, *The Art of Dramatic Writing*
_____, *Screenplay: The Foundations of Screenwriting*
Fitz-Randolph, Jane, *How to Write for Children and Young Adults*
Forester, E.M., *Aspects of the Novel*
Franklin, Jon, *Writing for Story*
Giblin, James Cross, *Writing Books for Young People*
Goldberg, Bonni, *Room to Write*
Goldberg, Natalie, *Writing Down the Bones*
Greenberg, David, *Inspire the Desire for Writing*
Heacock, Paul, *Which Word When?*
Henderson, Kathy, *Market Guide for Young Writers* (book for children who want to write)
Hopkins, Lee Bennett, *Pass the Poetry, Please!*
Hughes, Elaine Farris, *Writing From the Inner Self*
Janeczko, Paul, *The Place my Words are Looking For*
Janeczko, Paul, *Poetry from A to Z*
Karl, Jean, *Childhood to Childhood*

Kennedy, X.J., *Introduction to Poetry*
Keyes, Ralph, *The Courage to Write: How Writers Transcend Fear*
King, Stephen, *On Writing*
Lamott, Anne, *Bird by Bird*
Lerner, Betsy, *The Forest for the Trees*
Levine, Donna, *Get That Novel Written*
Levine, Mark. L., *Negotiating a Book Contract: A Guide for Authors, Agents, & Lawyers*
Litowinsky, Olga, *Writing and Publishing Books for Children in the 90's*
Livingston, Myra Cohn, *Poem-Making*
Lubbock, Percy, *The Craft of Fiction*
Manhard, Stephen J, *The Goof Proofer*
McKee, Robert, *Story*
Marcus, Leonard, *Dear Genius*
Meredith, Robert C. & Fitzgerald, John D., *Structuring Your Novel*
Mettee, Stephen Blake, *The Portable Writer's Conference*
_____, *The Fast-Track Course on How to Write a Nonfiction Book Proposal*
Newman, Leslea, *Writing from the Heart*
New York Public Library's Book of Chronologies
Olmstead, Robert, *Elements of the Writing Craft*
The Concise Oxford English Dictionary (book and CD Rom)
Palmer & Fowler, *Fieldbook of Natural History*
Peck, Robert Newton, *Secrets of Successful Fiction*
Perry, Dick, *One Way to Write Your Novel*
Provost, Gary, *Make Your Words Work*
Random House, *Webster's Pocket Rhyming Dictionary*
Ray, Katie Wood, *Wondrous Words*
Roberts, Ellen, *The Children's Picture Book: How to Write it, How to Sell it*
Rodale, J.I., *The Synonym Finder*
Rubey & Provost, *How to Tell a Story*
Scholastic, *The Scholastic Rhyming Dictionary*
Seger, Linda, *Making a Good Script Great*
Seuling, Barbara, *How to Write a Children's Book and Get it Published*
Shaw, Fran, *50 Ways to Help You Write*
Shepard, Aaron, *The Business of Writing for Children*
Shulevitz, Uri, *Writing with Pictures*
Silber, Lee, *Time Management for the Creative Person*
Society of Children's Book Writers and Illustrators, *The Very Best of Children's Book Illustration*
Time Warner, *Time Warner's Instant Spelling Dictionary*
Tobias, Ronald, *20 Master Plots*

Ueland, Brenda, *If You Want to Write*
Vogler, Christopher, *The Writer's Journey*
Von Oech, Roger, *A Whack on the Side of the Head*
Welty, Eudora, *One Writer's Beginnings*
White, E.B.& Strunk Jr., William, *The Elements of Style*
Winokur, Jon, *Advice to Writers*
Writer's Digest, *Children's Writers and Illustrator's Market*
Wyndham, Lee, *Writing for Children and Teenagers*
Yolen, Jane, *Writing Books for Children*
Zinsser, William, *On Writing Well*

Recommended Periodicals

Byline Magazine
Children's Book Insider
Children's Writer
Publishers Weekly (spring and fall issues)
The Writer
Writer's Digest

Closing Thoughts

When I asked one author to give a last bit of advice or philosophy, she said, "Tell them to go away! *Don't* want to write for kids. There's no money in it and there are already too many other people trying to do it. I don't need the competition!"

Actually, she's right! The financial rewards are often scarce, and the competition is fierce. Many authors freelance in the adult world of writing, or they become teachers or find another secondary job to support themselves. One author calculated that she receives ten cents an hour writing!

But if you have a deep need to connect with children, have talent, are willing to learn and don't give up, you'll be rewarded in ways you won't be able to predict.

Invitation to the World

"Writing for young readers is a matter of sending out invitations, invitations to the world. Like many other invitations, ours are often declined, but we keep sending them out.

"Invitations to grow up anyway, even though it isn't a peer-approved activity. Invitations to stop shifting blame and taking charge of your life. Invitations to ask uncomfortable questions, even of yourself."

Richard Peck

Try Nonfiction and Hang in Through the Difficult Places

"For people who want to break into the field, they should try writing nonfiction. People don't often realize they have information that is interesting and fascinating. It might be a basis for a nonfiction book. It's easier to break in this way, and it's worth it to spend time talking to librarians. *What's out there? What hasn't been covered that kids might be interested in?* The field is open to new people who have a great vision and who are willing to really work hard at learning the craft and refining it.

"My son is a professional saxophone player. He went to a college of music in Boston, and he plays with bands. I remember a time when he was eight. He wanted to give up the sax. I said, 'Please, hang in there over this difficult place.' He did. Then it got fun! You have to master the tools. Once you get there and it's fun, you'll learn because it's fun.

VOICES

"A true voice for children's stories is as rare as a counter-tenor's in professional singing. Everyone and his brother think they can do this. Editors' desks are loaded with thirty new manuscripts a day in a big pile of mail called the 'slush.' Nonetheless, if you are good, publishers are looking for you all the same, and they will find you eventually."

Rosemary Wells

"When writing is going well, you disappear into some other place. That's an incredibly great reward. Another reward of writing children's books is the appreciation you get from kids and parents. You *do* change lives. You get kids into reading. It's the most important skill anyone can have. Adult writers may get more money or more fame, but they don't get that reward. We have a fun and honorable profession. People involved with children's books are some of the best people I've ever met."

Stephen Mooser

Don't Pay. Get Paid.
"Don't ever pay to get published. Writers get paid—writers don't pay."
David Lubar

Listen to Yourself and Others
"To get book ideas, ask booksellers and librarians what book-topics are needed in the marketplace. Listen to real kids. Ask them what books they like and why. Ask them what books they dislike (and hope they don't name yours) and why. You probably won't succeed as a writer if your only goal is to be published. Look beyond that. Ask yourself: Do I have something to say as a writer? What do I care about? What interests me? What interested me as a child? Write the book that only you could write."

Joan Holub

The Child in You

"Writing for children taps into the big kid inside of me who refuses to grow up, and delights in injecting fantasy and magic into the normally logical—and mundane—framework of life. When all my corporate clone friends are sitting in their cubicles during the day, working on company business, I'm home playing with poltergeist pugs, the Queen of Halloween, and other fun and fantastical characters I've created.

"Author Budd Schulberg (*What Makes Sammy Run*) once said, "Life isn't a stairway to the stars. You just keep walking.' But being a children's book writer helps you bypass the stairs to take the escalator."

Ellen Leroe

Make Kids Feel Better

"Those of us who write for children are lucky. We're putting books into the hands of children. Giving children comfort. Books close doors as well as open them. If a kid is miserable, it gives him or her a way of being happy. I'm proud I'm a writer when I get a letter from a child that says, *'I used to feel bad, but now I realize someone else has this problem.'*"

Marilyn Sachs

Be True to You

"I don't write specifically for children or young adults. I write what I write, and would write it no matter what it was called. I don't think a lot about my young audience when I'm writing a book. I don't think 'I can't use this word because it's too big.' They can look it up! On the other hand, I don't dwell on sex or violence, not because it's not appropriate for kids—it's not appropriate for me! I like writing for young people because I am allowed—and even encouraged—to end books, if not happily, at least with hope."

Karen Cushman

Get the Ticket

"My advice to playwrights, is to go to the theater as much as possible—and see as many different kinds of plays as you can."

Joanna H. Kraus

Read

"Read. Every time I sit down to write a new book, I read two or three of my favorites in that genre to get me in the mood and to be thinking along the lines what goes into a story like that. I've been known to take a picture book and type out the whole text so it gives me a feel of the language, length, and balance of description, dialogue, action, etc."

Suzanne Williams

Roller Coaster

"We're in a wonderful business but you have to totally love it to deal with the daily ups and downs. For every wonderful moment there are several rejections. It's a lot of work. The shorter the book, the harder it is! Writing is a fantastic job and I treasure every bump and bliss along the way."

Linda Joy Singleton

Movie Time

"Look at good films to get a sense of dramatic structure."

Marilyn Singer

Don't Give Up

"If you really want to write, don't give up. It's not easy to get published, but it is worth all the struggles once you get there. One of the best quotes I've ever heard is, 'The difference between a published author and an unpublished writer, isn't necessarily the quality of the writing. It's that the published author never quits.'"

Verla Kay

Obsession

"The only people who should really attempt to get published, are people who are completely and obsessively impassioned by writing and illustrating children's books. If you're doing it for the money, or fame, turn around and run in the opposite direction! It's frustrating. It can be really tough, but it is the most rewarding and blessed career I've ever had. I will do everything in my power to be able to keep doing this. I've never been so professionally fulfilled in my life. School visits and conference speaking is an added bonus to this job I never knew about before I started. How wonderful it is to talk to people who love books as much as I do!"

Katie Davis

Gotta Love It!

"If you have no passion for doing it, don't do it. It requires passion."

Sue Alexander

Proofread

"As an editor (for Children's Press) I had a view of what worked for the author. Manuscript presentation is very important. Clean, orderly, correct punctuation."

Ruth Radlauer

"Respect the child."

Ed Radlauer

Optimism

"I don't believe in Unhappily-Ever-Afters. No, not every day is a sunny one. But I think stories for children should offer honesty and hope. Your protagonist should always triumph, should always get what she deserves—(or close to it)—and so should your villain! The philosopher Aristotle once said that history shows us things as they are, whereas fiction shows us things as they could be or ought to be. Offer children stories in which hope plays a paramount role: that they have the power to change their lives to what could be...and should be."

Lee Wardlaw

No Fooling

"I write kid's books because I've never been good at pretense. I hate writing things that are false. If you're interested in writing for children, make certain what you write is absolutely authentic. You can fool adults. You can't fool kids."

Gennifer Choldenko

Write for You

"Connect the commercial part of writing to something that's important to you. It has to have depth. I don't think it's a good idea to write just because you think something will sell. My best writing has been when *I* figured out what *I* needed. What would *I* have liked to read as a child? There must be integrity of the writing. When I stay true to that, things work."

Ellen Jackson

A Calling

"I think children's books all have a mission. Most of the writing I respect. It seems to stand for deeply imbedded principles—not preachy stuff—but simple stuff. The trend of books talk about interpersonal relationships and respecting each other— the glory and beauty of the world. My profession allows me to be a little kid. I'm a nine-year-old trapped in a fifty-three-year-old body!"

Patricia Polacco

Celebrate!

"Children's books are basically a celebration of life. The best children's books contain universal truths in a context that is easy to understand but brings us all closer to our own humanity."

Sarah Wilson

Be Crazy! Have Fun!

"If you have a degree of insanity, you might make a go of it. It's acquired. Don't take yourself too seriously, for then you'll stop having fun!"

Kelly Milner Halls

Remember
"When I get discouraged, I always remember how wonderful it was to read my favorite books as a kid. If I can hold on to that, it usually pulls me through."
Bruce Balan

Why?
"Don't ever stop asking *why* or *if.*"
Nancy Barnet

Get Style
"Think about what children know and explain what they do not know. I think that I use the *People Magazine* style of writing: as sensational as I can get away with. I read that children look for dialogue in books, and so I use a lot of quotations, put into my text, so that they read like dialogue."
Angelica Carpenter

Dear Celebrity
"For the celebrity-turned-children's writer: Having experienced childhood doesn't necessarily mean you are practiced enough to write for children. For people who are driven to write for this special audience and who have done their homework: Believe in yourself and your ability to breathe life into worlds other than the tangible one. The rest will follow."
Larry Dane Brimner

Make a Difference
"People complain that they can't make a difference in the world. I think that writers are in a unique position to make a huge difference in the future. Kids read fiction to vicariously explore who they are and who they will become by experiencing the events, feelings, decisions the fictional character makes. Creating these characters, we are able to impact upon thousands of kids. It's wonderful and a little scary. We have a responsibility in what we write."
Elaine Marie Alphin

Ode to Joy
"Writing for me is a joy. Being able to bring my artists and writers to life is a privilege. I once read that writing a biography is a little like falling in love—it's important to care about your subject because you're going to live with him or her for at least a year."
Beverly Gherman

Be Unique
"Read the new books that are coming out and read the books that have come

out this past century. You don't want to be derivative or a copy cat, but you want to see the major scenes so you can become part of the body of literature without replicating it. This way you won't write a book that's too much like another one."
Kathryn Reiss

Write from Your Heart

"My philosophy of writing for children is that authors should write from the heart. If you don't write what is meaningful to yourself, then you're producing the literary equivalent of white bread—possibly filling, but devoid of nutrition. Kids deserve the best and deepest parts of us, to help them grow into whole human beings—rather than the robotic consumers that most mass culture tries to make them."
Aaron Shepard

Be Kid-Like

"Remember what it's like to be a kid. Write to that."
Wendelin Van Draanen

Be Astonishing

"I've been asked, 'What do preteens want to read?' That is the wrong question to be asking! Write what you want to write; the truest and best stuff you can write. Don't write to the market. Every book needs to season. Let your books marinate. I give myself six months off from every book. Then I can start a new project. If I'm writing a book, it's because something comes from me. Have the courage of your convictions to write what you want to write. Then it will be fresh, astonishing and original. You will succeed if you stick with it!"
Franny Billingsley

Excite You

"I think it's important to write about something you personally think is interesting and exciting. Your own enthusiasm and excitement is going to come out in the way you put the words on the page."
Caroline Arnold

Connect with Kids

"Remember what you loved as a kid. I write books I'd like to read. I think we're responsible for giving children hope; not false promises, but encouragement and connection."
Elisa Kleven

Writer Growth

"Writing for children is fun, satisfying, and educational. I have learned so much

about many subjects from all of my research and have grown as a writer and a person because of it."
   Loretta Ichord

Give It Your All
   "Whether your first or your tenth book has just been published, it deserves a focused promotional strategy to insure a long and healthy shelf life."
   Evelyn Gallardo

Golden Nuggets
   "If the strongest voice in your head, the strongest memories in your mind, the strongest feelings in your heart, come from your childhood, then writing for children may be for you. Tune in to the child inside you. Write the stories only you can tell. Don't be afraid to embroider, to make your experiences better, bigger, more interesting. That's what writers do, they tell stories that contain a nugget of truth!"
   Stephanie Jacob Gordon

Listen to Your Voice
   "If you aren't in touch with being five, but you can't forget what it's like to be nine, don't force yourself to write picture books when your voice is probably in the short chapter or middle grade story. Too often beginning writers think they HAVE TO write a picture book and try to squeeze a longer story into that tiny space; it doesn't work. They are so relieved to learn that they actually belong in an older genre and that it's okay to write for the 'bigger' kids."
   Judith Ross Enderle

Exploration
   "Even in this age of TV, video and hi-tech, high-speed communication, the time children spend being read to or reading, can still be the most precious, nurturing time in their day. By writing children's books, I feel that I help open children's eyes to the world, give them a gift of imagination they can share with their family and friends, and encourage them to 'fly' on wings of wonder—exploring ideas and possibilities that will carry them into healthy adulthood."
   Deborah Lee Rose

Children Come First
   "Have fun! Remember you're creating for children first, and adults second. Do something else no one else has done."
   Thacher Hurd

Go for It!

"The best advice I ever received about writing was the *first* advice I ever received. Just try it! No one ever has read it."
Debra Keller

"Keep it brief. Keep it moving. Keep it entertaining."
Sid Fleischman

"Read a lot of children's books and know who you're writing for, but write for yourself."
Debbie Duncan

Take a Break

"I think it's important to have passion for your subjects. If you're not passionate about what you write, chances are your readers are going to be drawn into the excitement of your subject or words. Also, it's okay. to take a break once in awhile to recharge your batteries. I've taken the last several months off to work on a novel and am finding it's helping me get excited about new nonfiction projects again."
Sneed B. Collard III

Straight to the Heart

"I'm very fortunate to do what I do. I'm able to touch the hearts of children with my books."
Eve Bunting

Stranger Than Fiction

"Today's nonfiction isn't the dry text that pops to mind from our school days. It can be filled with stories, anecdotes, facts; a delicious mental feast. Writing interesting, honest nonfiction at a child's level isn't always easy, but you spend time learning about things you love. You can entice children into the stranger than fiction world of real life. You offer them possibilities."
Suzanne Morgan Williams

Investment

"Be prepared to invest time and money to become a writer. After all, you didn't become a librarian, a teacher or a nurse without training. Join the Society of Children's Book Writers and Illustrators. Start up critique groups with other beginning writers. Attend conferences. Don't tell yourself you can't afford them; if you're serious about writing, you can't afford not to go. Enter contests held by book and magazine publishers, local libraries and writing clubs. Mingle, meet editors, agents and other writers. Consider writing for magazines; don't limit yourself at the beginning of your writing career. Everything you write, regardless of the target audience, will improve your skills."

Connie Goldsmith

Take Time

"Write things that you love and want to spend time with because it is a very long process from manuscript to finished book."

Susan Middleton Elya

Respect Your Audience

"Never write down to kids. Write up."

Jane Yolen

Remember Your Readers

"It's *for children*. So many books are done for adults."

Ashley Wolff

The Game of Pretend

"I think I write for children because part of me still wants to live in Magic Time in the Land of Great Pretend."

Laura Leonard

It Just Looks Easy

"Don't write for children because you think it will be easier or faster. You will be sadly disappointed. Poetry is one of the shortest genres, but also one of the most difficult in which to get published. Don't equate brevity with simpleness, or length with masterpieces. If that were the case, we would all write the New York City phone book and win Pulitzers. Write for children because it is your passion."

Mary Pearson

Dream Come True

"I've wanted to write for children all my life, and I am so, so happy to be doing it!"

Karen Romano Young

Hard Work

"Most producing writers learn this truth at one point or another: you have to put in the hours. You have to sit in the chair and stay with the story. If something isn't working, you have to be willing to throw it out and begin again. Some days, the hours will fly, but all too often, they will drag because, let's face it, the work is hard. If it comes too easily, then perhaps you're not stretching yourself.

"Try taking a story to the next level, or attempt something new rather than doing things the way you've always done them. Re-invent yourself with every story. As Natalie Goldberg says in *Writing Down the Bones*, 'Each time is a new journey with no maps.' And so it's worth it. The greatest thing is to walk into a school and have a child run up to you, clutching one of your books, and gush with utter admiration, *'Are you the author?'*"
Dian Curtis Regan

Pass it On

"I write to pass on the pleasure I've always derived from reading."
Mary Downing Hahn

The Hush

"Well-meaning people sometimes say, 'You write so well, why do you write for children?' The question always irritates me, but as a former professor, I feel obligated to educate.

"I think it's vital for young people to be exposed to significant issues, profound feelings and for the theater to awaken or heighten their curiosity about the world and their compassion for others. I respect those squirming, yelling pre-show audiences for the very reason that when the house lights dim, there is an instant hush, and they are totally open to the magic of the moment. Young people are receptive and vulnerable. Their innate optimism and sense of moral justice as well as their complete 'suspension of belief' demands my strongest passion, my full commitment and my best work."
Joanna H. Kraus

Get Real

"Nonfiction writers tell tales about tiny ants and gigantic mountains. In their books, young readers meet people who share today's world and others who lived in the past. Nonfiction is an exciting, fascinating genre for writers. It's the real world!"
Tekla White

I Believe

"When I read *Peter Pan* for the first time, I was totally smitten, and I just knew that if I wished hard enough, I could fly, too. I loved the magic of that story and I wanted so badly to be able to fly. I remember standing on the top bunk of my bunk bed with my eyes squeezed shut, ready to leap and whispering over and over, 'I can fly. I can fly!' I knew that, technically, I was missing the pixie dust, but I figured if I just wished hard enough, I'd fly anyway.

"Well, I jumped, and of course, crashed to the floor. But for one sweet second, I *was* airborne. This is not something I'd recommend doing, and fortunately for me,

I'd forseen the possibility that I might *not* fly, and had scattered pillows all over the floor to break my fall. But that feeling, wishing, believing, wanting something with every ounce of your young heart, that is what makes me a children's writer. Part of me is still a child inside, still wishing, hoping, believing and it's that part I tap into to write for children. If you can hang on to that, or remember it, really remember it, you will touch the hearts of your readers."

Maureen Boyd Biro

Joy

"I believe writing for children is a wonderful thing. Through writing, we are part of literature, of culture, of values. And in writing for young people, we are a part of the next generation. That's pretty important, isn't it? That's why I think we all need to do our very best work and, as Jane Yolen writers, take joy in the process."

Caryn Yacowitz

Bridge Building

"The illustrations in a book work like a bridge between the story and the child's mind. If you can excite a child with the illustrations so you get him to read, it's a marvelous thing to do. Not only do I enjoy illustrating books for children, I feel it's a very worthwhile thing to do."

Daniel San Souci

Humor Is the Key

"I broke into this profession through the influence of my wife, a kindergarten teacher at the time. So I brought with me many of her 'teacherly' concerns about the often-dismal reading performance of children today.

"At first, to get published, I submitted whatever ideas seemed to make a complete story. But as I continued to work, I soon felt it was not enough to simply get published. I wanted to hear that kids were demanding to read and re-read the books until the poor read-aloud parents could no longer stand it. I wanted to see kids hugging the book. I wanted no less than to be a part of the monumental, nationwide effort (bring up the music) to get our children reading again and loving it. Of the many tools in the toolbox that work, the tool I personally have found most effective in cranking up that reading machine in children, is humor. When I'm asked the lofty question of what I was trying to accomplish with this or that story, I answer, it's just a funny book that I hope kids will read."

Tedd Arnold

Feelings

"Don't write for trends or to impress someone. Truly write what you feel."

Marisa Montes

Discipline

"Don't quit your day job! However, if you want to make a living writing and illustrating picture books, you have to give yourself the pleasure of some business sense. For many of us, that means changing slowly from the admired and courted artist, to a business person. It also means setting up a schedule and a commitment to a regular writing pattern—maybe two hours a day, maybe in summers—but something you feel obligated to. Get an agent, look in *Writer's Market* for peoples names, get to know other writers who are professional children's book writers. Go to conferences and bookstores for author visits. Join Society of Children's Book Writers and Illustrators and attend their summer conference."

Teri Sloat

No Right or Wrong

"Writing should be fun! There's no right or wrong way to do it. Teachers always say, write a great story. I tell people, let's write lousy stories and then rewrite them. Have fun with it!"

David Adler

Today's Child

"Write from the heart and know today's child. We live in a fast-changing society that changes by the moment. It's important to keep up with societal trends, to know what's happening in the lives of children"

Lee Bennett Hopkins

Aim High

"I have lofty aims for my books. I always want them to be worth the high price they cost. This means they need to be good enough to read again and again. Every word is tried out and chosen for the best possible contribution it can make to this aim. Whether a poem is telling a story, making a concept clear, teaching new information, seeing the funny side of things or jingling with jump-rope rhythm, I want it to delight the reader as well as the listener, no matter what the age. I include many dimensions and levels of learning that can be enjoyed both for their sound and their sense. I hope a reader's life has been made better in some small way by enjoying what I have written.

"I would be less than honest if I did not include some of the negative aspects of what it is *really* like to be a children's book writer. For me, it is a life full of uncertainty, long decision delays, many more manuscript revisions, inaccurate illustrations contradicting accurate information, editorial changes and company mergers that often end in canceled contracts. I can never be sure a book will really happen until I hold it in my hand. Even though I claim that writing is my *profession*, I could never live on the income. I have fourteen books with ten publishers and am still hoping to find an editorial 'home.' It takes a tough cookie to hang in there and survive all the rejection. But when I hear that *Bubble Trouble* is the favorite book of two of my great grandchildren, it is all worth the effort."

Joy N. Hulme

Have Purpose

"I think writing for young people is a true responsibility. It's a tough world out there that kids are exposed to. I'm not advocating we should only write stories about kittens with sunhats. I think we need to show that life can be hard, but we need to show how things can be overcome through emotional strength and getting help. I see being a writer to young people as a bearer of light. We are teaching whether we think about it that way or not. You can teach by all kinds of examples. It's one of the things humor can do, too. You can have the message and humor makes it light. I think about when my daughter was in middle school. I'd ask myself, what would I like her to read? What do I want her to know? I think through the eyes of a mother.

"I try to show how great adversity, if it's addressed, can really make us stronger. Having traveled some difficult roads myself as a teenager, I can underscore the importance of strategically placed adults in my life. And I learned how to overcome things through a sense of humor. The combination of those things fuels my writing. I have faith in God and believe he has a purpose for all of us. I wish I had a better sense, as a teenager, that there was a purpose for me. It would have made things easier. Now as an adult, I revisit some of the pain I had, but I layer on some of the things I learned as an adult. I find the process amazingly redemptive."

Joan Bauer

Crabby? Write!

"If you don't love it, if you don't *have* to do it, if you don't get crabby when you're not writing—don't do it! If you can't bounce back from rejection, if you're in it for the money—don't write! If you love adventure, if you love nice people—write for children! There are no nicer people than those who write for children. As for adventure—how far can your imagination fly?"

Tricia Gardella

Love of Reading

"The written and published word takes on its own life. Books are read and reread by children. Even an old out-of-print book is a new book to a reader picking it up for the first time. Writing for children is a great responsibility. I am thrilled by my audience and don't want to ever write anything that could direct them towards harm. I want to make them laugh and perhaps learn a thing or two. Mostly however, I hope they learn to love reading."

Johanna Hurwitz

Sanity

"I like to keep a balance between writing my own poetry and picture books and compiling the work of other writers. My own writing keeps me sane, and the anthologies are a way of giving back."

Betsy Franco

BE A KID

"To write for children, you must still be a child. You can't be an adult thinking like a child; you must actually still be a child inside. My writing room is full of teddy bears, stuffed bunnies, troll dolls and other critters. I also have stacks of picture books and other books for children. If you truly are still a child, you can write the stories you—I mean they—want to hear."

Linda Kay Weber

Different Kind of Richness

"When children ask me if I am rich, I always answer 'yes.' I explain that children's authors don't make much money, but we do what we love, which is writing for children and meeting children through school visits and fan mail, so that is the best kind of 'richness' in my mind."

Ginger Wadsworth

Write What You Like to Read

"I write for children because children are the best readers. When a child loves a book, she *really* loves it. Children dive into stories, becoming part of them; taking on the persona of Mary Lennox or Huck Finn or Jo Marsh, in a way that adults, with all the responsibilities and distractions of the adult world, cannot.

"Another answer is that I never fully grew up. In many ways, including my reading tastes, I just never quite entered the adult world. I write what I like to read. Since I generally prefer children's literature, that's why I write for young people."

Ann Manheimer

Working, Watching and Worry

"I can only believe writing for children is like writing for anyone else. The process is the same. You worry about working when you're not working. When you're not working, you're thinking about writing. Writing is so much a part of my life. It's part of my everyday existence. When I'm not doing it, I'm watching people. I get on public transit and stare at people and wonder if I'll find characters."

Angela Johnson

"There are a lot of ways in which children's lives are just as challenging and complex as those of adults. And there are a lot of ways in which children are wiser and more moral than adults. If you want to write good children's literature, never forget that."

Nancy Etchemendy

Poem a Day

"Poetry for children is the best genre for me, my favorite to write and my favorite to read. I love the fact that most children's poems are short, yet say a lot in such a little space. And give us something to think about, or talk about, later. In this age of constant hurry, a poem is the perfect way to start and end my day."

Janet Wong

Entertainment Value

"Entertain yourself or the child *within* yourself. Make sure that whatever you write will be appreciated by the audience you're writing for."

Bernard Waber

Story Portrait

"Writing is a wonderful thing. Words are strong, words paint pictures just as much as a sweep of a brush across a canvas. It's in creating the story portrait, that you discover a piece of art with the way you dream your words together."

Margaret O'Hair

Work at it!

"The successful writer isn't necessarily the one with the most talent, or the most time, or even the most ideas. The successful writer is one who believes passionately in the dream of being a writer and is willing to do the work needed to make that dream come true."

Susan Taylor Brown

Make Them Think

"I think stories for adolescents are among the most important stories there are, because it's in those early teenage years that we are deciding who we are going to be for the rest of our lives. It's important to give kids as much perspective as possible on the world, because the broader one's perspective, the more informed one's decisions and choices will be. I try not to propose easy answers, but rather to pose as many questions as I can."
Neal Shusterman

One and Only

"I try to remember, with each nonfiction book I write, that this may be the only book on the subject that a child reads—so what I say has to be accurate."
Kathy Pelta

The Bottom Line . . .

"I write to entertain. That's all. I think a lot of people think that when kids read, they have to be uplifted. There's a rule that characters have to learn and grow. My characters don't learn and grow—they mostly run! Kids have the right that they can turn to books just for entertainment."
R. L. Stine

In It Together

"Teachers, librarians, children's authors, editors and publishers pass on the torch of human literacy. The light cast by that torch is the reason we are no longer trying to crack coconuts with rocks. It illuminates our shared experience, knowledge, humanity. I am just pleased and proud to take my own little place in this long parade of committed literates."
Kathleen Duey

Purpose

"You can't write for children out of any rational calculation that you'll make money. Most of us make little. I write for children, and I surmise that most other writers are like me, out of passionate, deep impulse to do so. I just love to do it. I want to do it. I can't imagine not doing it. It's a glorious thing to do and gives glorious purpose to life."
David Greenberg

Rebellion

"One reason I became an illustrator was that my parents didn't want me to! It's not that my folks thought that I couldn't be an illustrator. It was more that I shouldn't be an illustrator because it was such an uncertain life. I think that uncertainty made it very attractive to me. Also, I couldn't think of anything else I felt good about working so hard.

"The other reason is that I always wanted to tell stories. If I hadn't been able to draw, I'd have become a writer. Drawing is an easier way for me to express myself. I also like being an illustrator because you get to see stories that you never would have made yourself. Being an artist is as much of a way of life as it is a job."

R.W. Alley

Closer and Closer

"All manuscripts have a rejection factor of X. So, when you get a manuscript back in the mail, rejoice! It means that you're one step closer to publication."

Alexis O'Neill

Books I Would Have Loved

"My mom was a great lover of poetry and children's books and instilled the same in me from the time I was very small. I wanted to be a writer before I could even read. As I got older, I was deeply disappointed by the number and quality of novels about my favorite subjects: Indians, wilderness survival, animals, etc., especially novels with girl characters who got to be part of the action. It seemed that a lot of authors thought that we kids wouldn't notice if a book was simplistic or unrealistic, and I considered that lazy and insulting. So I decided to make my first task when I got old enough, was to write some of the books I wish I'd had as a kid. I intended to write for middle-grade but seem to turn everything into YA."

Diane Matcheck

Building Blocks

"I like writing stories that show children they are not alone in their feelings. I also like planting little seeds that can build character. I think writing for children occupies a very noble place in our society. Through our writing we get to teach and broaden horizons."

Karen English

Don't Be Afraid

"I'm always amused when people make a distinction between 'novelist' and 'children's author' as if one is more legitimate than the other. Grown-ups seem so afraid that some sort of uncool, kid-cootie will rub off on them and make them unworthy as adults. What a shame. We children's book people have so much fun doing what we love to do—and it isn't just playing in the sandbox!"

Susan Hart Lindquist

Solitude

"Don't consider a career as a writer if you aren't given to a certain amount of optimism. If there is any place for optimism in this occasionally hopeless world, it must be when you are young and growing. Also don't write for children if you aren't able to enjoy a certain amount of time spent in solitude. Writing is seldom a social endeavor."

Zilpha Keatley Snyder

Be the Best You Can Be

"In Fall 1996, my first book was published. A year later, my second. That winter, I had a baby; one I'd waited years and years for and had just about given up on ever having. I was overjoyed. More than anything—even more than publishing books—I wanted to be her mother. And, for a while, I wanted to be nothing else. And I was blissfully happy...until a little voice in my head suggested that I couldn't possibly be so.

"'Hurry, write another book,' it urged me. 'You don't want to lose your momentum.' Now I'm ready to work on book manuscripts again. For the first time, I have a clear sense, as a writer, of my own personal philosophy towards my craft. I write to compete only with myself. That's the only way I can make this career choice work for me. In other words, I don't worry about being a better or more prolific writer than someone else; I only try to be the best writer I can be. My goal is to mature into a more polished writer with each story I write—to outdo the writer I have been in the past. I've never been good at races. I much prefer a journey that will see me quicken my pace at times, as well as slow down to smell the wild flowers."

Haemi Balgassi

Read and Reread

"The single most important bit of advice any writer can be given is to read. A writer of poetry reads poems—lots of them. If you want to write picture books, then read picture books. Many people who write are given manuscripts to look at by first time writers. I am often struck by how clearly these manuscripts come from people who don't read the kinds of books they are trying to write. Read the current books, the ones in the bookstores today. Read the older, long-loved books as well. Then read them all over again. You're going to have a ball doing it!"

Alice Schertle

Art + Books = Happiness

"I've always loved art and I've always loved books. It took art school to show me that I could combine these two loves into the perfect occupation of children's book illustrator. For those of you who dream of getting published, what I've learned is that fame isn't likely, fortune even less, so if you're not doing it for love, you might want to stick with banking.

"I strongly suggest joining The Society of Children's Book Writers and Illustrator's. Go to their workshops. Take a kids' book writing/illustrating class. Not only will you learn a lot, but you can come away with a great critique group, whose support will help you immeasurably with your work as well as with the inevitable 'bad hair' days."

Eve Aldridge

It's Not Easy

"I take my work seriously. It's not easy—contrary to what some people think. Don't quit your day job until you know what you're doing. After years of struggling to get my career going, I was finally able to quit my day job."

Paul Brewer

Ex-Library Worker Tells All...

"I've been able to support myself by writing children's books for the last ten to fifteen years. Things that have helped: working seven days a week, keeping up with current children's literature, Society of Children's Book Writers and Illustrators, my writer friends, the stimulating people who work in this field, and a basic love of books.

"As a child, I thought books were the most important thing in the world, and that perception is actually more intense right now. I'm grateful, for so many reasons, to be able to work in a vital and exhilarating field; preserving literacy. One of a writer's perks is that I can't be fired. Especially for reading too much! Which is what happened when I tried to work in a library!"

Kathleen Krull

Full Circle

"My middle name should be Perseverance. I never gave up, even when I got nothing but rejections. I studied the craft, kept trying, and finally broke in. Now I'm actually being published by a press called Perseverance Press! I've come full circle, it seems. My advice to every writer—keep at it and don't give up. And write what you love. For me, that's mysteries for adults and kids, an activity and parenting books for parents."

Penny Warner

Head over Heels

"I had no intention of writing for children until I had my own. I was working on a novel for adults, at the time, and had published poetry and short stories in literary magazines. When I was haunting the library and reading aloud to my kids, I fell in love with children's literature and never looked back."

Jane Kurtz

New Worlds

"When you write a good book, you create a whole new world for a child to explore."

SuAnn Kiser

What They Need

"Children will not always get out of a book exactly what you thought you put into it. Don't worry about that. If you have written the book well, they will always get what they need from it."

Kevin Kiser

Keep Company

"Nothing is more important than our children. Turning them on to language is one of the best gifts we can give. If we can get them to love words on a page at an early age, we'll have book lovers forever.

"Poetry can creep up on you when you least expect it, but when you more than ever need it. It can wiggle its way into your heart and get cozy there, ready to keep you company on the brightest day or the darkest hour."

Rebecca Kai Dotlich

Make a Difference

"I think I work in the children's field because I believe it's a place where you can influence or touch people at the deepest part of their development. A child has been on the earth five or ten years, so he or she doesn't have a lot of comparisons. If you reach children with a creative experience, you have a chance to penetrate and form something inside them that means something. Odds are better than if you work in the adult field. When you reach children, it goes into a place that stays with them their whole lives."

Lin Oliver

"I'd rather write for kids because they still view optimism as making sense."

Bruce Coville

Be Fearless!

"I don't write *for* children. I write *about* them. If I try to write for them, I'd ask myself all of those non-story questions and I'd tell a bad story. I hate it when some great character tries to preach to others. Kids don't like moralizing. Readers don't. The best piece of advice is, the most important thing about writing, is the *story*. You can figure the theme later. You don't pick a book apart until you've put it together. If it fits the story, do it. You can fix anything in editing. If you don't put out your best story, then you don't have a good body to edit from. Be fearless!"

Chris Crutcher

Love 'em!

"I write because my life has always involved children. I really like kids! They're great!"

Jacque Hall

Write!

"Writers write. I love to punctuate that sentence several different ways. For example: Writers, write. So many people are 'going to write' when they retire, when they get a computer, when they have time, when... Remember, writers write! If you have a pencil and the back of an envelope you can write. Eve Bunting said that she wrote one of her books in an airplane on the back of a barf bag. It was the only paper she had. You can write anywhere, any time, any place and almost any age. So, writer! Write!"

Pat McKissack

Glossary

advance: amount of money an author receives from selling a book to a publisher; this amount is deducted from the royalties earned.

backlist: publishing houses books, from their previous lists, still in print.

board book: picture book made of sturdy cardboard (must withstand chewing and drooling!) for the youngest child, typed length is generally Â½ - one typed manuscript page.*

book proposal: what an author sends a publisher to pitch an idea for a book; usually includes an outline, sample chapters (and synopsis if it is a work of fiction).

camera copy: (or camera ready); finished art and text ready to be printed.

chapter books: books for children generally ages 5-10, who have accomplished read aloud books but aren't ready for a children's middle grade novel; chapter books usually have at least one illustration per chapter; 35-50 manuscript pages, and occasionally up to 80 pages.*

copyright: legal protection of an author's work; under U.S. law, copyright is automatically secured when the piece is written; publisher should (and usually does) assign this to the author; before signing a contract, the author holds the copyright.

creative nonfiction: real facts incorporates fiction elements such as dialogue, scenes, and characterization.

double-page spread: side by side pages; presentation of art and text intended to be read as a unit.

dummy: handmade picture book by an author and/or illustrator, showing a rough guide of illustration and text.

F & G's: folded and gathered loose sheets; final proofs of finished book.

flat fee: author writes a book for a specified amount of money; the author will not receive any royalties.

galleys: first typeset proofs of a manuscript; these are sent to reviewers a few months prior to publication date.

gutter: where the book will be sewn together.

high-low books: books written with a limited vocabulary, but with topics that appeal to older children.

mass market: paperback books, sold through school book clubs, and sometimes supermarkets and drugstores, as well as bookstores; print runs are much larger than trade publishers.

middle grade: books for children ages 8-12, generally 90-150 manuscript pages.*

ms: abbreviation for manuscript.

net royalty: percentage of the amount a publisher receives for a book after wholesale discounts have been granted.

packager: a company that puts together a book, working with writers, editors and artists; doesn't market the book, but instead sells the package to a publisher. Often they create book series, and books with gimmicks, such as pop-up books.

picture books: books with an illustration on every page or every other page; generally run 2-5 manuscript pages.*

picture story books: a longer picture book that runs 6-9 typed manuscript pages*; many folk tales are picture story books.

pop-up books: books with cardboard or other material that "pops up" when the reader turns the pages.

primary source: Original works such as diaries, letters, and interviews used for research.

read aloud/easy reader: books for the beginning reader with specific guidelines that vary from each publishing house, usually 10-20 manuscript pages.*

royalty: Money—generally not much, in this business, unfortunately—a percentage the author receives on each book sold.

secondary source: books, book reviews, periodical articles used for research.

SASE: self-addressed stamped envelope, which should be included with the manuscript when sent to a publisher.

SCBW: Society of Children's Book Writers; began in 1968 by Steve Mooser and Lynn Oliver.

SCBWI: Society of Children's Book Writers and Illustrators; the "I" was added in 1992.

synopsis: summary of a novel; one or two pages in length.

trade books: paperback and hardcover books sold in bookstores and libraries.

trim size: shows where pages will be cut; the final size of the pages in the book.

work-for-hire: writer or illustrator gets paid a fee for a project the publisher assigns; no royalty will be paid.

young adult books: books for ages 12 to 18, usually 100-150 typed manuscript pages.*

*There are always exceptions to the manuscript length rules.

Resources

Organizations and Periodicals

American Book Producers Association
156 Fifth Avenue
New York, NY 10010
800-209-4575
www.abpaonline.org

American Booksellers Association
560 White Plains Road
Tarrytown, NY 10591
800-637-0037
www.ambook.org

American Library Association
50 East Huron Street
Chicago, IL 60611
312-944-6780
www.ala.org

Association of Authors Representatives
10 Astor Place 3rd Floor
New York, NY 10003
212-353-3709

Authors Guild
330 W. 42nd Floor
New York, NY 10036
212-563-5904
www.authorsguild.org

Booklist Magazine (Published by ALA)
Box 607
Mr. Morris, Il 61054
888-350-0949
http://www.ala.org/booklist/index.html

Byline Magazine
P.O. Box 130596
Edmond, OK 73013
http://www.bylinemag.com

Children's Book Council
CBC Features (Periodical)
12 West 37th St.
2nd Floor
New York, NY 10018
800-999-2160
www.cbcbooks.org

Children's Book Insider (Newsletter)
901 Columbia Road
Ft. Collins, CO 80525
www.write4kids.com
Children's Writer's Institute
Children's Writer Newsletter
95 Long Ridge Road
West Redding, CT 06896
www.childrenswriter.com

The Horn Book (Review Journal)
56 Roland St., Suite 200
Boston, MA 02129
800-325-1170
www.hbook.com

International Reading Association
800 Barksdale Road
Newark, DE 19714
302-731-1600
www.reading.org

Kirkus Reviews
200 Park Avenue South, Suite 1118
New York, NY 10003
212-777-4554

Kliatt Children's Review Magazine
33 Bay State Road
Wellesley, MA 02481
781-237-7577

Mystery Writers of America
17 E. 47th St. 6 Floor
New York, NY 10017

National Council of Teachers of English
111 W. Kenyon Road
Urbana, IL 61801
800-369-6283
www.ncte.org

Once Upon A Time Newsletter
553 Winston Court
St. Paul, MN 55118
http://members.aol.com/ouatmag/index.html

Poetry Society of America
15 Gramercy Park
New York, NY 10003
212-254-9628
www.poetrysociety.org/

Poets and Writers (Magazine)
72 Spring Street
3rd Floor
New York, NY 10012
www.pw.org

Publisher's Weekly (Magazine)
245 W. 17th Street
New York, NY 10011
800-278-2991
http://publishersweekly.reviewsnews.com/

Riverbank Review
1624 Harmon Place, Suite 305
Minneapolis, MN 55403
612-486-5690
www.riverbankreview.com

Romance Writers Association
13700 Veterans Memorial Dr. Suite 315
Houston, TX 77014
713-440-6885
www.rwanational.com

School Library Journal
245 W. 17th St.
New York, NY 10011
http://slj.reviewsnews.com

Science Fiction and Fantasy Writers of America
1436 Altamont Ave
Schenectady, NY 12303
www.sfwa.org/

Society of Children's Book Writers
and Illustrators (SCBWI)
SCBWI Bulletin
8271 Beverly Blvd.
Los Angeles, CA 90048
818-888-8760
www.scbwi.org

Voice of Youth Advocates (Library Magazine)
Scarecrow Press
4720 Boston Way
Lanham, MD 20706
888-486-9297
www.voya.com

Western Writers of American
209 E. Iowa
Cheyenne, WY 82009
http://westernwriters.org/membership.htm

The Writer
Kalmbach Publishing Company
Box 1612
Waukesha, WI 53187
www.writermag.com

Writer's Digest Magazine
1507 Dana Avenue
Cincinnati, OH 45207
http://writersdigest.com/

Writers Guild of America
7000 West Third Street
Los Angeles, CA 90048
800-548-4532
www.wga.org

Writers' Journal
Val-Tech Media
Box 394
Perham, MN 56573 http://
www.writersjournal.com

Writers Guild of America
Written By (Periodical)
7000 W. Third Street
Los Angeles, CA 90048
www.wga.org/

Web sites

Artist Resource
www.artistresource.org/

Biography
www.biography.com

Book Browse
www.bookbrowse.com

Book Events Calendar
http://lcweb.loc.gov/loc/cfbook/bkevents.html

Book News
www.bookwire.com

Children's Opinions
www.childrens-express.org

Children's Writer's
and Illustrator's Resource List
http://www.pfdstudio.com/cwrl.html

Classroom Connect - Author Chats
http://www.authorchats.com

Educational Publishers
http://www.textbook.com

Encyclopedia Britannica
www.britannica.com/

Graphic Arts Guild
http://www.gag.org

Health Information
www.medscape.com

Hollywood Creative Directory
www.hcdonline.com

Illustration Internet Site
www.thispot.com

Independent Bookseller's Association
http://www.booksense/com

Independent Book Publishers
http://www.bookmarket.com/101pub.html

Author Verla Kay
http://www.verlakay.com/

Library of Congress
www.loc.gov

Librarian's Index to the Internet
http://www.lii.org/

Loose Leaf Book Company (weekly radio show
for adults about children's books)
http://www.looseleafbookcompany.com/

Movie News
www.imdb.com

News Site
http://www.researchbuzz.com

Nostalgia - Want help in remembering your
childhood?
http://www.sweetnostalgia.com/
rememberwhen.html

Personal Historians
www.personalhistorians.org

Photo Research
www.corbis.com

Prof Net Find professional,
free sources on many topics
http://www3.profnet.com/profnet_home/
index.html

Publicity Online Interviews
www.GuestFinder.com

Publishing News
http://www.authorlink.com

Reference Site
http://about.com/

Reference Questions?
http://ask.elibrary.com

Susan Salzman Raab Children's Book Promotion
http://www.raabassociates.com/authors.htm

Science Resource
http://www.mediaresource.org/

Author Aaron Shepard
http://www.aaronshep.com/

Author Cynthia Leitich Smith
http://www.cynthialeitichsmith.com

Editor Harold Underdown
http://www.underdown.org/
welcome_popup.htm

Virtual Library
http://vlib.org/

Writing Online Newsletter
http://www.writing-world.com

Yearbook Reference
http://www.yearbook.com/

Used Book Sites

http://www.addall.com
http://www.alibris.com
http://abebooks.com

The Authors and Illustrators

Adler, David is the author of more than 150 books including the *Cam Jansen* mysteries, the *Andy Russell* books, the *Picture Book Biography* series, various other picture books, math and science books and books on the Holocaust.

Aldridge, Eve has a masters degree in the fine art of procrastination as well as a BFA in illustrations from the California College of Arts and Crafts. Her picture books include *Hurry Granny Annie* by Arlene Alda and *Sarah's Story* by Bill Harley.

Alexander, Sue is the author of more than twenty books for young people. Among the books she's written are *Witch, Goblin and Sometimes Ghost*, *One More Time, Mama*, and *Behold the Trees*. She's a very valuable member of SCBWI.

Alley, R.W. has illustrated nearly fifty books, including the new Paddington Bear picture books, *Little Flower* by Gloria Rand, and *The Real, True Dulcie Campbell* by Cynthia DeFelice. He lives in Rhode Island with his family.

Alphin, Elaine Marie has published fourteen books and over 200 magazine articles. Her books for children include *A Bear For Miguel*, *Counterfeit Son*, and *The Ghost Cadet*.

Arnold, Caroline has written more than 100 books for children including *Stories in Stone: Rock Art Pictures by Early Americans*, which was named a Notable Book in the Field of Social Studies by the Children's Book Council, and *Easter Island*, a School Library Journal Best Book of the Year. A teacher at UCLA Extension, she is also known for her books about animals, including *Australian Animals* and *Shockers of the Sea*.

Arnold, Tedd began to dream of creating the kid of books his wife, Carol was collecting for her kindergarten class. After studying fine art and working in advertising, Tedd now has more than forty books bearing his name, including *No Jumping on the Bed*, *Green Wilma*, and *Parts*.

Balan, Bruce is the author of thirteen books for children including *Balloon Man* and *The Cherry Migration*, which was inspired by the time he spent working as a soda jerk in England. *Buoy, Home at Sea*, reflects the thousands of miles he has sailed across the ocean.

Balgassi, Haemi is the author of the chapter book, *Peacebound Trains* and the middle-grade novel, *Tae's Sonata*. *Tae's Sonata* won the National Christian Schools Association's 2000 Lamplighter Classic Award.

Barnet, Nancy is the illustrator of *Dream Meadow*, *Where's The Fly*, *Reef Count* and several other titles. Working under the careful supervision of three cats, she creates her colored pencil, pastel or digital artwork for a variety of clients and markets in addition to publishing.

Bauer, Joan is the author of the Newbery Honor-Winning *Hope Was Here*, as well as many other award-winning novels for young adults, including *Rules of the Road* and *Squashed*.

Billingsley, Franny retired from the practice of law in 1983 and began writing children's books. Her books include *Well Wished* and *The Folk Keeper*. The *Folk Keeper* is the winner of the 2000 Boston Globe-Horn Book Award.

Biro, Maureen Boyd has written articles for magazines and newspapers and is the author of a picture book, *Walking With Maga*. She was an associate publisher for Manfit Press and teaches cooking classes in her spare time.

Brewer, Paul is the illustrator of the "*Robert*" books by Barbara Seuling and *Clip, Clip Clip: Three Stories about Hair* by Kathleen Krull. He also wrote and illustrated the infamous, out-of-print, *Grossest Joke Book Ever*.

Brimner, Larry Dane is the author of almost one hundred books for children. His titles include *The Littlest Wolf*, *Cat on Wheels*, and *Angel Island*.

Brown, Susan Taylor is the author of several books for children, including the non-denominational picture book *Can I Pray With My Eyes Open*? She is an instructor for the Institute of Children's Literature.

Bunting, Eve is an award-winning author who has written hundreds of books including novels, picture books and chapter books. Three of them are: *Riding the Tiger*, *Jin Woo*, and *Terror of the Seven Seas*.

Carpenter, Angelica is the Curator of the Arne Nixon Center for the Study of Children's Literature, California State University, Fresno. With her mother Jean Shirley, she wrote *Frances Hodgson Burnett*, *L. Frank Baum* and *Robert Louis Stevenson*.

Chin-Lee, Cynthia is the author of three picture books: *Almond Cookies and Dragon Well Tea*, *A is for Asia*, and *A is for the Americas* (with Terri de la Pena). *A is for Asia* was named by Ruminator Review as one of the Best 100 Children's Books of the Century and *A is for Americas* is a Children's Book Council Outstanding Social Studies Book for Young People.

Choldenko, Gennifer is the author of *Moonstruck: The True Story of the Cow Who Jumped Over the Moon*, a book reviewers called hilarious and hysterical, a middle grade novel, *Notes From a Liar and Her Dog*, a Junior Library Guild Selection and an easy reader entitled, *Tales of a Second Grade Giant*.

Collard III, Sneed B. is a former marine biologist and the author of more than twenty award-winning nonfiction children's books. His titles include *Animal Dads*, *1,000 Years Ago On Planet Earth* and *The Forest in the Clouds*.

Coville, Bruce is a prolific author whose works include music, songs & lyrics, science fiction, Shakespeare retellings, and plays. His books include the *My Teacher is an Alien* series, *Space Brat* series and *The Dark Abyss*. He collaborated with Jane Yolen on *Armageddon Summer*.

Crutcher, Chris majored in psychology in college and became a high school teacher and a school administrator before becoming a therapist and author. His award-winning books for young adults include *Running Loose*, *Chinese Handcuffs* and *Staying Fat for Sarah Byrnes*.

Cushman, Doug is the author and illustrator of the popular *Aunt Eater* books and *Inspector Hopper*. He is illustrator of the best-selling *What Dads Can't Do* and *What Moms Can't Do*.

Cushman, Karen won the Newbery Honor Award for her first book, *Catherine Called Birdy*, and the Newbery Medal for her second book, *The Midwife's Apprentice*. Her third book, *Lucy Whipple*, became a television movie. Karen holds an M.A. in Human Behavior and an M.A. in Museum Studies.

Davis, Katie is a book reviewer and a writer/illustrator of several picture books, including the award-winning *Who Hops?*, *Who Hoots?*, and *I Hate to Go to Bed!*

Dotlich, Rebecca Kai is a poetry consultant and the author of *Lemonade Sun and Other Summer Poems*, *Sweet Dreams of the Wild: Poems for Bedtime*, and *Riddles Come Rumbling: Poems to Ponder*. She has also written a series of photographic concept books and her poetry has appeared on *Reading Rainbow*.

Duey, Kathleen has written and created several series including:: *American Diaries* (19 titles), *Survival* (11 titles), and *The Unicorn's Secret* (4 titles).

Duncan, Debbie is the author of *When Molly was in the Hospital: A Book for Brothers and Sisters of Hospitalized Children* and her book for adults, *Joy of Reading: One Family's Fun-filled Guide to Reading Success*. Debbie reviews children's books and writes essays for local and national media as well as National Public Radio.

Elya, Susan Middleton is the author of many picture books, including *Say Hola to Spanish*, *Say Hola to Spanish, Otra Vez (Again!)* and *Say Hola to Spanish at the Circus*. Before she began her writing career, Susan taught Spanish to junior high school students.

Enderle, Judith Ross has written *Nell Nugget and the Cow Caper*, *What's the Matter, Kelly Beans?*, and *Something's Happening on Calabash Street* with coauthor Stephanie Jacob Gordon. She and Stephanie are authors of over fifty books for young people.

English, Karen is a second grade teacher and the mother of four grown children. She is the author of the novel, *Francie*. She has been writing stories since she was seven.

Etchemendy, Nancy is the award-winning author of several children's books and numerous short stories for both children and adults including *The Power of Un*. Her work has appeared in magazines and anthologies both in the U.S. and in translation abroad, including *The Year's Best Fantasy and Horror* and Joyce Carol Oates' definitive compendium of dark fiction, *American Gothic Tales*.

Fleischman, Sid is a screenwriter, a children's author, and a magician. He won the Newbery Award for *The Whipping Boy*. His other award-winning books include *By the Great Horn Spoon!* (A Walt Disney feature film), *The Ghost in the Noonday Sun* and the *McBroom* series.

Franco, Betsy has over forty books, including picture books, poetry, and young adult anthologies. Her titles include *Grandpa's Quilt, Why the Frog Has Big Eyes,* and *You Hear Me?* Betsy has a B.A. in Studio Art from Stanford University and a Masters in Education from Lesley College.

Gallardo, Evelyn is an award-winning author, wildlife photographer, and consultant to children's authors. Her books include *Among the Orangutans, Endangered Wildlife,* and *How to Promote Your Children's Book—A Survival Guide for Published Writers.*

Gardella, Tricia is the mother of three, grandmother to her "Magnificent Seven," loves to write, cook and bake, garden and run her ice cream parlor in Jamestown, California. Her books include *Just Like My Dad, Casey's New Hat* and *B*lackberry *Booties.*

Gherman, Beverly books include *Norman Rockwell, Storyteller with a Brush*; *E. B White Some Writer!;* and *Robert Louis Stevenson Teller of Tales.*

Goldsmith, Connie is the author of *Lost in Death Valley, The True Story of Four Families in California's Gold Rush* and *Neurological Disorders.* She works part time as a nurse, while freelancing for magazines.

Gordon, Stephanie Jacob has written *Two Badd Babies, Six Creepy Sheep,* and *Dear Timothy Tibbits* with coauthor Judith Ross Enderle. Stephanie loves writing and sharing stories that make kids laugh.

Greenberg, David is the author of many books for children including *Slugs!, Bugs!, Skunks!,* and *Whatever Happened to Humpty Dumpty?*

Hahn, Mary Downing was born in Washington, D.C. and grew up in Maryland. She graduated from the University of MD with a degree in fine art and a master's degree in English. Beginning work on a Ph.D, she discovered that children's books were much more fun! She's the author of many award-winning books including *Anna All Year Round, Promises to the Dead,* and the ghost stories, *Wait Till Helen Comes and Time for Andrew.*

Hall, Jacque is the author of *What Does the Rabbit Say?* She freelances, writing numerous articles in magazines and anthologies.

Halls, Kelly Milner has written more than 1500 articles and reviews for *Writer's Digest, Family Fun, Booklist, Highlights for Children,* the *Chicago Tribune,* the *Den-*

ver Post and other publications. *I Bought a Baby Chicken* is her latest children's book.

Heller, Ruth is the author-illustrator of more than 30 books for children. Her books include *A Sea Within a Sea: Secrets of the Sargasso, Galapagos' Means "Tortoise,"* and *Colors.*

Holub, Joan is the author and/or illustrator of more than forty-five children's books, including *Cinderdog and the Wicked Stepcat, I have a Weird Brother Who Digested a Fly,* and *Eek-A-Boo! A Spooky Lift-the-Flap Book.* Joan was formerly a graphic designer at a PR firm, and an Associate Art Director at Scholastic.

Hopkins, Lee Bennett is the award-winning author of many poetry books and anthologies including *Marvelous Math,* a Reading Rainbow feature selection, *Been to Yesterdays* and *Pass the Poetry Please!,* a book for teachers and poetry lovers. He founded the Lee Bennett Hopkins Poetry Award, and the Lee Bennett Hopkins/ International Reading Association Promising Poet Award.

Hulme, Joy N. combines her life-long love of learning, her unique, often humorous viewpoint, with her skills as a poet to create joyful picture books with words that waltz, sounds that sing and refrains that jingle like jump-rope rhymes. Her books include *Sea Squares, Sea Sums,* and *Counting by Kangaroos.*

Hurd, Thacher was born in Vermont but has lived most of his life in California. He is the author and illustrator of many books, among them *Art Dog, Mama Don't Allow* and *Mystery on the Docks.* He and his wife Olivia founded Peaceable Kingdom Press, which publishes cards and posters from well-known children's books.

Hurwitz, Johanna is the author of more than fifty books, fiction and nonfiction, for young readers. Among these are *Russell Sprouts, Baseball Fever,* and the biography *Astrid Lindgren: Storyteller to the World.*

Ichord, Loretta has written articles, short stories, and middle-grade non-fiction historical books. Her titles include *Hasty Pudding, Johnnycakes and Other Good Stuff: Cooking in Colonial America, Toothworms and Spider Juice: An Illustrated History of Dentistry,* and *Skillet Bread, Sourdough, and Vinegar Pie: Cooking in Pioneer Days.*

Jackson, Ellen has worked as a teacher, curriculum specialist, and freelance writer. She is the author of many books for children, including *Cinder Edna, Turn of the Century,* and *Scatterbrain Sam.*

Johnson, Angela lives in Northeastern Ohio and spends her time traveling and gardening. Her recent books, *Those Building Men*, *When Mules Flew on Magnolia Street* and *Heaven* are out there somewhere on bookshelves.

Kay, Verla is the author of many picture books including *Gold Fever*, *Iron Horses*, and *Tattered Sails*. She hosts children's author chats on the Internet, and her web site was named one of *Writer's Digest's* Best 101 Web Sites.

Keller, Debra is the author of the picture book, *The Trouble with Mister*, and several adult books including *The Spiritual Garden* and *My Best Friend*. In her earlier career, she was an advertising copywriter, where her first job was to write dog food coupons!

Kiser, Kevin has been writing since he learned to read and writing well since he met his wife and writing partner, SuAnn. He is the author of *The Birthday Thing*, *Sherman the Sheep* and *Buzzy Widget*.

Kiser, SuAnn is the author of books for children, including *The Catspring Somersault Flying One-Handed Flip-Flop*, *The Hog Call to End All*, and *Hazel Saves the Day*. She is also a writing consultant, teaches classes in writing for children, and operates a manuscript critique service with her husband, Kevin.

Kleven, Elisa is a former teacher and toymaker. Her popular books include *The Paper Princess*, *The Lion and the Little Red Bird*, and *The Puddle Pail*.

Koehler-Pentacoff, Elizabeth is the author of books including *Louise the One and Only*, *Wish Magic*, and *Help! My Life is Going to the Dogs*. She's written over 300 articles for magazines and newspapers, is *Byline* magazine's children's columnist, and teaches educators workshops through California State University Hayward's Extension Department.

Kraus, Halpert Joanna, Professor Emeritus of Theatre at State University of New York, is an award-winning playwright of fifteen published and widely produced plays, including *The Ice Wolf* and *Remember My Name*. Her books include *Women of Courage* and *Tall Boy's Journey*.

Krull, Kathleen is the author of the *"Lives of"* series, such as *Lives of Extraordinary Women: Rulers, Rebels (and What the Neighbors Thought)*, *Lives of the Writers: Comedies, Tragedies (and What the Neighbors Thought)*, and *Wilma Unlimited: How Wilma Rudolph Became the World's Fastest Woman*, and many other popular books for young readers.

Kurtz, Jane is the author of many books including *Jakarta Missing*, *Faraway Home* and *River Friendly, River Wild*. She speaks to schools and conferences in the United States and in East Africa.

Lattimore, Deborah is the author and illustrator of *Why There is No Arguing in Heaven*, *The Dragon's Robe* and *I Wonder What's Under There?: A Brief History of Underwear*. A noted historian, she is also the life of every party.

Leonard, Laura is the author of the historical middle grade novels *Finding Papa* and *Saving Damaris*. She lives in Northern California.

Leroe, Ellen has worked as a fashion buyer and corporate newsletter editor before writing for children. She's the author of over 25 books for readers aged 7 to 17, including the young adult novel, *Confessions of a Teenage TV Addict*, the chapter book, *Ghost Dog*, and a nonfiction middle grade, *Disaster! Three Real-Life Stories of Survival*.

Lindquist, Susan Hart is a poet and an author of popular novels including *Walking the Rim*, *Wander*, and *Summer Soldiers*. She has a B.A. in African and Middle Eastern History from University California Santa Barbara.

Lubar, David writes books and games. He's still waiting for them to write back. His books include *Hidden Talents* (an ALA Best Book for Young Adults), *The PsychoZone The Witches Monkey and Other Tales*, and *Monster Road*.

McKissack, Patricia has cowritten over fifty books with her husband, Fred. These include biographies, religious stories, and folktales, such as *Flossie and the Fox*, *The Dark Thirty: Southern Tales of the Supernatural*, and *A Picture of Freedom: The Diary of Clotee, A Slave Girl*.

Manheimer, Ann has worked as a journalist, a lawyer, a substitute teacher and a librarian. Her work has appeared in magazines and anthologies, such as *Ghosts and Golems*, and she is the author of *Seeds of Dreams: The Story of Martin Luther King, Jr.*

Matcheck, Diane a young adult author of *The Sacrifice*, about a Crow Indian girl in the mid-1700's and the wilderness adventure, *Survival School*.

Montes, Marisa was born in Puerto Rico but now lives in California. A former lawyer, she is the author of *Something Wicked's in Those Woods*, *Juan Bobo Goes to Work*, and *Egg-Napped!*

Mooser, Stephen is the cofounder and President of the Society of Children's Book Writers and Illustrators. A former freelance treasure hunter and film-maker, he is the author of nearly 60 books including *The Ghost With The Halloween Hiccups*, *Elis Is Back And He's In the Sixth Grade!* and *The Thing Upstairs*.

O'Hair, Margaret's first picture book is, *Twin to Twin*, and she is currently writing a children's novel and several other picture books. She teaches by day and writes books by night.

O'Neill, Alexis is the author of *Loud Emily*, *The Recess Queen* and *Estela's Swap*. She also writes for a variety of children's magazines and teaches writing for the UCLA Extension Writers' Program.

Oliver, Lin has written, developed and produced films, movies and series for television. Her projects have included E.B. White's *The Trumpet of the Swan*, *Finding Buck McHenry*, and *Aliens Ate My Homework* by Bruce Coville. She is cofounder and Executive Director of SCBWI and has also written numerous books for children.

Pearson, Mary E. is a writer and a teacher whose books include the young adult novels, *Scribbler of Dreams* and *David v. God*. She lives in Southern California.

Peck, Richard is the award-winning author more than twenty-five novels, including the *Blossom Culp* series, *The Last Safe Place on Earth*, *A Year Down Yonder* and the sequel, the Newbery Award winner, *A Long Way from Chicago*.

Pelta, Kathy is an award-winning author who has written nearly twenty books that include biographies, career books, and histories, such as *Discovering Christopher Columbus*, *Rediscovering Easter Island*, and *Bridging the Golden Gate*.

Polacco, Patricia is the author and illustrator of many popular books for children, including *Meteor*, *Rechenka's Eggs* and *Thank You, Mr. Falker*. She holds a Ph.D. in Art History and is a Member of the Virginia Kitteridge Society. Many of her stories honor her Russian, Ukrainian and Irish heritage.

Radlauer, Ed has written over 200 books for children. Ed was honored by the National Hot Rod Association with their special Award of Merit for his three books: *Drag Racing*, *Drag Racing Funny Cars*, and *On the Drag Strip*. He wouldn't trade this NHRA for anything—even the Newbery Award!

Radlauer, Ruth is the author and coauthor of over 200 books, and two musicals. An editor of Elk Grove Books Division of Childrens Press for sixteen years, she is most proud of her book, *Molly Goes Hiking* and her series on national parks, including Shenandoah National Park.

Regan, Dian Curtis is the author of 40 books for young readers, including *Princess Nevermore*, the *Monster of the Month Club Quartet*, and the *Friendship of Milly and Tug*. Originally from Colorado, Dian has recently repatriated to the USA after three years in Venezuela, and presently resides in Kansas.

Reiss, Kathryn is a writing instructor and author of several mystery novels for children including *Time Windows*, *Riddle of the Prairie Bride*, and *Paint by Magic*.

Rose, Deborah Lee is the author of the environmental folktale, *The People Who Hugged the Trees*, which has been published in nearly a dozen languages and included in major school anthologies. Inspired by her love of marine wildlife, she has written several ocean picture books, including *Into the A,B Sea*, and *One Nightime Sea*.

Sachs, Marilyn has written over 35 books, and won numerous awards. Her books include *The Bears' House*, *Veronica Ganz* and *Four Ugly Cats in Apartment D*.

San Souci, Daniel is the illustrator of many books, including *Two Bear Cubs*, by his brother, Robert San Souci, *Antelope, Bison Cougar, A National Park Alphabet Book*, by Steven P. Medley and *North Country Night* by Robert San Souci.

Schertle, Alice was an elementary school teacher before she became a prolific author. Her titles include *I am the Cat*, *How Now Brown Cow?* and *A Lucky Thing*.

Shahan, Sherry researched her middle-grade adventure novel, *Frozen Stiff*, by camping and kayaking in a remote Alaskan wilderness. Other assignments have led her hiking through a leech-infested rain forest in Australia and riding in a dogsled for the first part of the Iditarod Trail Sled Dog Race, which resulted in her nonfiction photo-essay book, *Dashing Through the Snow: The Story of the Iditarod*.

Shepard, Aaron is the award-winning author of *Master Man, The Sea King's Daughter*, and many more picture book retellings of traditional literature. He is also author of the best-selling *The Business of Writing for Children*.

Shusterman, Neal is the author of more than a dozen-award winning books, including *The Dark Side of Nowhere, Downsiders*, and *What Daddy Did*. His books have received honors from The American Library Association and The International Reading Association, as well as receiving numerous state awards.

Singer, Marilyn loves the word "versatile." She's written over sixty books for children and young adults: realistic novels, ghost stories, fantasies, mysteries, fairy tales, nonfiction, and picture books, including such titles as *Turtle in July*, *The Circus Lunicus*, and *Didi and Daddy on the Promenade*. She enjoys writing different books because it's so challenging to do, and it keeps her from getting bored.

Singleton, Linda Joy's, *Regeneration* series has been optioned by Fox TV and was selected for the Young Adult Library Services Association 2001 Quick Pick List. She has two middle grade e-books from New Concepts Publishing: *Mail-Order Monster* and *Melissa's Mission Impossible*.

Sloat, Teri wrote and illustrated bi-lingual materials in rural Alaska, and later, trade books based on her family's anecdotes. Her books include *Farmer Brown Shears His Sheep*, *There was an Old Lady Who Swallowed a Trout*, and *Patty's Pumpkin Patch*.

Snyder, Zilpha Keatley is the award-winning novelist whose many titles include three Newbery Honor books. Her recent books are *Gib Rides Home*, *Gib and The Gray Ghost* and *Spyhole Secrets*.

Soto, Gary is the author of many books for young people and adults, including *Buried Onions*, *Living Up the Street*, *Chato's Kitchen*, and *Jessie De La Cruz: A Profile of a United Farm Worker*. He is presently Distinguished Professor of Creative Writing at the University of California at Riverside.

Stine, R.L. has been recognized by the Guinness Book of World Records as the best-selling children's author in history. *His Fear Street*, *Goosebumps* and *The Nightmare Room* series of scary books have sold more than 300 million copies from around the world. Recent titles include: *The Nightmare Hour*, *The Haunting Hour*, and *The Nightmare Room Thrillogy*.

Sturtevant, Katherine is the author of *Our Sisters' London: Feminist Walking Tours*, a book for adults and the historical novel for young adults, At the Sign of the Star. She received a B.A. and M.A. in creative writing from San Francisco State University, and writes articles and reviews for various publications.

Van Draanen, Wendelin has been everything from a forklift driver to a computer science teacher. Her critically acclaimed *Sammy Keyes* mystery series includes *Sammy Keyes and the Hotel Thief*, a 1999 Edgar Award winner, *Sammy Keyes and the Sisters of Mercy*, a nominee for the California Young Reader Medal, and *Sammy Keyes and the Curse of Moustache Mary* is one of the Booksellers of America's Best Book of the Year nominee.

Waber, Bernard attended the University of the Arts and lives in New York with his wife, Ethel. His popular books include *Lyle, Lyle Crocodile, Ira Sleeps Over,* and *Bearsie Bear and the Surprise Sleepover Party.*

Wadsworth, Ginger is a native California who likes to write about people, places, animals - anything to do with the environment. She has published numerous children's books including *John Muir, Wilderness Protector, Desert Discoveries,* and *One Tiger Growls.*

Wardlaw, Lee is the author of more than twenty books for children, ranging from picture books to young adult novels. She has won numerous reader's choice awards for her titles such as *Punia and the King of Sharks, 101 Ways to Bug Your Parents,* which has been optioned for a TV movie, and *101 Ways to Bug Your Teacher.*

Warner, Penny is the author of the adult mystery series featuring Connor Westphal. Her children's books include *The Mystery of the Haunted Caves, The Mystery of the Missing Mustangs* and *The Mystery of the Disappearing Dolphins.*

Weber, Linda Kay is an editor and author of *Louie Larkey and the Bad Dream Patrol.* She lives in Nevada.

Wells, Rosemary began her career in children's books working as a designer for MacMillan. Since then she has authored and/or illustrated over sixty books for children. She is the award-winning author and illustrator of the Max series, *Noisy Nora, Morris's Disappearing Bag: A Christmas Story,* and *Shy Charles.*

Wetzel, Joanne Stewart has written CD ROMS, travel articles and a magazine column as well as the nonfiction book, *Onstage/Backstage* and a picture book, The *Christmas Box. The Christmas Box* was named one of the noteworthy books for children by Bank Street College of Education.

White, Tekla is the author of *Missions of the San Francisco Bay Area* and *The Flight of the Union.* She has written a variety of workbooks, stories and educational materials.

Williams, Suzanne is a children's book author and a former elementary school librarian. Her books for children include *Library Lil, My Dog Never Says Please,* and *Mommy Doesn't Know My Name.* She lives in Washington State, and is a frequent author visitor at schools.

Williams, Suzanne Morgan's books include *Made in China: Ideas and Inventions* from Ancient China, and *Pinatas and Smiling Skeletons: Celebrating Mexican Festivals*. She gives teacher workshops and school presentations on multi-cultural subjects.

Wilson, Sarah is the author and/or illustrator of more than twenty books for children. Her titles include *The Day That Henry Cleaned His Room, Big Day on the River,* and *George Hogglesberry, Alien.*

Wolff, Ashley majored in printmaking and illustration at the Rhode Island School of Design. She has illustrated the *Miss Bindergarten Goes to Kindergarten* series (written by Joseph Slate), *Raffi Songs to Read* (by Raffi) and has written and illustrated her own books, including *Only the Cat Saw.*

Wong, Janet, a former lawyer, is the author of several picture books and poetry collections, including *A Suitcase of Seaweed, The Trip Back Home,* and *This Next New Year.*

Yakowitz, Caryn writes picture books and poetry for young people. Her books include *Pumpkin Fiesta, The Jade Stone, A Chinese Folktale* and *Onstage/Backstage.*

Yolen, Jane is the award-winning author of over 200 books for children, including Caldecott winner, *Owl Moon, Sleeping Ugly,* and *The Devil's Arithmetic,* which was made into television movie. She collaborated with Bruce Coville to write the young adult novel, *Armageddon Summer.*

Young, Karen Romano is the author of *Outside In, Small Worlds: A Book About Maps and Mapmakers,* and *The Beetle and Me: A Love Story.*

Index of Authors

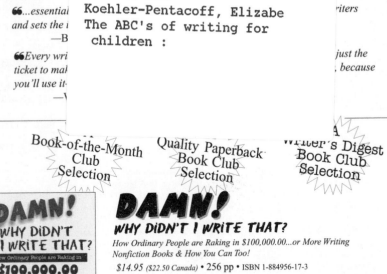